Schriftenreihe des Europäischen Zentrums für Föderalismus-Forschung Tübingen (EZFF)

Herausgegeben vom Vorstand des EZFF:

Prof. Dr. Gabriele Abels (Sprecherin des Vorstands)
Prof. Dr. Jochen von Bernstorff, LL.M.
Dr. Martin Große Hüttmann (Geschäftsführendes Vorstandsmitglied)
Prof. em. Dr. Rudolf Hrbek
Prof. Dr. Sebastian Kinder
Prof. Dr. Martin Nettesheim
Prof. Dr. Barbara Remmert (Stellv. Sprecherin des Vorstands)
Prof. Dr. Josef Schmid
Prof. Dr. Gunter Schubert
Prof. Dr. Christian Seiler

Band 52

Gabriele Abels [Ed.]

The Conference on the Future of Europe

National and Regional Participation
in an Innovative Reform Process

Printed with the kind support of *Universitätsbund e.V.* of the University of Tübingen.

The Deutsche Nationalbibliothek lists this publication in the
Deutsche Nationalbibliografie; detailed bibliographic data
are available on the Internet at http://dnb.d-nb.de

ISBN   978-3-7560-0435-5   (Print)
        978-3-7489-3797-5   (ePDF)

British Library Cataloguing-in-Publication Data
A catalogue record for this book is available from the British Library.

ISBN   978-3-7560-0435-5   (Print)
        978-3-7489-3797-5   (ePDF)

Library of Congress Cataloging-in-Publication Data

Abels, Gabriele
The Conference on the Future of Europe
National and Regional Participation in an Innovative Reform Process
Gabriele Abels (Ed.)
177 pp.

ISBN   978-3-7560-0435-5   (Print)
        978-3-7489-3797-5   (ePDF)

Onlineversion
Nomos eLibrary

1st Edition 2023
© Nomos Verlagsgesellschaft, Baden-Baden, Germany 2023. Overall responsibility for manufacturing (printing and production) lies with Nomos Verlagsgesellschaft mbH & Co. KG.

This work is subject to copyright. All rights reserved. No part of this publication may be reproduced or transmitted in any form or by any means, electronic or mechanical, including photocopying, recording, or any information storage or retrieval system, without prior permission in writing from the publishers. Under § 54 of the German Copyright Law where copies are made for other than private use a fee is payable to "Verwertungs gesellschaft Wort", Munich.

No responsibility for loss caused to any individual or organization acting on or refraining from action as a result of the material in this publication can be accepted by Nomos or the authoreditor.

Preface: The future of Europe starts in its regions and cities

"*A leading and active part in building the future of our Union*" for all European citizens: that was what the President of the European Commission, Ursula von der Leyen, aimed to achieve when she announced the Conference on the Future of Europe in her opening statement as candidate in front of the European Parliament in July 2019.

Since the start of the process, the European Committee of the Regions – the assembly of elected regional and local representatives in Europe – has supported this democratic experiment, ensuring that regions and cities are fully involved in this endeavour.

As stated in the Resolution of the Committee on the Conference on the Future of Europe adopted in February 2020, "*democratic legitimacy of the European Union lies with the trust of citizens in their representatives elected at European, national, regional and local levels.*" Studies demonstrate that people have most trust in their mayors, local councillors, governors, and regional leaders as their actions have a more visible impact on their lives. This is why they are and must remain a key component of the European policy- and decision-making process, in line with the principle of subsidiarity. The Conference on the Future of Europe has come to an end and it is now time to turn its conclusions into reality.

Across the nine thematic fields tackled by the Conference[1], the resulting recommendations show a clear need to reinforce the regional and local dimension of European policies. As regards European democracy in particular, the conclusions are a clear call for increased citizen participation and a stronger contribution by regions and cities in European policymaking, with an enhanced role for the European Committee of the Regions.

Another significant outcome of the Conference was the call for a convention to revise the European treaties; that call was endorsed by the European Parliament and the President of the European Commission and supported by the Committee of the Regions.

With this in mind, we need to focus our efforts on three key strands. First, we need to deliver. The Conference on the Future of Europe will be only another exercise in pretty words unless its conclusions become reality. All the European institutions have to be committed to ensuring to a follow-up. The Committee of the Regions, building on its active contribution to the process, takes full ownership of the recommendations and is working on implementing them. Greening our cities, facilitating rural and inter-island connectivity, ensuring better access to local food, facilitating cross-border healthcare, fostering innovation, developing internet connectivity in rural areas, increasing support for the integration of refugees and migrants – these are all challenges and solutions on which local and regional authorities can work from day one. They will deliver regardless of the debate on treaty change.

Follow-up and accountability are key for ensuring that the Conference's conclusions are not simply filed away. The European Committee of the Regions is a key player in showing how local and regional authorities are implementing the recommendations of the Conference on the Future of Europe.

---

1   Climate change and the environment; Health; A stronger economy, social justice and jobs; EU in the world; Rule of law, values and rights, security; Digital transformation; European democracy; Migration; Education, culture, youth and sports.

Second, we are opening a new chapter for European democracy. Hundreds of Europeans actively and willingly involved, representatives from all levels of government and from all parts of civil society, thousands of ideas on online platforms, hours of discussions: the Conference cannot be a footnote in the history of EU democratic engagement.

Sometimes criticised for its perceived democratic deficit, the European project can only benefit by embracing deliberative democracy as a complement to its representative structure. Building on regional success stories such as Ostbelgien or national ones like the citizen assemblies in Ireland, mainstreaming the use of citizen panels and other exercises in participatory democracy will strengthen the legitimacy of European legislation and, ultimately, reinforce its impact.

For years, the European Committee of the Regions has been advocating for a permanent dialogue with citizens in order to build a bridge between EU institutions and people. More citizens' panels are the way forward, provided that they are organised in our regions and cities. A permanent dialogue with Europeans will prove the truth of what Jean Monnet once said: *"Nothing is possible without people, nothing lasts without institutions."*

Third, we need to start mapping out the shape and inner workings of the future of the European Union. While many measures proposed during the Conference on the Future of Europe can be implemented directly, some – more ambitious and more long term in scope – will require a revision of our constitutional framework.

Since the adoption of the Lisbon Treaty, the notion of reopening negotiations on the European Union's founding texts has often been seen as taboo or a far-fetched dream on the part of a small group of euro-enthusiasts. It can be argued that this has been the case since the Maastricht Treaty was adopted 30 years ago, establishing the Committee of the Regions and enshrining the principle of subsidiarity – whereby decisions must be taken at the appropriate level – in the European policy approach. However, there comes a time when we need to overturn taboos and take action to ensure that we have a more efficient European Union.

Today's challenges, such as the climate and energy crises, the fallout of Russia's war against Ukraine, mastering the digital transformation and reducing inequalities, require complex and multifaceted responses.

To begin, we need to involve local and regional authorities in the policy- and decision-making process, from design to implementation. Then, we need to admit that our rules, our procedures, our treaties do not always allow to reach the desired outcome. From unanimous voting to budgetary capacity, from the division of competences to the role of citizens and the power of institutions and bodies such as the European Parliament and the European Committee of the Regions, now is the time to overhaul our Union to make it fit for purpose: delivering a stronger and fairer Europe for its people.

The Committee of the Regions will take a constructive approach to the preparations on a Convention, the constitutional body which would be tasked with the reform of the EU treaties. The Committee must be an active part of this exercise as the voice of local and regional authorities.

Only by involving all parties – Member States, European institutions, local and regional representatives, civil society, trade unions, the general public – can we define the shape and inner workings of a European Union that can deliver solidarity, hope, and progress for all.

By building on the achievements of the Conference on the Future of Europe we will be heading in the right direction to secure meaningful results.

Delivering where we can, strengthening our democratic functioning and reforming the Union to make it fit for purpose: these are the three strands that must steer our work in the wake of the Conference on the Future of Europe. These three dimensions will require work, debates, courage, and determination both on the political stage and in civil society and the academic world. I welcome this book because it brings together the lessons learned from the Conference on the Future of Europe in various Member States, shows the sheer range of initiatives across regions and cities and offers food for thought on the future of the European project.

We have our heading: we must ensure that we follow it to deliver a better life for Europe and for everyone.

Ponta Delgada, December 2022

Vasco Alves Cordeiro
President of the European Committee of the Regions

Contents

Preface: The future of Europe starts in its regions and cities   5
    Vasco Alves Cordeiro

National and regional participation in the Conference on the Future
of Europe: Introduction   11
    Gabriele Abels

The Conference on the Future of Europe and the involvement of the
European Committee of the Regions   39
    Wolfgang Petzold

French perspective on the Conference on the Future of Europe   55
    Servane Metzger/Mattéo Torres-Ader

The Belgian experiments of deliberative democracy –
An analysis of the institutionalisation of deliberative citizen participation
in multi-level Belgium   67
    Ann-Mireille Sautter/Min Reuchamps

The Conference on the Future of Europe in Germany: Activities at
federal and Länder level   78
    Gabriele Abels

The Conference on the Future of Europe – Personal experiences and
expectations from the perspective of state parliaments   97
    Muhterem Aras

The contribution of Baden-Württemberg to the Conference on the
Future of Europe – Taking the conversation to the people   108
    Timo Peters/Florian Ziegenbalg

Austria in the Conference on the Future of Europe   119
    Sarah Meyer/Lukas Böhm/Anna Dermitzakis/Leopold Kernstock/
    Oskar Kveton/Patrick Steindl/Melina Weilguni/Jasmin Zengin

The Conference on the Future of Europe and the Autonomous
Communities in Spain 135
  Mario Kölling

Italian perspective on the Conference on the Future of Europe 148
  Susanna Cafaro

Conference on the Future of the EU in Czechia: Achievements and setbacks 159
  Jarolím Antal

Authors 169

Annex I: *Timeline of the Conference on the Future of Europe* 171

Annex II: *List of Key Documents* 173

Annex III: *Conference Charter* 176

National and regional participation in the Conference on the Future of Europe: Introduction[1]

Gabriele Abels

1. Introduction

After a late and rocky start, the Conference on the Future of Europe (CoFoE) started on 9 May 2021, and it was recently concluded on 9 May 2022 by a major event in the European Parliament's Louise Weiss building in Strasbourg. The CoFoE can be labelled as an experimental, transnational endeavour in deliberative democracy – "an out-of the box initiative" (Fabbrini 2021: 402). It was originally proposed by French President Emmanuel Macron in spring 2019 before the European Parliament election. The idea actually builds on French national experiences with the "grand débat" in response to social protest and the climate crisis (see Metzger and Torres-Ader in this volume). In order to push for his conference vision, the French President took an unprecedented step by directly addressing the European citizens in an open letter as of March 2019. In this letter, which was published in many national newspapers in many member states, President Macron calls for a "Conference for Europe" to discuss "with an open mind" the need for change and to "define a roadmap" for translating "key priorities into concrete actions" (Macron 2019). This conference "will need to engage with citizens' panels and hear academics, business and labour representatives, and religious and spiritual leaders" (ibid.).[2]

The European Parliament had already on 13 February 2019 adopted a resolution "on the state of the debate on the future of Europe", in which it speaks out for initiatives to renew and revive European integration (see Johansson/Raunio 2022: 23). Hence, the upcoming European Parliament election clearly provided "a 'policy window' open for debates about engaging with citizens and improving the democratic credentials of the EU" (ibid.: 24).

After the May 2019 election and the failure of the Spitzenkandidaten (lead candidate) mechanism[3], the idea was then quickly and warmly adopted by the surprise candidate for Commission Presidency, Ursula von der Leyen. In her speech as presidential candidate for the European Commission in the European Parliament on 16 July 2019 von der Leyen was

---

1 I am grateful to Martin Große Hüttmann for his valuable comments on a previous version of this chapter and to Mirjam Zillober for her thorough copy-editing.
2 For an overview of how CoFoE has evolved see also Johansson/Raunio 2022; Maurice 2022.
3 In 2014, Jean-Claude Juncker was running as lead candidate for the conservative European People's Party (EPP). After intense discussion among governments, the European Council (EUCO) finally nominated Juncker as candidate for the post of Commission President; the European Parliament elected him with a broad majority. In 2019, however, EUCO opposed to all lead candidates running for the political groups in the European Parliament elections. The French President had strong objections against the EPP lead candidate Manfred Weber, even though the party came in strongest, while the social democratic candidate Frans Timmermans faced opposition especially by CEE governments. In the end, Ursula von der Leyen was the out-of-the-box candidate nominated by EUCO. This nomination was strongly criticized in the European Parliament as violating the – legally non-binding – "lead candidate principle." Von der Leyen was elected with only a close majority of nine votes in the European Parliament (for details see Armstrong 2019).

aware that there was as "broad partisan consensus" (ibid.: 29) in the Parliament, on whose support in the election she depended, favoured such an initiative. Once elected by the Parliament, she included the plan in her political agenda for the European Commission as part of the broader objective of "a new push for European democracy". In her agenda she proclaims that she wants

"Europeans to build the future of our Union. They should play a leading and active part in setting our priorities and our level of ambition. I want citizens to have their say at a Conference on the Future of Europe, to start in 2020 and run for two years." (ibid.: 19)

Consequently, she made CoFoE a core issue in her mission letter as of 1st December 2019 to Commissioner Dubravka Šuica, a former MEP, who then became the Commission Vice-President responsible for the future conference. The CoFoE was hence on the agenda – "designed to relaunch the project of European integration after a decade of crisis" with the aim to build a more resilient Europe (Fabbrini 2021: 402). Yet, in the month to come this plan and how to implement it was contested.

Originally, the CoFoE was intended to last for two years from May 2020 to May 2022 to bridge symbolically the German Council presidency in the second half of 2020 to the French Council Presidency in the first half of 2022. Furthermore, this timing would allow for a follow-up process and potential reforms before the next European Parliament elections in 2024. These elections were then meant to be a vote by the citizens on the way forward. However, the Covid-19 pandemic kicked in in March 2020 and forced EU institutions to change their mode of operation and their priorities. This, however, is only part of the answer for the delay in the CoFoE start.

Indeed, from the very start the conference was met with great expectations and reservations alike – by policymakers as well as by scholars. Many conditions and criteria were discussed for making the CoFoE a success. Some observers see CoFoE as a window of opportunity for opening the debate, bringing in citizens' voices and eventually leading to a constitutional convention aiming at substantial treaty reforms. Simultaneously, it was met with suspicion not least because of the conflict over the objective and the governance structure of the conference. On the one hand, there was a strong *inter-institutional* power play among the Commission, the Council and the European Parliament over the mandate, the composition and governance structure of the conference. Ålander et al. (2021b: 1) state that "[w]hile the Parliament embraced the Conference from the start and is prepared to go as far as citizens want to take it (including treaty change), and the Commission has taken on the managerial tasks of facilitating citizen participation, the Council has been rather more reticent, albeit with significant variations among individual member states." The main conflict was between the Council and the European Parliament. "The European Parliament and its main party groups had actively campaigned for the 'conference format'" in both various documents and in interaction with other actors (Johansson/ Raunio 2022: 25). Parliament perceived the CoFoE as an opportunity to have for the first time a direct and equal involvement in steering a reform process which, as it hoped for, was meant to result in a formal convention for treaty changes which could be used to strengthen the powers of the European Parliament similar to previous treaty changes.

In addition, there was a strong *intra-institutional* conflict especially inside the Council. Member states had different preferences in relation to conducting such a deliberative experiment at all as well as in relation to it specific goals and its proceedings (Ålander et al. 2021b). This latter conflict was indeed the main reasons why it lasted until May 2021 for the CoFoE to start: the Council of the EU adopted its revised position in February 2021. It was not until last minute that the inter-institutional conflict was then somewhat settled in a Joint Declaration in mid-March 2021 (Official Journal C 91 I). In this Declaration the European Parliament, the Council and the Commission emphasized the participatory nature of the event, by stating that it "is a *citizens-focused, bottom-up exercise* for Europeans to have their say on what they expect from the European Union" (ibid.: 1; emphasis in original).

"The Conference on the Future of Europe will open a new space for debate with citizens to address Europe's challenges and priorities. European citizens from all walks of life and corners of the Union will be able to participate, with young Europeans playing a central role in shaping the future of the European project.

We, the Presidents of the European Parliament, the Council and the European Commission want citizens to join the conversation and have their say on the future of Europe. We hereby jointly commit to listen to Europeans and to follow up on the recommendations made by Conference, in full respect of our competences and the subsidiarity and proportionality principles enshrined in the European Treaties.

We will seize the opportunity to underpin the democratic legitimacy and functioning of the European project as well as to uphold the EU citizens support for our common goals and values, by giving them further opportunities to express themselves" (ibid.).

However, many of the contested issues were not resolved when the Joint Declaration was adopted – including the raison d'être (Alemanno 2022). Many questions regarding the concrete organizational structure and the actual working of the different bodies involved were only discussed and decided on as the Conference process unfolded, underlining the experimental nature of the whole endeavour.

While there is certainly a lack of scholarly analysis of the CoFoE thus far, some observers argue that the CoFoE is more than a window of opportunity. Blokker (2021) argues that it could be a real "constitutional moment" which entails the potential for addressing the EU's "constitutional deficit". Also Alemanno and Nicolaïdis (2022) see CoFoE and its outcome as a starting point for developing a stronger pan-European public sphere and citizens' empowerment.

Others are much more sceptical, especially with a view on institutional conflicts. In a first analysis Fabbrini et al. (2021) conclude that to the European Parliament (and other supporters) the CoFoE provides a "vehicle for reform" whereas the Council considers it merely as a "forum for reflection". Hence, many observers see the risk that CoFoE could in the end be only window dressing without real institutional and policy impact – just as too many of the reform processes in the past.

Obviously, unlike previous instruments for discussing reforms such as the Constitutional Convention (see, for many, Cahill et al. 2019) or the numerous "reflection groups" (Abels 2010), which have accompanied European integration from the early days onwards, the core innovation of the CoFoE is that it aimed to bring citizens in. Moreover, it does so via different channels and innovative methods (see also discussion in Alemanno 2022). The core elements are

(1) direct involvement of 800 randomly selected citizens in the four European Citizens Panels (ECP) plus the participation of 80 of these citizens drawn by lot from these ECPs to act as "citizens ambassadors" in the Conference Plenary and its thematic working groups, and

(2) participation open to everybody via the digital Multilingual Digital Platform, which was equipped to automatically translate between all 24 official languages.[4]

The implications of this citizen-driven format and its success are still subject of discussion and require further analysis. For this volume it is most important that the conduct of deliberative events was not restricted to the supranational level only but was aimed to take place at all levels of the EU multi-level polity. The Joint Declaration contains a commitment that

"we [i.e. Council, Parliament and Commission] will organise events in partnership with civil society and stakeholders at European, *national, regional and local level*, with national and regional Parliaments, *the Committee of the Regions*, the Economic and Social Committee, social partners and academia. *Their involvement will ensure that the Conference goes far beyond* Europe's *capital cities and reaches every corner of the Union*" (Official Journal C 91 I: 2; emphasis added).

To ensure linkages to CoFoE and coherence of the process, organizers of events at national, regional, and local level were required to follow the Conference Charta and were asked to upload the results of the decentralized events onto the Multilingual Platform so that other can respond to them and for the results to be taken into account in the Conference Plenary's ten thematic working groups. It is against this background that the *core questions* underlying this collection of articles becomes evident: *If and how did member states – at national and at regional level – respond to and participate in the CoFoE? If and how was the role of actors at national and regional level discussed in the deliberative events?* While, as mentioned, a fundamental gap regarding research on CoFoE exists, this is even more so the case regarding the analysis of the numerous decentralized events that were conducted in a number of member states and its regions and municipalities. The focus of any academic analysis so far is clearly on the events at supranational level. Yet, given the multi-level nature of the EU polity, innovative instruments which aim at strengthening democratic resilience of the EU system also need to be rooted in and accompanied by developments at national and regional (and essentially also local) level.

In this introduction I will first sketch out the key conflicts regarding the governance structure and the main decisions taken regarding the role of the EU institutions in the CoFoE (section 2). This is not limited to the three key legislative institutions, but it also includes the role of the European Committee of the Regions (CoR) to which I will pay particular attention. The CoR is a key institution for the representation of territorial, i.e., subnational interests in the EU system. Besides the European Parliament also the CoR unfolded unprecedented institutional activism. It clearly regarded the CoFoE as a "window of opportunity" to strive for a stronger role in the EU polity (see Abels et al. 2021; see also the contribution by Petzold in this volume). Second, I will focus on the multi-level nature of the CoFoE. I will discuss in more detail why it is important to include the national *and* the regional level in this deliberative experiment and the response to and participation in the CoFoE at this level (section 3). In section 4 I will give an overview of the contributions in

---

4   See https://futureu.europa.eu/ (01.08.2022).

this volume before, finally, drawing some conclusions in relation to the follow-up of the CoFoE on the one hand and the gap for future research on the other hand (section 5).

2.   Looking back: How CoFoE got started and its core governance features

"The Conference is a *joint undertaking* of the European Parliament, the Council and the European Commission, *acting as equal partners* together with the Member States of the European Union. As signatories of this Joint Declaration, we commit to *working together throughout the Conference* and to dedicating the necessary resources to this endeavour" (Official Journal C 91 I: 1; emphasis added).

This compromise laid out in the Joint Declaration was anything but clear given the conflicts which have shaped the early days of CoFoE.

As already mentioned, the French Presidential initiative, which was then taken up by the new Commission President von der Leyen, was the starting point (see above). This was followed by a joint Franco-German initiative outlined in a non-paper as of November 2019. Both governments called for a future conference and a two-step process. In a first phase a discussion of "issues related to EU democratic functioning" (including the electoral system for the European Parliament and citizens' participation) should take place, then followed by a second phase devoted to policy priorities. The non-paper favours a "bottom-up process" with "EU-wide participation of our citizens on all issues discussed" (Franco-German non-paper 2019: 2). Yet, the non-paper with its intergovernmental underpinning neither specified the topics nor the composition in more detail. However, it did set the path for the summit of the European Council (EUCO) on 12 December 2019.

Despite differences among the heads of state and government, CoFoE was addressed in the summit conclusions. EUCO "considered the idea of a Conference on the Future of Europe" and asked the Croatian Council Presidency incoming in 2020 "to work towards defining a Council position on the content, scope, composition and functioning of such as conference" (EUCO 2019a: 3). The resolution also demanded that "priority should be given to implementing the Strategic Agenda" for 2019–2024 of the Council (ibid.), which contained four areas: "protecting citizens and freedoms; developing a strong and vibrant economic base; building a climate-neutral, green, fair and social Europe; promotion European interests and values on the global stage" (EUCO 2019b). In line with this EUCO conclusion, the Croatian Presidency then declared the future conference to be part of its priorities. With this decision, the CoFoE train has left the station – even if a number of hurdles were still to come.

At this point in time, in autumn 2019, the European Parliament was already discussing the idea and set up a special high-level working group consisting of one person per political group[5], plus members of the AFCO Committee for Constitutional Affairs. Having had a committee hearing on 4 December 2019 AFCO presented an opinion on 10 December 2019. In this opinion, the committee claimed a "leading role" for the European Parliament given that it is the only EU institution directly elected by the citizens. AFCO, and the European

---

5   Besides the President of the European Parliament, David Sassoli, who chaired the group, it consisted of Paulo Rangel (EPP), Gabriele Bischoff (S&D), Guy Verhofstadt (Renew), Daniel Freund (Greens/EFA), Gunnar Beck (ID), Zdzisław Krasnodębski (ECR), and Helmut Scholz (GUE/NGL); see EPRS 2019.

Parliament in general, welcomed the Conference as an opportunity for stronger, bottom-up involvement of citizens in a "meaningful dialogue" (European Parliament/AFCO 2019: 2). Moreover, it called for "an inclusive approach" and explicitly mentioned "age, gender, socio-economic diversity, and geographic balance in different pillars, of Members of the European Parliament, Members of national parliaments, the European Commission, the Council, civil society, social partners and citizens" (ibid.). As for the choice of topics, AFCO advocated "a mandate to identify and discuss a wide range of topics and policy areas that are of major importance for the future of Europe in the 21st century and represent core concerns of EU citizens" (ibid.: 3). It then went on to propose a not exhaustive list of topics. Unlike the Council in its EUCO conclusion, the European Parliament also included the option of treaty changes and a formal convention as a potential outcome of the future conference.

Based on the AFCO opinion, the plenary adopted a resolution on 15 January 2020 outlining the European Parliament's position on the future conference (European Parliament 2020). The "rather detailed resolution" was adopted with an overwhelming majority of 494 votes in favour, 147 against (mainly the Eurosceptic political groups) and 49 abstentions (Johansson/Raunio 2022: 29). This illustrates the building of a grand coalition and the salience of the future conference for the European Parliament. The resolution by and large followed the AFCO opinion, yet it developed much more detailed suggestions for the governance structure, organization, and composition of the different bodies. What is more, it also claimed Parliament leadership for the conference (with the liberal Guy Verhofstadt as Chair).

A few days later also the European Commission published it position. On 20 January 2020 it issued its communication arguing that CoFoE is essential to give a "new push for European democracy" and that citizens' participation must be at the heart (European Commission 2020: 1). It must be "a major pan-European democratic exercise" providing "*a new public forum for an open, inclusive, transparent and structured debate with citizens ...* from all walks of life, and from all corners of the Union" reflecting "*Europe's diversity*" (ibid.; emphasis in original). The Commission followed the line of the Franco-German non-paper by proposing an organization that follows two strands: one focusing on policy, the other on institutional matters – again the lead candidate system and transnational list are explicitly mentioned. The Commission's Political Guidelines plus the EUCO Strategic Agenda (EUCO 2019b) should frame the topics.

Regarding participation, according to the Commission the CoFoE can build on a rich experience with different forms of citizens' participation in Europe and previous dialogues organized by the Commission. Yet, the CoFoE should take participation "to the next level" via "the connection between citizens' views and practical policy-making" (European Commission 2020: 4). The Commission specifically proposed a "European citizens' panel" which must be "representative of geography, gender, age, socio-economic background and/or level of education of citizens" tasked to develop policy recommendations (ibid.).

The Commission emphasized that "*All Europeans should be given an equal opportunity to engage* – whether young or old, whether living in rural or urban areas and whether knowledgeable about the Union or not" (ibid: 4; emphasis in original). The conference should reach out to "the silent majority of Europeans, empowering them and giving them space to speak up" (ibid.). What is striking is the Commission's strong commitment to the outcomes: "The Commission is ready to *take into account citizens' feedback and proposals in the setting of its legislative agenda.*" (Ibid.: 6; emphasis in original).

In the aftermath of the Commission's communication the Covid-19 pandemic kicked in and it has, as mentioned, changed the timetable for the CoFoE. In addition – or rather: moreover – contestation among the national governments in the Council led to substantial delay, leading in the European Parliament to another resolution as of June 2020 in which it urged the Council to finally adopt a position.

Among national governments interest diverged on several key issues, especially institutional reform (above all: lead candidate principle and transnational lists in European elections), option for treaty reforms, and the policy fields to be prioritized in the process. Social policy, for instance, was important for hardly any member state in contrast to climate policy and competitiveness (see Ålander et al. 2021a/b). There was also divergence about how far any outcome of citizens consultations should be considered in the EU policy process. Most member states were reluctant and wanted to stick to the European Council's Strategic Agenda.

Unsurprisingly, the Council's position as of 24 June 2020 was the usual "lowest common denominator". The common position explicitly excluded that CoFoE falls within the scope of Article 48 TEU – thereby excluding treaty changes, which was a priority for the European Parliament from the very beginning. Furthermore, it favours a "policy-first approach" (Council of the EU 2020) and linked the choice of policies to the EUCO's Strategic Agenda 2019–2024. While calling for "effective involvement of citizens and stakeholders" (ibid.: 6), the Council position remained silent on the composition of these citizens' panels. The Council declared under the topic "guiding principles for the CoFoE" that it wants a "broad debate with citizens in the course of the process" (ibid.: 4) and welcomes citizens' "active participation and contribution in framing our joint vision of Europe's future" (ibid.: 5). This should be achieved "in various fora … to ensure a wide representation of different groups in our society" (ibid.), especially of young people. Yet, this still leaves room for how to do this.

An important dispute among the three EU institutions – especially among the European Parliament and the Council – in the months to follow was the governance structure in general and, most importantly, the leadership. In its original common position, the Council stated

"that the Conference could be placed *under the authority of an eminent European personality as its independent and single chair*; this personality should be able to represent the joint interests of the three EU institutions and be selected by mutual agreement among them." (Council of the EU 2020: 5; emphasis added)

The structure and mandate were a key concern for the like-minded group of 12 member states, also called "the EU's dirty dozen" (Financial Times, 23 March 2021, quoted in Blokker 2021: 330), which lobbied for a more restrictive view. In a non-paper as of March 2021 this group of more Eurosceptical national governments[6] emphasized that "The Conference's structure should be lean, streamlined and avoid any unnecessary bureaucracy. It should not create legal obligations, nor should it duplicate or unduly interfere with the

---

6   Austria, Czech Republic, Denmark, Estonia, Finland, Ireland, Latvia, Lithuania, Malta, the Netherlands, Slovakia, and Sweden.

established legislative processes." (Non-paper 2021). Furthermore, "Safeguarding the inter-institutional balance, including the division of competences" is paramount (ibid.).

Yet, what a lean structure could look like was disputed. The European Parliament did clearly not support a lean, intergovernmental dominated structure but lobbied for equal participation. In the end, this goal was achieved which is a considerable success for the Parliament. When comparing the original June 2020 Council position with the revised Council position as of February 2021 the main difference is the move towards joint leadership:

> "The Council considers that the Conference could be placed under the authority of the three European Institutions, represented by the President of the European Parliament, the President of the Council and the President of the European Commission, acting as a Joint Chairmanship." (Council of the EU 2021: 5)

Against the background of this revised position, it finally became possible to compromise on a Joint Declaration with the European Parliament and Commission. This Joint Declaration of March 2021 outlined the concept, scope, and structure of the CoFoE, committing all three EU institutions to the conference. The Declaration confirms that the CoFoE must be "a *citizens-focused, bottom-up exercise* for Europeans to have their say on what they expect from the European Union" (European Commission 2021: 3; emphasis in original).

Fig. 1: Set-up and process of CoFoE

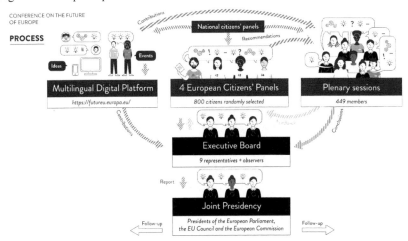

Source: Process of the Conference on the Future of Europe; see https://futureu.europa.eu/en/pages/information-material (15.12.2022).

At EU level European citizens' panels are considered a key tool (see Fig. 1). "These should be representative in terms of citizens' geographic origin, gender, age, socio-economic background and/or level of education" (ibid.). In addition, online participation should be a key bottom-up tool via the Multi-lingual Platform. Besides these tools, the Conference Plenary is established as a forum for thematic policy debates. It consists of a total of 449 members bringing together parliamentarians, stakeholders, EU institution representatives and citizens from the ECPs.

In addition to the joint presidency, the entire process was to be steered by an Executive Board co-chaired by all three EU institutions, each represented by three members. In addition, there was an observer status for other bodies and actors, among them national parliaments, social partners but also the European Committee of the Regions as well as the European Economic and Social Committee. For the monitoring of the CoFoE the Executive Board was the central body, while the Conference Plenary with its ten thematic groups became the main body for policy discussions and writing up of the final conference report. In terms of scope, the policy-first focus prevailed. Besides the EUCO's Strategic Agenda also the Political Guidelines of the von der Leyen Commission are mentioned while institutional reforms are side-lined.

The formal establishment has thereby ended and CoFoE was officially launched on "Europe Day", i.e., on 9 May 2021 – a year later than originally planned – resulting in an ambitious timeline (see Annex). Yet, also with its formal establishment not all organizational and political issues were resolved at this stage.

In sum, the analysis of the founding documents illustrates that CoFoE was strongly disputed among the EU institutions but also among the member states in many ways. Being "an out-of-the box initiative" (Fabbrini 2021: 402) it is not surprising that a lot of institutional activism was invested in the process and that the power play was intense. This is evident regarding the Council resp. EUCO and its internal dynamics, but also regarding the rivalry among the three EU institutions. Yet, the conference also provided an opportunity structure for EU bodies usually more at the margin. Of relevance for this special issue is the role of the Committee of the Regions in CoFoE – its origins, development, and follow-up (see also Petzold in this volume). The CoR was eager to fill this new format with life in the light of, firstly, previous experiences such as the constitutional convention in the early 2000s and, secondly, its manifold activities by which it has established itself as a policy-shaper "from below" (Piattoni/Schönlau 2015). Yet, when having a chance, the CoR also tries to influence *polity*-shaping in favour of a stronger role for subsidiarity concerns, for regions and for the CoR itself to expand the CoR's role "beyond mere consultation" (Schönlau 2017). In this sense, CoR turns to a strategy of "institutional acitivism" whenever a window of opportunity is perceived to be opened (see Abels et al. 2021).

In sum, over the course of two years during which the CoFoE was discussed and took shape, the various EU institutions and bodies tried to have an impact on the overall set-up in line with their specific but diverging preferences. Thus, in the end the CoFoE was – unsurprisingly – an inter- and intra-institutional compromise. Crucial issues were left unresolved and had to be discussed and solved as the conference unfolded.

3.   CoFoE – Why a national and regional perspective?

While the focus was on the EU level to give a new push to European democracy, CoFoE was more than just a supranational experiment. The multi-level nature of the EU polity must be considered in all discussion about democracy in resp. democratization of the EU. Hence, it also must be reflected in the CoFoE set-up. This becomes obvious when the Joint Declaration mentions

"Under the umbrella of the Conference and in full respect of the principles set out in this Joint Declaration, we will organise events in partnership with civil society and stakeholders at *European, national, regional and local level,* with national and regional Parliaments, *the Committee of the Regions*, the Economic and Social Committee, social partners and academia. *Their involvement will ensure that the Conference goes far beyond Europe's capital cities and reaches every corner of the Union*" (Official Journal C 91 I: 2; emphasis added).

This promise or announcement is at the heart of this special issue. The contributions to this special issue focus on the involvement of member states, and their regions, in relation to their CoFoE related activities. Before we address this in more detail, it is important to take a step back and ask why it is important to integrate this perspective.

Firstly, much has been written about the role of regions in European integration and about prospects of a "Europe of the regions" or "Europe with the regions". While these debates have been prominent in the 1980s and 1990s, they have been revived every now and then. The establishment of the CoR in 1992 is certainly an expression of the debates and of the demands of regions to play a stronger role in EU affairs (see Abels 2022a). With treaty changes since the mid-1990s and the Constitutional Convention of the early-2000s, not only the CoR but also the regions have often lobbied for a stronger role and increased competences (for a discussion see, for instance, Abels/Battke 2019; Große Hüttmann 2003; Hrbek 1996; Hrbek/Große Hüttmann 2002; Pahl 2003; Schakel/Massetti 2020). In this sense, the activism developed in the context of the CoFoE is neither new nor surprising, but it is intrinsically linked to the discourse over how to foster the democratization of the EU polity and which role regions can play (see Piattoni 2019). Strengthening the democratic functioning of the EU has been core to CoR activism since its inception. In its multi-annual work plan for 2020–2025 the CoR declared as a goal to "Rethink the EU democratic model to better reflect the role and responsibilities of regional and local authorities" in order to take decisions "as close as possible to citizens" (quoted in Abels 2022a: 387). Part of this initiative was, amongst other things, a campaign "reflecting on Europe" which involved local citizen's dialogues, surveys, and social media activities. The CoR's Draft Resolution VII/003 as of 11-12 February 2020 pointed to the need to integrate local and regional representatives to increase the visibility of the CoFoE on the ground (CoR 2020).

Against this background, the framing of the CoFoE by CoR representatives is telling. The CoR refers to the "house of European democracy" in which the municipalities and regions are the foundation. Furthermore, it refers to "1 million elected politicians" which it, the CoR, represents. The speech given by the then CoR President at the inaugural event of the Conference Plenary on place 19 June 2021 illustrates this quite well. President Apostolos Tzitzikostas said:

"The European Committee of the Regions (CoR) is the EU political Assembly representing one million local and elected politicians across Europe. Our priority is to make sure that the voice of our people in regions, cities and villages is heard. We will ensure that the proposals made by citizens during our local dialogues and the political input gathered via our Plenary sessions, via our Members' actions and via our key events will be taken up in the final report" (CoR 2021).

The CoR brought up a number of demands related to its own role in the EU polity as well as to the role of regions and municipalities. Towards the end of CoFoE the CoR adopted the "Marseille Manifesto of local and regional leaders" on 4 March 2022. In this manifesto it reinforces its expectations with regard to the CoFoE outcome and its own role, and it calls for more effective responses to the needs and aspirations of citizens (CoR 2022a).

In sum, the CoFoE offered the CoR and regional actors a window of opportunity to lobby for their cause of a stronger role in EU affairs – at domestic as well as at EU level. But the question is, how these actors made use of it and what were the effects? Were regional voices and preferences of regional actors represented in CoFoE and its outcome?

A clear success of regional lobbying was the change in the complex governance structure, especially the composition of the Executive Board and the Conference Plenary. These were the two main bodies to steer the CoFoE and to filter the debate and develop the final report. In response to lobbying, the CoR was included in the group of observers to the Executive Board. Furthermore, 18 members (out of a total of 449) in the Conference Plenary were then delegates of the CoR plus an additional 30 representatives from regional and local level (for details see Petzold in this volume).[7]

In addition, all national parliaments were represented in the Conference Plenary, both with a total of 108 representatives each (i.e. four representatives per national parliament) and COSAC (the body of European Affairs Committees from all national parliaments) received an observer status to the Executive Board along with the CoR.

A second strand of reasoning for considering national and regional perspectives comes from the development of the "deliberative wave" (OECD 2020) in Europe in the last two decades. CoFoE is indeed an expression of this turn towards experimenting with deliberative formats. The origins, however, come from the member states – and often from regional and local level developments. Deliberative formats, often called mini-publics, have gained prominence in many countries including Belgium, France, Germany or Ireland, and on a range of issues (see also Geissel 2019; Smith/Setälä 2018). At regional level, Baden-Württemberg is indeed one of the trailblazers (see Peters and Ziegenbalg in this volume) and so is Ostbelgien. Recently the citizen-driven model of participation adopted by the parliament of the German speaking community has gained international prominence (see Sautter and Reuchamps in this volume; see also Niessen/Reuchamps 2019). It has inspired development at local, national, and even supranational level.[8] With CoFoE we can now observe a remarkable adaptation of what started local now to the transnational level of the EU. Yet, CoFoE is not the first of its kind as far as it can build on deliberative formats, called Citizens' Dialogues, organized by the European Commission and private foundations especially in the aftermath of the constitutional crisis. Especially the Juncker Commission has expanded the use of this instrument since 2012 (see Johansson/Raunio 2022: 22). Hence, while there were forerunners, the overall design of CoFoE is new.

Member states involvement – at national and at regional level – happened in different forms. Regarding citizen participation, the European Citizens' Panels operated with national quota for the selection of citizens. The number of citizens randomly selected per member

---

7   Among these CoR delegates was also the President of the Land Parliament (Landtag) of Baden-Württemberg, Ms Muhterem Aras. For her experience and insights into the CoFoE and her expectations for the follow-up see her contribution in this volume.

8   For instance, the city of Aachen has recently decided to implement the model, Northern Ireland has developed an adapted version and finally it has inspired a proposal for institutionalizing citizen participation at EU level in the aftermath of CoFoE (see Abels et al. 2022).

states resembles the degressive proportionality principle in relation to the number of seats per member state in the European Parliament.

In addition, CoFoE aimed at mobilizing similar events in the member states – at national, regional, and local level. This happened to quite different degrees (see also the contributions in this volume). To do so, organizers of events in the member states had to commit themselves to the Conference Charta and to keep some of the design structures. Also, they were called to feed the results of their discussions into the Multilingual Platform. Yet, no legal requirement on the national governments existed to participate in CoFoE and to initiate national events. In the end, only a minority of member states conducted national events within the scope of CoFoE: Belgium, France, Germany, Italy, Lithuania, and the Netherlands. But also Austria was quite active. In addition, in several member states regions got engaged as for instance in Spain. In total, numerous decentral citizens' panels took place, some of which were transborder events bringing together regions from different member states. The CoR developed a programme to support the conduct of such decentral and trans-regional activities via providing resources and a toolbox.

Thirdly, the Multilingual Digital Platform was used in all member states. According to the official evaluation "a total of 7,005 events were registered on the platform" (CoFoE 2022a: 18) and in addition "48,530 contributions were collected" (ibid.: 15). Yet, there are vast differences regarding the number of entries coming from each member state (ibid.: 17). However, even if almost 50,000 contributions sound like a substantial number, in relation to the EU population it is small. The lack of attention for CoFoE in the media and the public at large in all member states is widely acknowledged and clearly one of the weak points.

4. Contributions in this volume

This volume builds on the contributions in the special section of the "Jahrbuch des Föderalismus 2022" (EZFF 2022). The collection of country reports has been expanded and the chapters were revised in light of the CoFoE follow-up in summer/autumn 2022. The contributions focus on how responses to CoFoE and strategies for participation in CoFoE were developed and implemented in select member states. In so doing they contribute to the analysis of CoFoE as a multi-level effort. The volume starts with a presentation on the involvement of the European Committee of the Regions (CoR) in the conference. *Wolfgang Petzold* analyses the process as well as the results of how the CoR participated in the CoFoE. He outlines that the CoR has become active early on, i.e. in 2019. It has hosted numerous meetings and has adopted several resolutions with the aim to play a role in the set-up and conduct of CoFoE and to lobby for recognition of regional aspects. It has – successfully – called for direct participation of representatives of the regional and local level to participate in the conference bodies, above all the Conference Plenary, but also for CoR participation – as observers – in the Executive Board. In addition, the CoR has hosted many "outreach events," it has commissioned surveys, and it has set up a High-Level Group on European Democracy chaired by Herman van Rompuy, the former EUCO President, to observe and give advice. The group published an analysis of the CoFoE (HLAG 2022). Finally, it has developed tools to empower regional and local actors to participate in CoFoE and to voice their concerns. Petzold argues that the final CoFoE report includes about "45 [measures] ... which appear to be of particular relevance for cities, regions, and the CoR", including measures to strengthen democracy. This is the effect of cross-partisan lobbying success. *Petzold* concludes that regions and cities are important in creating the "missing links" between citizens and the EU level, and that this can be done via different approaches.

Servane Metzger and *Matteo Torres-Ader* present the "French Perspective on the Conference on the Future of Europe". As said, the initiative goes back to an idea brought forward by the French President – and build on national experiences such as the *Citizens' Climate Convention* and the *Grand Débat National*. The national implementation was an important pillar of the French Council Presidency in 2022. The French national conference was aimed to be "complementary to the EU level exercise and enrich its results" and it was "100% citizen driven". Given the unitary nature of France, it come as a surprise that the approach was very territorial-based consisting of a total of 18 regional conferences. The regional panels were followed by a national panel leading to a synthesis report enclosing 14 proposals of what citizens want to see changed in the EU. A group of delegates from the regional events was then entrusted with the task to defend these overall ambitious and pro-integrationist French proposals in the Conference Plenary. The entire process and participatory methodology were monitored by a group of guarantors to enhance the credibility of the process.

Metzger and Torres-Ader see the CoFoE and its national implementation as a success. They call for deliberative events in the future to complement representative democracy and, hence establish a "hybrid model" aiming at "a renewed and truly political EU citizenship." However, they do see room for improvement in further events i.e. regarding the selection of participants, its timing in the EU policy process, the linkages between national and EU level events, the educational aspect and the transnational public discussion.

Belgium has become a trailblazer in pushing for new and, moreover, institutionalized forms of deliberative democracy in the last 20 years, starting at local level. This is the topic of the contribution "The Belgian experiments of deliberative democracy: An analysis of the institutionalisation of deliberative citizen participation in multi-level Belgium" by *Ann-Mireille Sautter* and *Min Reuchamps*. It is against this background that CoFoE was implemented and that it "was met with open arms" in Belgium, where a total of 26 events was organised.

Recently, a particular model has created great attraction – and even became a potential model for citizen participation at EU level (see Abels et al. 2022). In 2019 the parliament of the small German-speaking community has adopted the "Ostbelgien model" of Permanent Citizen Dialogue. Due to its innovative nature, it has met strong interest among scholars and policymakers in Belgium and beyond. While Belgium in general has followed a trend regarding deliberative democracy, the specific and citizen-driven model of institutionalization is a novelty, as the authors illustrate. The authors explain this trend using a "Three I's approach" according to which interests, ideas and institutions shape perceptions and formats of deliberation. A key aspect, which still requires more scholarly attention, is the role of Members of Parliaments within this process, which potentially challenges representative democracy.

Germany was one of the more active countries and one of the few member states where an official national citizens' panel was set up. In her contribution *Gabriele Abels* analyses the activities at federal and *Länder* level. Numerous actors involved in the supranational CoFoE governance structure were indeed from Germany. *Abels* situates the German response to CoFoE in the context of Franco-German relations and tensions of the past years. While the previous, Merkel IV government (2017–2021) was quite ambivalent towards CoFoE, the current "traffic light government" – consisting of the social democrats (red), the liberals (yellow) and the Greens – is more supportive towards the process and its outcome. Yet, given the overwhelming pro-integration stance in the German party system the differences are less relevant. The only exception is the right-wing populist or extremist AfD which was completely opposed to CoFoE as a biased form of citizen participation. The governmental activities at federal level were accompanied by parliamentary activities of the German *Bundestag* and the *Bundesrat* based on Article 23 of the constitution (Grundgesetz) outlining the right of participation of both actors in EU affairs. Simultaneously, a number of German *Länder* discussed CoFoE and adopted official positions. Many of them got engaged by organizing regional or transborder events, often emphasizing issues which are relevant for the regional level in regard to *Länder* involvement in EU affairs.

The most active state within Germany was clearly Baden-Württemberg. The state is a trailblazer regarding both regional involvement in EU affairs as well as citizens' participation. CoFoE allowed to combine engagement in both fields and to build on previous experiences. Therefore, its involvement in CoFoE is discussed in two separate chapters with different foci. *Muhterem Aras* participated in CoFoE in her capacity as President of the state parliament (Landtag) of Baden-Württemberg. Her active participation in the future conference builds on the long tradition of the *Landtag* of getting involved in EU affairs, which includes the representation of members of the *Landtag* – at least as alternates – in the CoR since its establishment almost thirty years ago. She was both a member of the CoR delegation to the Conference Plenary and of the Working Group on Climate Change and Environment, i.e. one of the ten thematic working groups in the Conference Plenary. In her contribution she elaborates on her overall very rewarding experiences of, and also her expectations about, the process – despite the strong time pressure of CoFoE.

Muhterem Aras is a strong advocate of CoFoE. She emphasizes that within CoFoE not only citizen participation was an absolute novelty, but also direct participation of regional politicians in a European institutionalised conference process. She praises the strong support and professionalism of the CoR for its delegation to the CoFoE. This direct involvement allowed regional actors to directly bring in their key demands, which she expects to be taken seriously in the ongoing follow-up process, i. e. the respect for the distribution of competences among the different levels in the EU system, and for the principles of subsidiarity and proportionality as enshrined in the Treaties. This is linked to institutional demands for changes in the so-called Early Warning System for subsidiarity control on the one hand and for strengthening the role and tasks of the CoR on the other hand. She welcomes that the final report included the demands raised by regional parliaments. They aim to improve the EU decision-making process in the direction of greater transparency for citizens and, in particular, of involvement of regional and local representatives to a greater extent.

In their article "The contribution of Baden-Württemberg to the Conference on the Future of Europe – Taking the conversation to the people" *Timo Peters* and *Florian Ziegenbalg* illustrate that Baden-Württemberg has been active as a European player since the 1980s; it has strongly supported the establishment of the CoR as a channel of influence for regional actors. Already before CoFoE the state government had initiated a "Dialogue on Europe" with citizens, resulting in a *Leitbild* establishing guiding principles for the state's approach to EU affairs. In this line not only the state parliament (see *Aras* in this volume), but also the state government welcomed the CoFoE and lobbied for regional actor involvement in the CoFoE via an initiative at domestic level in the German *Bundesrat* and at EU level. Also the Prime Minister himself, Winfried Kretschmann, participated in the CoFoE Executive Board from time to time as observer for the German COSAC presidency and State Secretary Hassler organized discussions and debriefings. Furthermore, the state government organized many citizens' dialogues in municipalities, but also cross-border – one of them being a six-region dialogue. Joint dialogues were conducted "with regions in France, Poland, the Czech Republic, Italy, Spain and in the Danube river region" in order to promote the development of "pan-European visions on the future of Europe". The findings were systematically evaluated and are included in a position paper of the state government. *Peters* and *Ziegenbalg* conclude that previous experiences were helpful and "indirectly served as a blueprint for the organisation" of CoFoE events. They consider CoFoE as "an incubator for a modern form of democratic participation at the European, regional, and local level" and call for more participation in the future; but resources mattered. In this sense, the support of the CoR and the program developed to facilitate local and regional participation was important.

The contribution by *Sarah Meyer, Lukas Böhm, Anna Dermitzakis, Leopold Kernstock, Oskar Kveton, Patrick Steindl, Melina Weilguni* and *Jasmin Zengin* on "Austria in the Conference on the Future of Europe" discusses CoFoE against the background of changes in the Austrian party system, changes in government, and strong Euroscepticism in the public. Based on document analysis, a survey and interviews, they illustrate that the development of the GAL-TAN cleavage (originally introduced by Marks and Hooghe) has an impact on Austria's European affairs politics and actors position towards CoFoE. Especially the role of the right-wing populist FPÖ is striking and resembles the populist response in other member states, i.e. while in favour of stronger citizens' involvement they strongly objected to CoFoE as a centralist, Brussels-based window-dressing show. But also the conservative ÖVP has taken on a much more Eurosceptical position than in the past.

The authors illustrate the range of activities at the national level and at the level of the *Länder*, including governmental as well as parliamentary responses to and participation in CoFoE. Clearly, for actors in the Austrian *Länder* CoFoE provided an opportunity to advocate for old claims again, i.e., for stronger regional involvement in EU affairs at domestic and at EU level. However, the authors conclude that "no major conflicts emerged in positioning towards and during the Conference between the federal and state levels." Finally, the chapter highlights some of the core issues for Austrian participation in CoFoE, such as its engagement for a role for accession countries from the Western Balkans as well as strong youth participation (Austria being the only member state where the general voting age is 16 years).

The contribution by *Mario Kölling* starts from the gap between the demands of the Spanish Autonomous Communities (AC) and their long-standing demands on stronger regional involvement in EU politics on the one hand and the (lack of) recognition of the territorial dimension and the subnational level in the official CoFoE final report on the other hand. Even if this gap did not come as a surprise given the citizen-focus of CoFoE, it still creates frustration – especially among regions with legislative competences such as the ACs in Spain. Overall, these regions have continuously called for stronger internal (i.e., domestic) as well as external (EU level) participation in EU affairs; the current systems is outlined by *Kölling* in his contribution. Almost all ACs made use of the numerous conferences organized by the national Spanish government within the CoFoE framework. AC government representatives voiced their demands regarding involvement of subnational actors, climate change policy, as well as their concerns about social and territorial cohesion. In addition, many contributions on CoFoE's digital platform on the issues of democracy come from Spanish commentators.

In addition, the Spanish ACs lobbied via different channels. Firstly, they networked with other legislative regions via RLEG to lobby via an open letter for stronger involvement of this group of 70 regional in the CoFoE governance structure, especially the Conference Plenary. Secondly, many of them signed the "Declaration on the place of regions in the European Union architecture in the context of the Conference on the Future of Europe," initiated in 2021 by an Alliance of Regions for European Democracy' together with, among others, the CoR. While acknowledging that the CoFoE was not intended to be "a framework for addressing the specific demands of subnational actors", this neglect due to the citizen-first and policy-first approach could explain the "low profile" all Spanish ACs have attributed to CoFoE.

Italy is another interesting case, since the country is one of the few which organized grand national events plus numerous additional activities. In her contribution *Susanna Cafaro*, who was one of the members of the Scientific Committee responsible for the national events, outlines the governance structure developed for CoFoE-related activities. The official objectives were two-fold: "(1) uploading of a significant number of contributions from Italy onto the platform and organizing many events; (2) spreading awareness of the democratic exercise". While the first goal was better achieved – Italy indeed came in second with regard to the number of events organised –, the second goal was less successful. However, with regard to the lack of media attention and awareness in the general public, Italy is not an exception.

Three aspects are particularly noteworthy in the Italian case: Firstly, the special committees established for the developing of a strategy; secondly, a dedicated budget for national (and regional) events; and, thirdly, the strong focus on young people. A number of creative tools and formats were developed and implemented in order to reach out to the young generation, including artist and creative competitions, TV commercials, events in universities and schools, involvement of social media influencers etc. Certainly, the diversified social media strategy is especially striking. *Cafaro* argues that "the focus on the younger segment of the population" was certainly "innovative for the Italian political experience". In that sense, CoFoE has fostered new opportunities for participation and involvement of younger people

26

in European politics. If this has a lasting effect remains to be seen. Italy was an outspoken advocate for treaty reforms under Prime Minister Mario Draghi. If this will continue to be the case with the new Meloni government is not so clear.

The Czech Republic is holding the rotating EU Presidency in the second half of 2022 and, hence, it must manage the immediate follow-up process. In this respect it is particularly interesting, how CoFoE was perceived and implemented in Czechia. This is the topic of the contribution by *Jarolim Antal*. He poses the question if CoFoE was a success or failure. In the Czech Republic, both parliamentary chambers, the Chamber of Deputies as well as the Senate, called for a strong involvement of national parliaments in CoFoE's Conference Plenary and the Executive Board. The observer status in the latter body was criticized as insufficient. The actual implementation of CoFoE was coordinated by the Office of the Government; overall, the government was skeptical and objected any need for treaty reform as a potential outcome. It supported the policy-first approach of the European Council (EUCO). The main aim was then "to verify whether opinions of citizens [in Czechia; GA] comply with" the EUCO policy agenda via a National Convention and the network of Eurocentres. A total of 114 events, including seven regional flagship debates plus three transnational (regional) debates were conducted focusing on four topics. The National Convention in the Czech Republic concluded "that COFE has been successful, as it engaged the citizens and triggered the discussion." Yet, it becomes clear that citizens' attitudes towards the EU are mixed.

5.   What's next? CoFoE follow-up

The Conference on the Future of Europe ended on 9 May 2022. The European Citizens' Panels prepared a total of 178 recommendations, only few of them addressing issues relevant to the territorial dimension of the EU. The recommendations were discussed in the Conference Plenary and – together with some input from the digital consultation platform – condensed to a report containing 49 proposals and 326 measures. The final report was prepared and adopted by the Executive Board (CoFoE 2022b). The rivalries among the main EU institutions have shaped the entire process towards the end; they have affected the discussions over the final report and now impact upon the follow-up. Credible commitment to the CoFoE process was a key concern and the institutions were aware that taking citizens' recommendations seriously was a key issue. Given the normal slow decision-making process in the EU, all three main institutions have developed a response in "warp speed" (see von Ondarza/Ålander 2022; see also Petzold in this volume).

The European Parliament was again the frontrunner. Early on, even before the final report was adopted and officially presented, it interpreted the Conference Plenary report as pointing towards treaty change via a convention (European Parliament 2022a). In its resolution as of 4 May, i.e. five days before the official closing ceremony, it proclaims that it "(s)tands ready to play its role and ensure proper follow-up to the Conference outcome" (European Parliament 2022c: point 15). It declares that it calls "for the convening of a Convention by activating the procedure for the revision of the Treaties provided for in Article 48 of the Treaty on European Union, and calls on its Committee on Constitutional Affairs to launch the necessary procedure accordingly" (ibid.).

This is an absolute novelty: for the first time the Parliament made use of this competence it gained with the 2009 Lisbon Treaty. Until then such conventions have been initiated by the Council only. A month after the end of CoFoE, on 9 June, the European Parliament adopted another resolution – with 355 votes in favour – whereby it calls on the European Council to agree to starting a process for treaty reforms on a number of institutional issues and social policy reforms (European Parliament 2022b). Ever since then the European Parliament's Committee on Constitutional Affairs (AFCO) is engaged in detailed stock-taking of the treaties based on Article 48, 2 TEU, which requires to "submit to the Council proposals for the amendment of the Treaties" as part of the ordinary revision procedure for treaty changes. These activities also involve the discussion as well as the commissioning of a study on establishing a permanent participatory mechanism to involve citizens (European Parliament/ AFCO 2022). It also comprises, for instance, activities of the European Parliament's Committee for Women's Rights and Gender Equality for drafting an explicit "EU Women's Rights Charter". Hence, the European Parliament has developed a remarkable degree of institutional activism to change the treaty, expand its mandate and emphasize crucial issues.

The situation and response are very different in the Council. Just from the very start, the Council was still split into two factions – with hardly any change between the two groups. On the same day when the final CoFoE report was published, a group of 13 member states – mainly CEE plus all Baltic and Scandinavian member states[9] – presented a short non-paper declaring: "We recall that Treaty change has never been a purpose of the Conference. What matters is that we address the citizens' ideas and concerns" (Permanent Representation of Sweden to the European Union 2022). Only a few days later, a group of six member states – Belgium, Germany, Italy, Luxembourg, the Netherlands, and Spain – published their own non-paper on 13 May 2022. Therein they declare to "remain in principle open to necessary treaty changes that are jointly defined" (Non-paper 2022). France has also voiced its support for the latter position. However, given its role as Council President in the first half of 2022 it formally stayed neutral. Concurrently, the Council's General Secretariat prepared a "technical assessment" scanning all measures proposed in the final report with a view on implementation (General Secretariat of the Council 2022). According to this assessment most proposals in the report do not require any treaty change while claiming that the EU is already active on a number of policy issues mentioned in the final report. Hence, further activities in line with the citizens' recommendations would only be necessary on few issues.

The last compromise adopted thus far was the Conclusion of the European Council (EUCO) Summit on 23–24 June 2022, which entails only a short reference to CoFoE. It emphasizes that it was a "unique opportunity to engage with European citizens" (EUCO 2022: 7). Furthermore, it states that the "EU institutions should ensure that there is an effective follow-up to the final report, each within the institutions' own spheres of competence and in accordance with the Treaties" (ibid.). The current (i.e. 2022) Czech Council

---

9 Bulgaria, Croatia, the Czech Republic, Denmark, Estonia, Finland, Latvia, Lithuania, Malta, Poland, Romania, Slovenia, and Sweden.

Presidency declares "resilience of democratic institutions" as a priority for its Council Programme in 2022 and promises to "continue the discussion in the Council of the EU on the implementation of its results" (Czech Council Presidency 2022: 14). Yet no concrete action is envisaged and the Presidency was is not actively supporting the follow-up.

Finally, the Commission issued a communication on 17 June 2022 on how it will organize the follow-up (European Commission 2022b). It declares that it considers the CoFoE successful with regard to citizen participation and that it intends to introduce a "new generation" (ibid.: 5) of Citizens Panels. These shall "enable Citizens Panels to deliberate and make recommendations ahead of certain key proposals, as part of its wider policy making and in line with Better Regulation principles" (ibid.). In addition, in the annex to the communication the Commission announces to "consider new areas of action" which include helping to "build capacity among national, regional and local actors to launch a new generation of decentralised citizens' dialogues built on deliberative approaches"; it also intends to: "Develop a European Charter for Citizens' Participation targeted at all those who participate in or organise citizen engagement activities promoting the general principles that are essential for successful citizen engagement" (European Commission 2022a: 25). This ambition of the Commission to act as the frontrunner for the promotion of citizens' deliberation and standard-setter is remarkable given the subnational origin of deliberative citizens' participation. In this spirit, Commission President von der Leyen announced in her State of the Union Address (SOTEU) on 14 September 2022 that "(t)he Citizens' Panels that were central to the Conference will now become a regular feature of our democratic life" (von der Leyen 2022). She announced that first European Citizens' Panels will be organized in 2023 on issues such as of food waste, learning mobility and virtual worlds (Greubel 2022: 4). The key to this new generation of deliberative panels is that citizens "can make recommendations before certain key policy proposals" are tabled (von der Leyen, quoted in Greubel 2022: 5).

On the controversial issue of treaty changes, which is most important for the European Parliament, the Commission is, however, reluctant:

"the Commission will always be on the side of those who want to reform the European Union to make it work better, including through Treaty change where that may be necessary … In this spirit, … (t)he Commission stands ready to fully play its institutional role in the procedure set out in Article 48 of the Treaty on European Union" (European Commission 2022b: 4).

Unsurprisingly, the CoR has also been active in discussing and defining the outcome and follow-up in line with its own institutional interest and its perception of the need for EU multi-level democratization. At its plenary session on 29–30 June 2022 the CoR adopted a resolution in which it supports citizens' calls for stronger democratic practices, including "more active inter-institutional cooperation" (CoR 2022b: point 2), and "highlights that many of the proposals made in the final CoFoE report refer to an active involvement of regions and local authorities, both in the design and the delivery of initiatives" (ibid.: point 3). It supports the European Parliament's call for a formal convention and the activation of Article 48 TEU and it calls for full involvement of the CoR in such a process (ibid.: point 4f.). It also supports, for instance, the proposals for "enhanced inter-institutional synergies involving the CoR" in a wider range of policy sectors (ibid.: points 7, 10).

This is certainly not the end of the story. What becomes clear is that the CoFoE was conducted in times of crisis for the EU and was meant to develop an impetus for future developments. Yet, it is also clear that the ambitions and preferences of the EU institutions and bodies regarding CoFoE varied strongly. Different ideas about the *raison d'etre*, about the mandate and the outcome dominated the entire process and led to intense rivalry among the institutions and disputes within the Council. In this sense, also CoFoE was clearly afflicted by the ubiquitous struggle over supranational vs. intergovernmental influence in and on the EU. Against this background, the contestation regarding the interpretation of the results and the way forward do not come as a surprise. In other words, the challenge is now "the complex implementation of high ambitions" (Maurice 2022). The institutionalization of citizens' participation, as promised by Commission President von der Leyen in her 2022 State of the Union Address, is just one out of many.

6.   Research perspectives

Given the novelty, research on CoFoE is still in its infancy. So far, only a handful of scholarly texts are published. More will certainly follow in the future. Clearly, for the years to come more in-depth research is needed on CoFoE's innovative nature, the politics behind it, its implementation, and its long-term effects on the EU polity. Scholarly analysis of the CoFoE will most likely focus on development at supranational level. Yet, as the papers in this volume illustrate, this research must reflect the multi-level nature of the EU. It must also include the involvement of the member states as well as of the subnational, regional level and its actors in the process. They were invited to contribute to CoFoE. Even if they did engage in different forms and to different degrees, this is an important aspect and must be considered in future research. The contributions illustrate that comparative research is needed to explain similarities and difference. Relevant factors could be, for instance, division of territorial competences, executive-parliamentary relations, European integration and party politics, level of activity and participation rights of parliaments in EU affairs, previous experiences with instruments of deliberative democracy, etc. Also the CoR certainly deserves further inspection. Its CoFoE-related activities and the way in which it supported the mobilization of regions can be linked to it manifold and remarkable "extra-curricular" activities (Hönnige/Panke 2016: 624).

This aspect is only one of the many research gaps which need to be addressed. Future research must study how CoFoE fits into the larger picture of European integration. CoFoE can and should be linked to previous constitution-making experiences and their interpretation in terms of theories of European integration. Useful starting points could be, for instance, Göler and Marhold (2005). They have discussed the deliberative nature of the Constitutional Convention and if the Convention, which was also considered to be of an experimental nature, has the potential to serve as a model for future reforms. In this sense, the deliberative nature of CoFoE is striking. Moreover, the composition of the Conference Plenary resembles the composition of the Convention – but develops it further with regard to "equal footing" among the three core EU institutions. Furthermore, it adds the group of citizens and, hence, expands the participatory nature.

30

Another inspiration comes from Christiansen and Reh (2009) who argue that constitutionalization has many faces. They distinguish between implicit and explicit, formal and informal constitutionalization as a more dynamic process. In this sense, CoFoE could be viewed as a process of a more implicit and informal constitutional nature. Also Blokker (2021: 330) argues in this line. He claims that even "if the Council denies the Conference's status of a convention, the endeavour nevertheless echoes the Convention on the Future of Europe of the early 2000s in name, but also in its set up". A difference to previous conventions is, however, the role of citizens and of strong civil society engagement.[10] This requires a more sociological interpretation of EU reform processes beyond the intergovernmental accounts which dominate the scholarly debates on treaty reforms.

CoFoE could be an interesting case for testing postfunctionalist interpretations of European integration, which contend that European integration is becoming increasingly contested – and even more so in response to the poly-crisis (see Kriesi 2016). In contrast to these findings the manifold recommendations and contributions to CoFoE point, by and large, into the direction of "more" and "stronger Europe". This leads right-wing populist parties to question the representative nature and random sampling of the citizens involved in the process. These observations could feed into discussions about politicization of European integration and how government can deal with it.

Also gender perspective can be fruitful. CoFoE is the first reform discussion in the EU with gender parity being implemented, at least in terms of numbers. This is already remarkable. Lombardo (2007) has analysed the Constitutional Convention as a constitutional moment which was really a disappointment regarding gender representation. In a preliminary analysis Abels (2022b) has adopted Lombardo's five dimensional analytical framework, which she applied to CoFoE. She illustrates the progress made in relation to gender representation in the last two decades. CoFoE provided for gender parity in terms of numbers of women participating in the citizens' panels as well as from the various political institutions; this is a great achievement (also in comparison to constitution-making on a global scale; see Rubio-Marín 2020: 237f.). However, this descriptive parity is hardly reflected in the discussions and the citizens' recommendations and the final CoFoE report, providing evidence that descriptive representation does not translate into substantive policy representations per se. Given "women's foundational exclusion and gradual inclusion into constitution-making" (Rubio-Marín 2020: 235) also in relation to European integration – the famous "founding fathers"[11], studies on gender and participatory constitutionalism can therefore provide insights of what would be required to achieve gender equality also in terms of outcomes and thereby women's equal citizenship (cf. Rubio-Marín 2020).

The multitude of old, new, and often critical approaches in the field of integration theories can certainly be useful for studying and making sense of CoFoE. Looking back, we can state that the previous "Convention on the Future of Europe" was taking place when the EU was still on fairly safe ground, i.e. before what has become known as the "poly-crisis" – or even "perma-crisis" – kicked in (for a detailed account see Riddervold et al. 2021). Starting with the Euro or debt crisis in 2009, the Schengen or refugee crisis in 2015, the rule

---

10 Such as the network Citizens Take Over Europe; see https://citizenstakeover.eu/ (14.08.2022).
11 For a critique and discussion of "founding mothers" see Abels/MacRae 2021.

of law crisis and democratic backsliding, the Brexit crisis in 2016, the Covid-19 pandemic in 2020, and now the return of war in Europe with the Russian invasion in Ukraine and a changing global order – all a major stress test for European integration intensified by their overlapping and dynamic nature and resulting in shifts in the EU power balance. Against this background CoFoE is an outstanding "European reform initiative that goes beyond crisis management" (von Ondarza/Ålander 2021), but which is clearly linked to crisis management and the search for the meaning of European integration. It certainly deserves theory-driven scholarly attention, but also political response by policy-makers, civil society, and citizens.

With regard to the CoR, its involvement in CoFoE is worth further in-depth analysis, for instance in comparison to previous processes of treaty reforms and the Convention on the future of Europe. The CoR's position could be characterized as strong "institutional activism" (cf. Abels et al. 2021), which was successful with regard to the inclusion of CoR representatives and CoR demands in the CoFoE process and the final report. CoFoE clearly provided the CoR with a window of opportunity to develop its role as a lobbyist for regions and municipalities in Europe. If this may have long-term effects e.g. on coalition-building, and division of competences remains to be seen and deserves further research.

Finally, CoFoE may be the start for stronger institutionalization of citizens' deliberations in the EU polity. The Commission announced to have three such transnational deliberations as part of its 2023 work programme; the first one on food waste in spring 2023. This fascinating development certainly offers opportunities for stronger linkages between the strong academic research on mini-publics and deliberation and EU studies. Further proposals for institutionalization (e.g. Abels et al. 2022) are on the table and need to be discussed in academia as well as by policy-makers.

7. References

Abels, Gabriele 2010: Reflexionsgruppen und ihr Einfluss auf den Integrationsprozess: Anmerkungen zu einem Instrument expertokratischer Politikberatung in der EU, in: *Abels, Gabriele/Eppler, Annegret/Knodt, Michèle (eds.)*: Die EU-Reflexionsgruppe „Horizont 2020–2030": Herausforderungen und Reformoptionen für das Mehrebenensystem, Baden-Baden, pp. 65–90.

Abels, Gabriele 2022a: The European Economic and Social Committee and the Committee of the Regions: Consultative Institutions in a Multichannel Democracy, in: *Hodson, Dermot/Puetter, Uwe/Saurugger, Sabine/Peterson, John (eds.)*: Institutions of the European Union, 5th revised edition, Oxford, pp. 369–390.

Abels, Gabriele 2022b: Gender, democracy and the Conference on the Future of Europe (CoFoE), paper presented at the 11th Biennial Conference of the SGEU, 8–10 June 2022 at Luiss University, Rome.

Abels, Gabriele/Alemanno, Alberto/Crum, Ben/Demidov, Andrey/Hierlemann, Dominik/ Renkamp, Anna/Trechsel, Alexander 2022: Next level citizen participation in the EU: Institutionalising European Citizens' Assemblies, Gütersloh.

Abels, Gabriele/Battke, Jan 2019: Regional Governance in the EU or: What Happened to the 'Europe of the Regions'? – Introduction, in: *Gabriele Abels/Jan Battke (eds.)*:

Regional Governance in the EU: Regions and the Future of Europe, Cheltenham, UK, Northampton, MA, USA, pp. 1–14.

Abels, Gabriele/Große Hüttmann, Martin/Meyer, Sarah/Lenhart, Simon 2021: The Committee of the Regions and the Conference on the Future of Europe, in: *Abels, Gabriele (eds.)*: From takers to shapers? Challenges for regions in a dynamic EU polity, EZFF Occasional Paper No. 43, Tübingen, pp. 23–44.

Abels, Gabriele/MacRae, Heather 2021: Whose Story is it Anyway? Studying European Integration with a Gender Lens, in: *Abels, Gabriele/Krizsán, Andrea/MacRae, Heather/ van der Vleuten, Anna (eds.)*: The Routledge Handbook of Gender and EU Politics. Abingdon, New York, pp. 1-14.

Ålander, Minna/von Ondarza, Nicolai/Russack, Sophia 2021a: Introduction, in: *Ålander, Minna/von Ondarza, Nicolai/Russack, Sophia (eds.)*: Managed Expectations: EU Member States' Views on the Conference on the Future of Europe, EPIN Report, Berlin, pp. 1–7.

Ålander, Minna/von Ondarza, Nicolai/Russack, Sophia (eds.) 2021b: Managed Expectations: EU Member States' Views on the Conference on the Future of Europe, EPIN Report, Berlin.

Alemanno, Alberto 2022: Unboxing the Conference on the Future of Europe and its democratic raison d'être, in: European Law Journal, https://doi.org/10.1111/eulj.12413, pp. 1–25.

Alemanno, Alberto/Nicolaidis, Kalypso 2022: Citizen Power Europe: The Making of a European Citizens' Assembly, in: Revue Européenne du Droit 3. https://papers.ssrn.com/sol3/papers.cfm?abstract_id=4000490 (02.08.2022).

Armstrong, Kenneth 2019: Has the Spitzenkandidaten System Failed and Should We Care? https://bit.ly/3cnpsPh (08.08.2022).

Blokker, Paul 2021: The Constitutional Deficit, Constituent Activism, and the (Conference on the) Future of Europe, in: *Blokker, Paul (ed.)*: Imagining Europe: Transnational Contestation and Civic Populism, Cham, pp. 303–340.

Cahill, Maria/Barber, Nicholas William/Elkins, Richard (eds.) 2019: The Rise and Fall of the European Constitution, Oxford, Portland.

Christiansen, Thomas/Reh, Christine 2009: Constitutionalizing the European Union, Basingstoke.

CoFoE 2022a: Multilingual Digital Platform of the Conference on the Future of Europe, Final Report, May 2022, https://bit.ly/3BLErNe (08.08.2022).

CoFoE 2022b: Report on the final outcome, May 2022. https://futureu.europa.eu/pages/reporting (02.08.2022).

Committee of the Regions 2020: Draft resolution on the Conference on the Future of Europe, RESOL VII/003, 138th plenary session, 11-12 February 2020. https://cor.europa.eu/en/news/Documents/Draft%20Resolution%20Conference%20Future%20of%20Europe.pdf (02.08.2022).

Committee of the Regions 2021: CoR delegation ready to represent 1 million regional and local elected politicians at the Plenary of the Conference on the Future of Europe. Press release, 16 June 2021. https://cor.europa.eu/en/news/Pages/CoFoE-plenary-19-June.aspx (02.08.2022).

Committee of the Regions 2022a: The Marseille Manifesto of local and regional leaders: "Europe starts in its regions, cities and villages". https://cor.europa.eu/en/summits/2022/Pages/Manifesto.aspx (05.12.2022).

Committee of the Regions 2022b: The outcome and follow-up on the Conference on the Future of Europe, Resolution adopted on 30 June 2022. https://memportal.cor.europa.eu/Public/Documents/MeetingDocuments?meetingId=2182079&meetingSessionId=22278 31 (04.07.2022).

Council of the European Union 2020: Conference on the Future of Europe, 9102/20, Brussels, 24.06.2020.

Council of the European Union 2021: Conference on the Future of Europe – revised Council position, 5911/21, Brussels, 03.02.2021.

Czech Presidency of the Council of the EU 2022: Europe as a Task: Rethink, Rebuild, Repower, Programme. https://czech-presidency.consilium.europa.eu/media/ddjjq0zh/programme-cz-pres-english.pdf (02.08.2022).

European Commission 2020: Communication from the Commission to the European Parliament and the Council: Shaping the Conference on the Future of Europe, COM(2020) 27 final, Brussels, 22.01.2020.

European Commission 2021: Conference on the Future of Europe – Joint Declaration. https://ec.europa.eu/info/sites/default/files/en_-_joint_declaration_on_the_conference_on_the_future_of_europe.pdf (02.08.2022).

European Commission 2022a: Annex to the Communication from the Commission to the European Parliament, the European Council, the Council, the European Economic and Social Committee and the Committee of the Regions, Conference on the Future of Europe: Putting Vision into Concrete Action, COM(2022) 404 final, Brussels, 17.06.2022.

European Commission 2022b: Communication from the Commission to the European Parliament, the European Council, the Council, the European Economic and Social Committee and the Committee of the Regions, Conference on the Future of Europe: Putting Vision into Concrete Action, COM(2022) 404 final, Brussels, 17.06.2022.

European Council (EUCO) 2019a: Conclusions of European Council meeting, EUCO 29/19, Brussels, 12.12.2019.

European Council (EUCO) 2019b: A new strategic agenda for the EU 2019-2024. https://www.consilium.europa.eu/en/eu-strategic-agenda-2019-2024/ (02.08.2022).

European Council (EUCO) 2022: Conclusions of the European Council meeting (23 and 24 June 2022) – Conclusions, EUCO 24/22, Brussels, 24.06.2022.

European Parliament 2020: European Parliament resolution of 15 January 2020 on the European Parliament's position on the Conference on the Future of Europe, P9_TA(2020)0010, Strasbourg, 15.01.2020.

European Parliament 2022a: Future of Europe: Conference Plenary ambitious proposals point to Treaty review. Press release 30 April 2022. https://www.europarl.europa.eu/

news/en/press-room/20220429IPR28218/future-of-europe-conference-plenary-ambitious-proposals-point-to-treaty-review (07.05.2022).

European Parliament 2022b: Parliament activates process to change EU Treaties, Press Release 9 June 2022. https://www.europarl.europa.eu/news/en/headlines/priorities/eu-future-conference-follow-up/20220603IPR32122/parliament-activates-process-to-change-eu-treaties (02.08.2022).

European Parliament 2022c: Resolution of 4 May 2022 on the follow-up to the conclusions of the Conference on the Future of Europe, P9_TA(2022)0141, Strasbourg, 04.05.2022.

European Parliament Research Service (EPRS) 2019: Preparing the Conference on the Future of Europe, EPRS Briefing, PE 644.202 – December 2019.

European Parliament/Committee on Constitutional Affairs (AFCO) 2019: Opinion on the Conference on the Future of Europe, adopted 10 December 2019. https://www.europarl.europa.eu/cmsdata/194307/Adopted%20opinion%20CoFoE_10122019-original.pdf (02.08.2022).

European Parliament/Committee on Constitutional Affairs (AFCO) 2022: Towards a permanent citizens' participatory mechanism in the EU. Study authored by Alberto Alemann, PE 735.927. https://www.europarl.europa.eu/RegData/etudes/STUD/2022/735927/IPOL_STU(2022)735927_EN.pdf (14.11.2022).

EZFF (Europäisches Zentrum für Föderalismus-Forschung) 2022: Jahrbuch des Föderalismus 2022, Baden-Baden.

Fabbrini, Federico 2021: The Conference on the Future of Europe: Process and prospects, in: European Law Journal 26 (5–6), pp. 401–414.

Fabbrini, Sergio/Fossum, Jan Erik/Góra, Magdalena/Wolff, Guntram 2021: Conference on the Future of Europe: Vehicle for reform or forum for reflection? EU3D Policy Brief No. 1, Oslo: ARENA Centre for European Studies.

Franco-German non-paper 2019: Conference on the Future of Europe: Franco-German non-paper on key questions and guidelines. https://www.politico.eu/wp-content/uploads/2019/11/Conference-on-the-Future-of-Europe.pdf (30.04.2022).

Geissel, Brigitte 2019: Democratic innovations in Europe, in: *Estub, Stephen/Escobar, Oliver (eds.)*: Handbook of Democratic Innovations and Governance, Aldershot, pp. 404–420.

General Secretariat of the Council of the EU 2022: Conference on the Future of Europe - Proposals and related specific measures contained in the report on the final outcome of the Conference on the Future of Europe: Preliminary technical assessment, 10033/22, Brussels, 10.06.2022.

Göler, Daniel/Marhold, Hartmut 2005: Die Konventsmethode. Institutionelles Experiment oder Modell für die Zukunft?, in: *Jopp, Mathias/Matl, Saskia (eds.)*: Der Vertrag über eine Verfassung für Europa. Analysen zur Konstitutionalisierung der EU, Baden-Baden, pp. 453–472.

Greubel, Johannes 2022: A new generation of European Citizens' Panels – Making citizens' voices a regular part of policymaking, European Policy Centre (EPC) Discussion Paper, October 2021, https://bit.ly/3PmMAwd (17.11.2022).

Große Hüttmann, Martin 2003: Der Konvent und die Neuordnung der Europäischen Union: Eine Bilanz verschiedener Verfassungsvorschläge aus Sicht der Länder und Regionen, in: *Europäisches Zentrum für Föderalismus-Forschung (ed.)*: Jahrbuch des Föderalismus 2003, Tübingen, pp. 423–443.

High-Level Advisory Group (HLAG) 2022: Conference on the Future of Europe: What worked, what now, what next?, HLAG Report, Conference on the Future of Europe Observatory, 22.02.2022. https://bit.ly/3HwyiqY (02.08.2022).

Hönnige, Christoph/Panke, Diana 2016: Is anybody listening? The Committee of the Regions and the European Economic and Social Committee and their quest for awareness, in: Journal of European Public Policy 23 (4), pp. 624–642.

Hrbek, Rudolf (ed.) 1996: Regionen und Kommunen in der EU und die Regierungskonferenz 1996, EZFF Occasional Paper No. 13, Tübingen.

Hrbek, Rudolf/Große Hüttmann, Martin 2002: Von Nizza über Laeken bis zum Reformkonvent: Die Rolle der Länder und Regionen in der Debatte zur Zukunft der Europäischen Union, in: *Europäisches Zentrum für Föderalismus-Forschung (ed.)*: Jahrbuch des Föderalismus 2002, Tübingen, pp. 577–594.

Johansson, Karl Magnus/Raunio, Tapio 2022: The partisan dimension of the Conference on the Future of Europe. Agenda-setting, objectives and influence, SIEPS Report No 2. https://bit.ly/3QKSWWa (02.08.2022).

Kriesi, Hanspeter 2016: The Politicization of European Integration, in: JCMS Annual Review of the European Union in 2015 54 (S1), pp. 32–47.

Lombardo, Emanuela 2007: Gender Equality in the Constitution-Making Process, in: *Castiglione, Dario/Schönlau, Justus/Longman, Chris/Lombardo, Emanuela/Pérez-Solórzano Borragán, Nieves/Aziz, Miriam (eds.)*: Constitutional Politics in the European Union. The Convention Moment and its Aftermath, Basingstoke, pp. 137–152.

Macron, Emmanuel 2019: For European renewal, 04.03.2019. https://www.elysee.fr/en/emmanuel-macron/2019/03/04/for-european-renewal (20.04.2022).

Maurice, Eric 2022: Conference on the Future of Europe: the complex implementation of high ambitions, European issues no 636, Fondation Robert Schuman Policy Paper.

Niessen, Christoph/Reuchamps, Min 2019: Designing a Permanent Deliberative Citizens' Assembly: The Ostbelgien Modell in Belgium, Working Paper Series of the Centre for Deliberative Democracy and Global Governance. https://pure.unamur.be/ws/portalfiles/portal/43760057/Niessen_Reuchamps_2019_Designing_a_permanent_deliberative_citizens_assembly.pdf (02.08.2022).

Non-paper 2021: Conference on the Future of Europe: Common approach amongst Austria, Czech Republic, Denmark, Estonia, Finland, Ireland, Latvia, Lithuania, Malta, the Netherlands, Slovakia and Sweden. https://bit.ly/3wuOHpI (23.07.2022).

Non-paper 2022: Non-paper submitted by Germany, Belgium, Italy, Luxembourg, the Netherlands, and Spain on implementing the proposals of the Plenary of the "Conference on the Future of Europe" 2022, 13.05.2022. https://twitter.com/alemannoEU/status/1526922932970262528 (02.08.2022).

OECD 2020: Innovative Citizen Participation and New Democratic Institutions: Catching the Deliberative Wave. https://bit.ly/3YnuSx0 (02.08.2022).

Official Journal 2021: Joint Declaration of the European Parliament, the Council and the European Commission on the Conference on the Future of Europe – Engaging with citizens for democracy – Building a more resilient Europe, OJ C 91 I/01, Brussels, 18.03.2021.

Pahl, Marc-Oliver 2003: Die Rolle der Regionen mit Gesetzgebungskompetenzen im Konventsprozess, in: *Europäisches Zentrum für Föderalismus-Forschung (ed.)*: Jahrbuch des Föderalismus 2003, Tübingen, pp. 462–479.

Permanent Representation of Sweden to the European Union 2022: Non-paper by Bulgaria, Croatia, the Czech Republic, Denmark, Estonia, Finland, Latvia, Lithuania, Malta, Poland, Romania, Slovenia, and Sweden on the outcome of and follow-up to the Conference on the Future of Europe, 09.05.2022. https://twitter.com/swedenineu/status/1523637827686531072 (07.07.2022).

Piattoni, Simona 2019: The contribution of regions to EU democracy, in: *Abels, Gabriele/Battke, Jan (eds.)*: Regional Governance in the EU. Regions and the Future of Europe, Cheltenham, pp. 16–32.

Piattoni, Simona/Schönlau, Justus 2015: Shaping EU Policy from Below. EU Democracy and the Committee of the Regions, Cheltenham, UK/Northampton, MA.

Riddervold, Marianne/Trondal, Jarle/Newsome, Akasemi (eds.): The Palgrave Handbook of EU Crises, Cham.

Rubio-Marín, Ruth 2020: Women and participatory constitutionalism, International Journal of Constitutional Law 18 (1), pp. 233–259.

Schakel, Arjan H./Massetti, Emanuele 2020: Regional institutions and the European Union, in: *Laursen, Finn (ed.)*: The Oxford Encyclopedia of European Union politics, Oxford/New York. https://doi.org/10.1093/acrefore/9780190228637.013.1236.

Schönlau, Justus 2017: Beyond mere "consultation": Expanding the European Committee of the Region's role, in: Journal of Contemporary European Research 13 (2), pp. 1166–1184.

Smith, Graham/Setälä, Maija 2018: Mini-Publics and Deliberative Democracy, in: *Bächtiger, Andre/Dryzek, John S./Mansbridge, Jane/Warren, Mark (eds)*: The Oxford Handbook of Deliberative Democracy, https://doi.org/10.1093/oxfordhb/97801987 47369.013.27.

von der Leyen, Ursula 2019: A Union that strives for more: My agenda for Europe. Brussels.

von der Leyen, Ursula 2022: A Union that stands stronger together. State of the Union Address 2022. https://ec.europa.eu/commission/presscorner/detail/ov/SPEECH_22_5493 (14.11.2022).

von Ondarza, Nicolai/Ålander, Minna 2022: After the Conference on the Future of Europe: Time to Make Reforms Happen. Four lessons for a European Union again requiring a new balance between deepening and widening, SWP comment No. 49, Berlin.

von Ondarza, Nicolai/Ålander, Minna 2021: The Conference on the Future of Europe: Obstacles and Opportunities to a European Reform Initiative That Goes beyond Crisis Management, SWP Comment No. 19, Berlin.

8. Annex: Timeline of the Conference on the Future of Europe

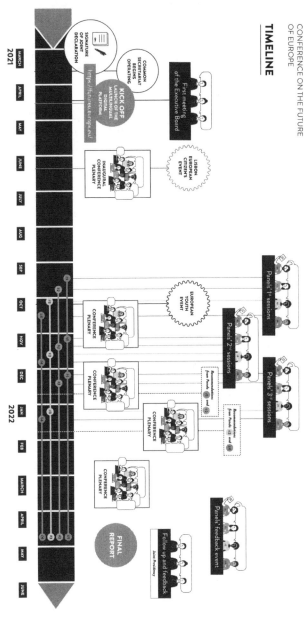

Source: https://futureu.europa.eu/uploads/decidim/attachment/file/14587/CoFoE_Timeline__3_.jpg (14.08.2022).

The Conference on the Future of Europe and the involvement of the European Committee of the Regions

Wolfgang Petzold[1]

On 9 May 2022, the Conference on the Future of Europe (CoFoE) ended with the presentation of a final report in the European Parliament in Strasbourg. For one year, citizens were at the centre of EU policy-making and methods of transnational deliberation were applied at a grand scale, which had never been tested before. As one of the results, the European Commission will continue to hold EU citizens' panels discussing new legislative proposals as of 2023.

In July 2019, the then designated President of the Commission, Ursula von der Leyen, had announced the Conference in the European Parliament as a project in which "the citizens of the European Union (should) play a leading and active role in shaping the future of our Union." In this article, the process and results of the Conference are presented with the focus on how the European Committee of the Regions (CoR) and regions and cities in general participated and what possible impact the Conference could have on them. Key questions to be answered are:

- How has the CoR positioned itself in the process?

- What results of the Conference matter to the CoR more specifically?

- What are the current positions of the EU institutions in the follow-up on the Conference?

- How can one imagine the future of citizens' participation across levels of democracy and government?

To answer these questions, documents presented by EU institutions and other bodies, as well as academic and other contributions are analysed, and first conclusions are drawn.

1. The CoR and the Conference on the Future of Europe

Activities and involvement of the European Committee of the Regions (CoR) related to the Conference on the Future of Europe in 2021 and 2022 have been manifold and are presented here with regards to (a) activities of the CoR delegation to the Conference, (b) activities of the CoR plenary and commissions, (c) activities reaching out to third parties, and (d) the works of a High-Level Group on European Democracy.

---

1 The author has been an EU official working for the European Commission (1992–1995 and 2001–2008) and the European Committee of the Regions (2008-2022). The views presented here are his own.

1.1 Activities of the CoR delegation to the Conference

Initially, in April 2021, the CoR delegation to the CoFoE was composed of 17 CoR members and one non-member, the president of the regional parliament of Bavaria.[2] Following an intervention by the CoR president, the delegation was completed by another 12 locally and regionally elected politicians in July 2021, some of whom being presidents of European associations representing local and regional interests, among them another three CoR members. By definition of the 'Rules of Procedure' adopted by the Executive Board of the Conference on 9 May and adapted on 19 July 2021, these 30 local politicians belonged to the Conference Plenary, the 450-strong body composed of 108 delegates each from the European Parliament, national parliaments and European and national Citizens' Panels, as well as representatives from governments (54), the European Commission (3), the CoR and the European Economic and Social Committee (18 each), local and regional politicians (12) and representatives from social partner (12) and civil society organisations (8). The Plenary had six meetings between June 2021 and April 2022 before it concluded on the recommendations from the European and National Citizens' Panels and the digital platform and adopted the draft final report during its final session on 29/30 April 2022. Due to the pandemic, the first sessions of the Plenary were held in hybrid mode, while the last two were in-person meetings. The level of participation of the CoR delegation and the local and regional politicians in the Plenary Session was about 70% on average and delegates delivered more than 60 statements during the sessions.

Fig. 1: CoR activities during the Conference on the Future of Europe

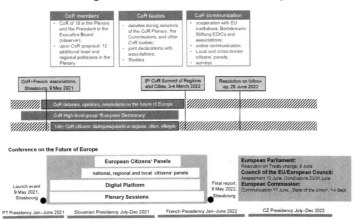

Source: Own depiction.

The deliberations of the Plenary were supported by working groups of about 50 members each, which met seven times between October 2021 and April 2022, usually ahead of the

---

2 All names and political affiliations can be found here: https://cor.europa.eu/en/engage/Pages/conference-future-of-europe.aspx (15.07.2022).

Plenary sessions, to discuss proposals and measures related to the topics of the Conference. Delegates met with respect to their organisational affiliation and role in the Conference ("components") in nine such groups, eight of which chaired by the European Parliament, the Council, the European Commission, and national parliaments, one by the European Youth Forum. For the members of the CoR delegation, these working groups were crucial to present their ideas and suggestions to the final report (see European Committee of the Regions 2022a). The CoR administration supported the 30 regional and local politicians by offering background information and briefings before and after the Plenary sessions as well as an online platform presenting documents. Moreover, an internal taskforce included members of the administration and the political groups in the CoR in order to guarantee a constant flow of information.

1.2 Activities of the CoR plenary and commissions

Since the second half of 2019, the CoR plenary, commissions and other bodies as well as its political groups discussed the set-up, works and follow-up of the Conference with great intensity. The Conference was on the agenda of almost all CoR plenary sessions between 2020 and 2022, during which no less than four resolutions and 15 opinions related to it were adopted.

On 12 February 2020, the CoR adopted its first resolution, in which it highlighted, among others, that the "democratic legitimacy of the European Union lies with the trust of citizens in their representatives elected at European, national, regional and local levels" referring to the increased voters' turn-out in 2019 European elections and stated its belief that "the Conference is an opportunity to identify measures that the EU needs in order to increase its capacity to deliver and enhance its democratic functioning in line with the new principle of active subsidiarity" (European Committee of the Regions 2020).

On 7 May 2021, just ahead of the formal launch event of the Conference in Strasbourg, the CoR adopted its second resolution, regretting that the launch had been delayed, highlighting the need to address regional aspects of the issues to be discussed "including through a number of local citizens' dialogues that the CoR will organise throughout the EU" (European Committee of the Regions 2021e).

On 27 January 2022, the CoR adopted a third resolution on the contribution of the local and regional authorities to the Conference on the Future of Europe, which addressed all the nine topics debated. With a focus on 'European democracy', the text suggests a more important role for citizens, regions, and cities in EU policy-making and to "develop a permanent and place-based dialogue with citizens as a participatory mechanism that would better link the EU with the realities at local, regional and national levels", which "would prove its added value in the context of European, national and regional/local elections" (European Committee of the Regions 2022e). The fourth resolution, adopted on 29 June 2022, is referred to further below.

In 2021 and early 2022, all six Commissions of the CoR organised regular debates and events on the CoFoE. Together, they held 24 such debates involving almost 50 experts, prepared 15 opinions, and issued four academic studies. Among the CoR Commissions, the one dealing with Citizenship, Governance, Institutional and External Affairs (CIVEX) started debating the Conference already in late 2019, held a total of 15 debates held and prepared six opinions. CIVEX also commissioned two studies on "The Conference on the Future of Europe: Putting local and regional authorities at the heart of European democratic renewal", published in October 2021, and on "The territorial dimension of the Conference on the Future of Europe and its follow-ups", published in June 2022 (European Committee of the Regions 2021b and 2022f).

1.3 Activities reaching out to regions, cities and European associations

Between the end of 2020 and June 2022, the CoR held a variety of outreach events in the context of the CoFoE, with the double objective of informing citizens and local politicians and developing its position with regard to the future of Europe. In so doing, the CoR worked together with local and regional administrations, associations representing local and regional interests and EU institutions. More than 140 events – local, regional, and cross-border citizens' dialogues – were held reaching out to 10 000 citizens, local politicians, and stakeholders. The ideas and recommendations from these events were uploaded to the digital platform of the Conference.

Among these, the following high-level events were organised, mostly attended by CoR members, local politicians, citizens, and representatives of the EU institutions:

- On 9 May 2021 in Strasbourg, the CoR launched a series of events on the CoFoE, together with the French Ministry for Territorial Cohesion, the City of Strasbourg, the French association *Régions de France*, the Assembly of *Départements de France*, and the association of French Mayors.

- On 29 June 2021, representatives from the EU and 57 national and regional parliaments and governments and European associations discussed during an online event the future role of regions in the EU, adopted a declaration on "The place of regions in the European Union architecture in the context of the Conference on the Future of Europe" and suggested to establish an "Alliance on European Democracy" (European Committee of the Regions 2021c).

- On 14 October 2021, the CoR together with "Eurocities" and the Council of European Municipalities and Regions discussed about "cities fostering democracy in the European Union - urban perspectives for the Conference on the Future of Europe" during an online event (European Committee of the Regions 2021a).

- On 3 December 2021, the High-Level Group on European Democracy set up by the CoR, held a hybrid conference attended by 150 stakeholders.

- On 26 January 2022, the CoR plenary discussed about the "vision for rural areas and the future of the EU".

- Finally, on 3 and 4 March 2022, 1 500 participants attended the CoR's 9th European Summit of Regions and Cities in Marseille, France. Under the headline "Citizens at the heart of Europe", a 12-points manifesto was adopted calling for the CoR be gradually upgraded beyond its current consultative function towards a having "binding role in a limited number of policy areas with a clear territorial dimension" and being granted "better access to negotiations between the EU institutions on legislative proposals (trilogues)" and enhanced access to "regional parliaments, in duly defined circumstances, a formal role in proposing EU legislation" (European Committee of the Regions 2022b).

Launched in spring 2021 by the CoR and the German Bertelsmann Stiftung, the objective of the joint project "From local to European" was to involve regional and local politicians and authorities in holding local or transnational citizens' panels in autumn 2021 and early 2022 to give a voice and visibility to regional and local concerns in line with the Conference Charter. Following two online information events in May 2021 attended by about 100 participants each, a total of 23 applications were received by June 2021, all partners were invited to attend online planning workshops and training seminars held between end of June and early July, with some 400 participants in total. Results can be summarised as follows (Bertelsmann Stiftung/European Committee of the Regions 2022):

- 19 partnerships materialised, most of which held online events, in accordance with the Conference Charter, between September 2021 and January 2022;
- the final project included 32 regions and 11 cities from 12 EU member states and one candidate country;
- most partners were German cities or regions (13), followed by France (8) and Czechia, Poland and Spain (4 each);
- three projects were delivered by one region or city, while 16 involved between two and six regions and cities;
- in total, all the partners together held 38 citizens' panels involving 1 400 citizens, who developed about 400 proposals;
- among the topics chosen for the panels, nine partners chose "a stronger economy, social justice and jobs", followed by "climate change and the environment", and "education, culture, youth and sport" (seven each), "European democracy" (six), and "health" and "values and rights, rule of law, security";
- all projects were supported by local or regional politicians, 13 of whom were CoR members;
- 14 Europe Direct Centres were involved in the organisation of events.

In addition, 30 local information events were carried out by CoR members in their constituencies in the context of the CoFoE, often in cooperation with local and regional authorities, non-governmental organisations and in partnership with EU institutions. The events reached out to 2 400 citizens. Moreover, a series of 67 local dialogues took place alongside the European Week of Regions and Cities in October and November 2021, which were attended by citizens, stakeholders, and politicians. Most of them were held by the Week's event partners and 58 CoR members were involved. In addition, 350 participants attended seven events organised as part of the CoR's Young Elected Politicians Programme between May and November 2021. As a result of their Forum in November, the young politicians agreed on 19 recommendations covering four topics, namely building resilient and inclusive communities; digital transformation; a lively local democracy for a healthy European democracy; jobs and education for young people (European Committee of the Regions 2021f).

2.   The views of local politicians on the future of Europe

Between July and September 2021 and 2022, the CoR carried out two surveys among the 1.2 million politicians elected at subnational level in the 27 member states of the European Union on the views on the future of Europe and European affairs more broadly. (European Committee of the Regions 2021d; 2022g). These surveys aimed at the representativeness in terms of the given national division of the levels of their responsibility (regions/federal states; provinces/counties; municipalities), age, political affiliation and gender. The results, in a nutshell, were:

- 93% of local politicians share the view that regions, cities, and villages should have better access to EU policy-making: 90% think that this should happen through more influence at the national level, 84% would see the EU level as important in this respect, and 83% see more cooperation among cities and regions as the right way forward.

- 65% agree that the future of Europe should be continuously discussed at regional and local levels and 27% would see a permanent citizens' assembly as the right tool to support the debate – including on a Convention to change the EU Treaties.

- Of the topics discussed during the Conference on the Future of Europe, 56% considered "climate change and the environment" most important, followed by "a stronger economy, social justice and jobs" (55%) and "education, culture, youth and sport" (49%).

- On their awareness of and involvement in the CoFoE, one in two politicians replied that they were aware of it (53% vs. 51% in 2021), while 47% were not aware at all and only a small fraction was actively engaged (2%). Awareness was highest among local politicians in Portugal (63%) and Malta (60%), while 77% in Denmark and 67% in the Netherlands had not heard of the CoFoE.

- With regard to the future of European democracy, two thirds of local politicians agreed that they have sufficient information on how democracy works at EU level (66% vs 32% who disagree). Even so, in response to the question of what could improve democracy at EU level, most local politicians mentioned information on democratic systems at EU, national, and subnational level (90%), followed by strengthening the involvement of subnational/local government levels in EU decision-making (86%) and "strengthening elements of participatory democracy such as citizens' assemblies or panels" (75%).

- Finally, on how to achieve a Europe closer to the citizens, most local politicians favoured "EU support for partnerships among regions and cities facilitating citizens' contacts" (52%), followed by "partnerships between regional/local councils" (46%) and "information for/training of local politicians" (45%).

3.   The CoR's High-Level Group on European Democracy

Ahead of the CoFoE, the CoR had asked a High-Level Group on European Democracy chaired by the President Emeritus of the European Council and former Prime Minister of Belgium, Herman Van Rompuy, to develop innovative ideas on improving European democracy and reinforcing the impact and influence of regions, cities, and the CoR in EU affairs.

Presented in January 2022, the Group's final report examines the general challenges facing representative democracy and analyses their root causes. In so doing, it looks at the challenges for "democracy in Europe" and its member states as well as the "democracy of Europe" and its institutional system and discusses the relationship between local, regional, national, and European democracy, the development of the EU's legal order and the emergence of a de facto "transnational democracy". The report proposes ways and means of strengthening democracy in the EU, suggests reducing the gap between citizens and decision-makers ("input democracy"), and highlights the need for inclusiveness, participation, and the development of policies that are close to the needs and interests of citizens. Delivering more effectively on these needs ("output democracy") requires a more dynamic interpretation of the Treaties on EU policies such as health, migration, and climate policy, coupled with an improved EU decision-making capacity. The report concludes by highlighting the need to strengthen the role of local and regional authorities in EU decision-making ("active subsidiarity") as well as the role of citizens through, for example, "local hubs", improving the European Citizens' Initiative and taking on board the best outreach practices and lessons learned from the CoFoE (European Committee of the Regions 2022d).

4.   The final report of the Conference: What is in it for cities, regions and the CoR?

Following the adoption of the 178 recommendations by the four European Citizens' Panels between December 2021 and February 2022, the nine working groups and the Conference Plenary looked into them afterwards, while the latter concluded on a draft final report on 28/29 April 2022, which was adopted by the three presidents of the European Parliament, the Council of the EU, and the European Commission on 9 May 2022 (Conference on the Future of Europe 2022). The final report presents – by the order of the nine topics chosen – a total of 49 proposals and 325 measures, 45 of which appear to be of particular relevance for cities, regions, and the CoR.

The table below puts a selected number of these measures into the context of both, the report's structure and the Conference bodies from which they originated. The overview confirms that of the 25 measures selected, only about half stem from recommendations made by the European Citizens' Panels, while the remainder came from either National Citizens' Panels, debates, and reports of the working groups or the Conference Plenary.

The latter was the case in particular for issues, which matter to the CoR such as its reform (40.3), its better involvement in EU decision-making (39.2), the definition of subsidiarity (40.5), "active subsidiarity and multilevel governance" (40.1) and the role of regional parliaments (40.2). The formulation of these measures was the result of deliberations in the working group on "European democracy" and interventions made by the then CoR president Apostolos Tzitzikostas. The overview confirms as well that the most relevant proposals and measures made in qualitative terms and relevance for regions and cities were developed on the topic of "European democracy" with a focus on citizens' participation.

Tab 1: Final report: proposals of relevance for cities, regions and the CoR

Topic	Proposals	Measures	Measures of relevance for cities, regions, CoR	ECP	NCP	WG-Plen	DP
Climate change and environment	1-6	57	*8 in total* green transition (3.1) local consultations (6.3)	x	x (DE, FR, NL)	x x	
Health	7-10	24	*1 in total* subsidiarity (10.2)		x (NL)		
A stronger economy, social justice and jobs	11-16	61	*10 in total* European Semester (11.3) regional products (12.3) social housing (14.5) absorption of EU funds (16.6)	x	x (IT) x(LT)	x	
EU in the world	17-24	48	*5 in total* affordability of products (17.5) transparency (22.1) citizen participation (22.2)	x x x	xx (DE, IT)	x	
Values and rights, rule of law, security	25-30	24	*2 in total* Charter on Fundamental Rights (25.3)	x		x	
Digital transformation	31-35	40	*3 in total* cyber security (33.3)	x			
European democracy	36-40	33	*9 in total* citizens' participation (36.4, 36.5) local EU Councilors (36.6) local youth councils (36.8) citizens information/Houses of Europe (37.5) EU topics in elections (38.4) EU decision-making/CoR (39.2) subsidiarity/ active subsidiarity/multilevel governance (40.1) regional parliaments (40.2) CoR reform (40.3) subsidiarity definition (40.5)	x x	x(BE) x (BE, FR) x x x x		x x x
Migration	41-45	16	*2 in total* financial support (43.2) regional authorities' involvement (45.1)	x x	x (FR)	x x	
Education, culture, youth and sport	46-49	24	*5 in total* coordinate education programmes (46.1) exchange programmes, CoR (48.1)	x	x (FR) x (BE, DE, FR, IT, NL)		
Total	**49**	**325**	**45**				

ECP: European Citizens' Panels; *NCP*: National Citizens' Panels; *WP-Plen*: Working groups, Plenary Session; *DP*: Digital Platform.

Source: Own depiction.

One finds below some extracts, which refer to proposals and measures with regards to "citizens' participation". In particular, proposal no. 36 asks the EU institutions and also member states, regions, cities, and civil society organisations to make participatory democracy more accessible and effective, to enhance its quality and effectiveness, and to develop quality standards. The proposal suggests, among others, the following measures:

- "improving the effectiveness of existing and developing new citizens' participation mechanisms, in line with EU acquis, by better informing on them. Ideally, all the information about the participatory spaces should be summarized in an integrated official website with different features. A mechanism should be devised to monitor policy and legislative initiatives, which have emerged from participatory democracy processes;"

(…)

- increasing the frequency of online and offline interactions between EU institutions and its citizens through different means of interaction in order to ensure that citizens can participate in the EU policy-making process to voice their opinions and to get feedback, and creating a charter for EU officials on citizens' participation;

- offering a user-friendly digital platform where citizens can share ideas, put forward questions to the representatives of EU institutions and express their views on important EU matters and legislative proposals, in particular youth. The platform should also allow for online polls;

- improving and streamlining existing mechanisms at the European, national, and local level, to make them more secure, accessible, visible, and inclusive;

- include organised civil society and regional and local authorities and existing structures such as the European Economic and Social Committee (EESC) and the Committee of the Regions (CoR) in the citizens' participation process;"

(…)

- holding Citizens' assemblies periodically, on the basis of legally binding EU law. Participants must be selected randomly, with representativeness criteria, and participation should be incentivized. If needed, there will be support of experts so that assembly members have enough information for deliberation. If the outcomes are not taken on board by the institutions, this should be duly justified; Participation and prior involvement of citizens and civil society is an important basis for political decisions to be taken by elected representatives. The EU is founded on representative democracy: with European elections, citizens give a clear mandate to their representatives and indirectly express themselves on EU policies;"

(…)

- summarise elements of citizens' participation in an EU Charter for the involvement of citizens in EU-affairs" (Conference On the Future of Europe 2022: 79f.).

5. Follow-up by the EU institutions

In the aftermath of the final event of the CoFoE, works on its follow-up have begun in the European Parliament, the Council of the EU, the European Commission, which are yet to be finalised in autumn 2022. More specifically, the European Parliament and the Council of the EU appear to remain at odds on the question whether or not a Convention on the revision of the EU Treaties should be launched. Meanwhile, in her "State of the Union" address presented on 14 September 2022 in the European Parliament, European Commission President Ursula von der Leyen confirmed that Citizens' Panels will now become a "regular feature of the democratic life of the EU" and will be used to inform key legislative proposals as of 2023 (von der Leyen 2022). In September 2022, the three EU institutions agreed to hold a feedback event on 2 December 2022 on the CoFoE in the European Parliament in Brussels involving the citizens and representatives of the CoFoE plenary.

In its resolution of 4 May, the European Parliament (2022b) called on its Committee on Constitutional Affairs (AFCO) to launch the necessary procedure to establish a Convention with the aim of revising the EU Treaties in line with Article 48 of the Treaty on European Union. On 9 June, the European Parliament (2022a) voted in favour of a resolution suggesting a Convention on the revision of the EU Treaties in regard to issues such as the EU's institutional setup, the abolition of veto powers in the Council, more EU powers in health, energy, defence, and social and economic policies, the right of legislative initiative for the Parliament and better protection of founding values. In September, AFCO published a study outlining the design of a permanent citizens' participation mechanism (European Parliament 2022c). Moreover, AFCO held a follow-up debate with representatives from national parliaments on 26 October 2022, during which the latter presented their views on the outcome and follow-up of the CoFoE.

On the side of the Council of the EU, a non-paper was published by the governments of Bulgaria, Croatia, the Czech Republic, Denmark, Estonia, Finland, Latvia, Lithuania, Malta, Poland, Romania, Slovenia, and Sweden on 9 May 2022 presenting an assessment of the Conference, which would not favour Treaty change (Permanent Representation of Sweden to the European Union 2022), while the governments of Belgium, Germany, Italy, Luxembourg, the Netherlands and Spain presented yet another non-paper on 13 May 2022 with a more open position towards Treaty change (Non-paper 2022). On 23 May, the General Affairs Council had an exchange of views on the result of the Conference and its follow-up and on 10 June 2022. The General Secretariat presented a "preliminary technical assessment", in which it looked into the 325 measures suggested in the final report and the actions already taken, still to be taken or those requiring Treaty change (Council of the EU 2022a). Furthermore, on 23/24 June, the European Council (2022) adopted conclusions on the follow-up of the CoFoE, stating that it was a "unique opportunity to engage with European citizens", that the "EU institutions should ensure that there is an effective follow-up to the final report, each within the institutions' own spheres of competence and in accordance with the Treaties", while recalling "the importance of ensuring that citizens are informed on the follow-up to the report." On 1 July, the presidency of the Council of the EU was taken over by the Czech Republic. Among their five priorities, the Czech government has put "resilience of democratic institutions" confirming that the CoFoE "created a unique space for citizens and especially for young people" and that emphasis will be put "on improving dialogue with young people and promoting their participation in political/policy processes" (Czech Presidency of the Council of the EU 2022). On 18 October 2022, the General Affairs Council confirmed that it had received two proposals for Treaty amendments under Article 48(2) TEU from the European Parliament while taking account that the EP has asked its Committee on Constitutional Affairs to prepare proposals for further Treaty amendments. The Council agreed to wait until the Parliament has concluded this work before transmitting the two specific proposals it had already received (Council of the EU 2022).

On 17 June 2022, the European Commission (2022a) presented its first analysis of the proposals made by the Conference on the Future of Europe and a communication on its follow-up. The communication refers to a "European public space" to flourish and "democracy to be enriched at European, national, regional and local level" through "Citizens' Panels to deliberate and make recommendations ahead of certain key proposals". The first generation of the latter will be launched in the context of the European President's "State-of-the-Union" address to be given in the European Parliament in September 2022. In the 29-page annex to the communication, the European Commission sets out, by the nine topics of the Conference, the actions it has already taken or which are underway to follow-up on the proposals, those on which suggestions or new programmes will be presented as well as those requiring a change of the EU Treaties. With regards to citizens' panels, the annex suggests to dedicate "time and resources" to organise them on a selected number of topics to "help prepare particularly important sets of key initiatives" ahead of the legislative process, "help to build capacity among national, regional and local actors to launch a new generation of decentralised citizens' dialogues built on deliberative approaches" and to "develop a European Charter on Citizens' Participation targeted at all those, who participate in it or organise citizen engagement activities" (ibid.; annex pp. 23ff.). In its work programme for 2023, the European Commission announced that it would hold citizens' panels in 2023 on three legislative proposals concerning food waste, learning mobility and virtual worlds (European Commission 2022b: 4).

On 29 June 2022, the CoR plenary adopted a resolution on the outcome and follow-up on the CoFoE, which refers to the mentions of local and regional aspects in the final report and supports the view that several proposals made in it should trigger a Convention according to article 48 TEU with the objective to change the Treaties. The resolution states the need to develop a "permanent and place-based dialogue with citizens as a participatory mechanism that would better link the EU with the realities at local, regional and national levels" (European Committee of the Regions 2022c).

6.   Citizens' participation in EU policy-making: What role for regions and cities?

The CoFoE marked a move from communicating and listening to enabling co-creation and deliberative models and made citizens' engagement a truly open and proactive process. In Europe's cities and regions, one finds since a while a wealth of participatory processes to engage citizens, which vary with regards to the policy issues or controversies surrounding them, the methods applied as well as their level of "constitutionalistion". During the CoFoE, most of the 6 500 events were held locally by a variety of government bodies and civil society organisations. However, their impact on the outcome of the Conference remained rather limited. Moreover, many of these local events were purely informative and did not respect the principles laid down in the "Conference Charter" regarding the random selection of participants, the application of deliberative methods, and the political follow-up. With only six member states holding national citizens' panels – Belgium, France, Germany, Italy, Lithuania, and the Netherlands – the same assessment holds true for efforts made by national governments.

Such "missing links" between citizens' participation at local, regional, national, and EU level remain among the challenging aspects for the follow-up of the Conference. Consequently, the European Commission' communication of 17 June 2022 suggests to "to build capacity among national, regional and local actors to launch a new generation of decentralised citizens' dialogues built on deliberative approaches". Moreover, "a European Charter on Citizens' Participation targeted at all those who participate in or organise citizen engagement activities" shall be developed, thus responding to proposals made by the European Citizens' Panels (European Commission 2022a).

Making the distinct local and regional voices of citizens heard in the making of EU policies and politics could take various formats such as

- debates on selected topics, such as health, defence, security, which would be part of European citizens' panels proposed in the European Commission's annual work programme ("legislation approach") – as it is now planned for 2023;

- citizens' panels in regions experiencing common challenges such as cross-border regions, metropolitan or rural regions, regions on their way to green transition, facing demographic decline or similar threats to their industry and service sectors ("geographical approach");

- connecting regions and cities with a certain experience in citizens' participation, who volunteer to address EU issues and suggest, for example, topics to be treated by the European Citizens' Panel ("network approach").

Finally, a recent study by the Bertelsmann Stiftung (2022) analyses the existing channels of citizens' participation the EU and combines them with evidence from surveys and research. It concludes that in order to make citizens' participation work, the EU needs to move from a participation patchwork to a participation infrastructure by addressing three gaps: the awareness gap, the performance gap, and the political commitment gap. In a participation infrastructure, the individual instruments would not only work on their own but would collectively establish the basis for a functioning participatory EU democracy alongside the representative dimension of European policy-making.

7. Conclusions

To conclude, I would like to share the following personal thoughts and ideas.

First, with regards to the overall impact of the CoFoE and its meaning for the CoR, and regions and cities more generally, I think that the exercise has been an unexpected but also limited success. Unexpected, because it has put citizens at the centre of the process applying methods of transnational deliberation, which had never been tested before. And it worked. Unexpected, because there was a strong inter-institutional spirit among the three leading institutions, which made it possible to achieve results despite of the usual beauty contest. At least *during* the process. Unexpected, because the CoR, regions, and cities found their way into the final report, mostly through the working groups of the Plenary, to a degree that not many would have guessed before. No doubt, this has been the result of effective lobbying including within and across political party families.

Second, EU regions and cities have developed multiple approaches and experiments to innovate democracy, which should be more systematically linked to citizens' participation at EU level. Respecting some key principles, such as inclusiveness, deliberation and valuing the impact of citizens' assemblies, panels, and juries etc., will be an important condition for ensuring successful and sustainable citizens' engagement. A permanent citizens' assembly at EU level would be well advised to link the different levels of parliaments and governments, as they are important in terms of addressing specific territorial challenges that citizens face in e.g., border regions, regions in demographic decline, rural areas, and tourism destinations etc.

Third, looking into the final report and its analyses by both the Council of the EU and the European Commission, some may be surprised about how many of the proposals and measures suggested by the citizens, but also other components of the Plenary, are actually already in place or in preparation. The immediate idea – "the EU should communicate better" – falls short of a more in-depth explanation on why the citizens don't know. True, more EU communication could be done better with a view to what the EU means for the daily life of citizens. But neither "falling in love with a common market", as Jacques Delors once doubted to happen, through more or better communication, nor the argument "there are EU funds" have the potential to repair citizens' detachment from the EU or any other political institution (Lübbe-Wolff 2019). I would argue that the citizens do know or feel that the EU is not made for them in the first place. Such assessment would only change if the EU offered them true citizenship, including more social rights that would make them equal before the law (Guérot 2019). In this respect, it is not surprising that the European Citizens' Panels were quite outspoken on such rights, which are usually not part of the catalogue of exclusive EU competences but remain in the remit of member states.

Fourth, there have been a number of weaker points during the process concerning, for example, the rules of procedure for the Plenary and the working groups, the rather unequal interest of citizens in the digital platform, which made its results less meaningful, the lack of transparency on how certain formulations made it into the final report or were deleted thereof at the final stage of the Conference and, more generally, the lack of interest of the media in the whole exercise. These and other issues will without any doubt be subject to the evaluation, which is underway and should be available in autumn 2022.

Fifth, with a more critical view on the issues in the interest of regions and cities or the CoR, which made it into the final report, one could ask whether "active subsidiarity", "multilevel governance", better access to "*trilogues*" or the change of the CoR's name will stick. Being on the menu of the CoR's "*ceterum censeo*" since quite some time, these topics appear to be things of the past and the time may have come to reflect on more convincing and relevant issues for the future of an advisory body, which is requesting a more significant role in the EU's institutional architecture for itself. That request, the CoR itself, and the role of regions and cities in EU policy-making will be at stake as soon as the European Council and the European Parliament can agree on a Convention to change the Treaties. Not likely at the moment, but not at all impossible to happen.

Finally, what will remain from the Conference on the Future of Europe needs to be handled with great care. From the point of view as a communicator, my argument would be that citizens' participation in EU policy-making is there to stay and that the EU institutions, the CoR, and regions and cities should find a meaningful way to link the levels of government and democracy. This will require political learning and coordination within and between EU institutions, political parties, civil society organisations, and academia. It will not be easy but: why should it?

8. References

Bertelsmann Stiftung 2022: Next level citizen participation in the EU. Institutionalising European Citizens' Assemblies, 24.06.2022. https://www.bertelsmann-stiftung.de/de/ publikationen/publikation/did/next-level-citizen-participation-in-the-eu-all (04.07.2022)

Bertelsmann Stiftung/European Committee of the Regions 2022: Europe up close. Local, regional and transnational citizens' dialogues on the Future of the European Union, 23.02.2022, Gütersloh. https://www.bertelsmann-stiftung.de/en/publications/ publication/did/europe-up-close-en (04.07.2022).

Conference on the Future of Europe 2022: Final Report May 2022, 09.05.2022, Brussels/Strasbourg. https://futureu.europa.eu/pages/reporting (04.07.2022).

Council of the European Union 2022a: Conference on the Future of Europe - Proposals and related specific measures contained in the report on the final outcome of the Conference on the Future of Europe: Preliminary technical assessment. https://aeur. eu/f/23h (04.07.2022).

Council of the European Union 2022b: Main results of the General Affairs Council on 18 October 2022. https://www.consilium.europa.eu/en/meetings/gac/2022/10/18/ (27.10.2022).

Czech Presidency of the Council of the EU 2022: Programme of the Presidency, 01.07.2022. https://czech-presidency.consilium.europa.eu/en/programme/ (04.07.2022).

European Commission 2022a: Conference on the Future of Europe. Putting vision into concrete action, Communication COM(2022) 404 final, 17.06.2022. https://ec. europa.eu/info/sites/default/files/communication_1.pdf (04.07.2022) and its annex: https://ec.europa.eu/info/sites/default/files/annex_0.pdf (04.07.2022).

European Commission 2022b: Commission Work Programme 2023. A Union standing firm and united, Communication 548 final, 18.10.2022. https://ec.europa.eu/info/sites/default/files/com_2022_548_3_en.pdf (28.10.2022).

European Committee of the Regions 2020: Resolution on the Conference on the Future of Europe, adopted on 12 February 2020, in: Official Journal of the EU C 141, pp. 5–7.

European Committee of the Regions 2021a: Cities fostering democracy in the European Union - urban perspectives for the Conference on the Future of Europe, conclusions of an event held together with "Eurocities" and the Council of European Municipalities and Regions, 14.10.2021. https://cor.europa.eu/en/events/Pages/Cities_fostering_democracy_in_EU.aspx (04.07.2022).

European Committee of the Regions 2021b: The Conference on the Future of Europe: Putting local and regional authorities at the heart of European democratic renewal, study, October 2021. https://bit.ly/3artdSX (04.07.2022).

European Committee of the Regions 2021c: Declaration on "The place of regions in the European Union architecture in the context of the Conference on the Future of Europe", adopted on 29 June 2021. https://cor.europa.eu/en/engage/Pages/declaration-place-of-regions-in-the-EU-architecture.aspx (04.07.2022).

European Committee of the Regions 2021d: Local politicians of the EU and the future of Europe, Eurobarometer Flash Survey, October 2021. https://cor.europa.eu/en/our-work/EURegionalBarometerDocs/Survey%20Report.pdf (04.07.2022).

European Committee of the Regions 2021e: Resolution on the Conference on the Future of Europe, adopted on 7 May 2021, in: Official Journal of the EU C 300, pp. 1–3.

European Committee of the Regions 2021f: YEP Forum. Recommendations by the Young Elected Politicians, 17.–19.11 2021. https://cor.europa.eu/en/engage/Documents/YEPs/202111_YEPForum/YEP%20Forum_Recommendations.pdf (04.07.2022).

European Committee of the Regions 2022a: Citizens, local politicians and the future of Europe, final report, 24.02.2022. https://cor.europa.eu/en/engage/brochures/Documents/Citizens,%20local%20politicians%20and%20%20the%20future%20of%20Europe/4666-final%20report%20lowres%20FIN.pdf (04.07.2022).

European Committee of the Regions 2022b: The Marseille Manifesto of regional and local leaders: Europe stars in its regions, cities, villages, 04.03.2022. https://bit.ly/3PeNPfK (04.07.2022).

European Committee of the Regions 2022c: The outcome and follow-up on the Conference on the Future of Europe, Resolution adopted on 30 June 2022. https://memportal.cor.europa.eu/Public/Documents/MeetingDocuments?meetingId=2182079&meetingSessionId=2227831 (04.07.2022).

European Committee of the Regions 2022d: Report of the High-Level Group on European democracy, 31.01.2022. https://cor.europa.eu/en/engage/brochures/Documents/Report%20of%20the%20High%20Level%20Group%20on%20European%20Democracy/HLG%20Final%20report.pdf (04.07.2022).

European Committee of the Regions 2022e: Resolution on the contribution of the local and regional authorities to the Conference on the Future of Europe, 26.01.2022. https://

memportal.cor.europa.eu/Public/Documents/MeetingDocuments?meetingId=2182077& meetingSessionId=2227825 (04.07.2022).

European Committee of the Regions 2022f: The territorial dimension of the Conference on the Future of Europe and its follow-ups, study, June 2022. https://bit.ly/3yvRGhL (04.07.2022).

European Committee of the Regions 2022g: Local and Regional Barometer. Survey conducted for the European Committee of the Regions by Ipsos European Public Affairs (October 2022). https://cor.europa.eu/en/our-work/Pages/EURegional Barometer-Survey-2022.aspx.

European Council 2022: European Council meeting - conclusions, 23./24.06.2022. https:// www.consilium.europa.eu/media/57442/2022-06-2324-euco-conclusions-en.pdf (04.07.2022).

European Parliament 2022a: Resolution on the call for a Convention for a revision of the Treaties, adopted on 9 June 2022. https://www.europarl.europa.eu/doceo/document/ TA-9-2022-0244_EN.html (04.07.2022).

European Parliament 2022b: Resolution on the follow-up un the Conference on the Future of Europe, adopted on 4 May 2022. https://www.europarl.europa.eu/doceo/ document/TA-9-2022-0141_EN.html (04.07.2022).

European Parliament 2022c: Towards a permanent citizens' participatory mechanism in the EU. Study requested on behalf of the European Parliament's Committee on European Affairs (September 2022). https://www.europarl.europa.eu/RegData/etudes/ STUD/2022/735927/IPOL_STU(2022)735927_EN.pdf (27.10.2022).

Guérot, Ulrike 2019: Why Europe should become a republic. A political utopia, Bonn.

Lübbe-Wolff, Gertrude 2019: Narrativkur für die EU? Forget it! in: *Franzius, Claudius/ Mayer, Franz C./Neyer, Jürgen (eds.)* 2019: Die Neuerfindung Europas. Bedeutung und Gehalte von Narrativen für die Europäische Integration, Baden-Baden, pp. 195–206

Non-paper submitted by Germany, Belgium, Italy, Luxembourg, the Netherlands, and Spain on implementing the proposals of the Plenary of the "Conference on the Future of Europe" 2022, 13.05.2022. https://bit.ly/3Ith6RA (04.07.2022).

Permanent Representation of Sweden to the European Union 2022: Non-paper by Bulgaria, Croatia, the Czech Republic, Denmark, Estonia, Finland, Latvia, Lithuania, Malta, Poland, Romania, Slovenia, and Sweden on the outcome of and follow-up to the Conference on the Future of Europe, 09.05.2022. https://twitter.com/swedenineu/ status/1523637827686531072 (04.07.2022).

von der Leyen, Ursula 2022: State of the Union 2022 Address. A Union that stand strong together. (14.09.2022). https://ec.europa.eu/commission/presscorner/detail/ov/speech_ 22_5493 (07.11.2022).

French perspective on the Conference on the Future of Europe

Servane Metzger/Mattéo Torres-Ader

1. Introduction

On 29 May 2005, 17 years ago, the French people rejected the draft European Constitutional Treaty in a referendum. This moment marked a fundamental break in the relationship between the French and the European Union. Since then, and after nearly two decades of successive crises, the citizens' distrust of the EU is deeply rooted in national political debates. In the 2021 Eurobarometer, 49% of French people expressed a general distrust of the European Union, six points higher than continental average. While French governments were often at the forefront of European initiatives for greater integration, the French remain one of the most Eurosceptic nation in the EU (Chopin et al. 2021). Since 2005, this ambivalent relationship of France to the EU crystallised and is reflected in the binarity of national debates and the artificial opposition between pro-European and Euro-critic positions.

At the same time, driven by the observation of limits of representative democracy and the growing demand of French citizens to be involved more directly in public decisions, successive governments have supported and accompanied a national dynamic in favour of citizen participation. Since 2017 and the election of President Emmanuel Macron, French authorities launched several large-scale participatory exercises in response to a variety of issues. Among the best known are the *Grand Débat National* launched in the context of the "*Gilets Jaunes*" movement, or the *Citizens' Climate Convention* (CCC) whose objective was to formulate solutions to accelerate the fight against climate change.

At EU level, aware of the existing gap between European citizens and the Union – the so-called "democratic deficit" –, institutions launched the first European Citizens' Consultations in 2018. France took part in this exercise through thousands of events, which brought up shared areas of concerns for citizens across the continent. Building on this first experience of consultative democracy at EU level, President Emmanuel Macron proposed in 2019 to take it a step further and called for the setup of an EU-wide *Conference on the Future of Europe* (CoFoE). For the French President, who was inspired by an idea developed by former Minister of Foreign affairs Hubert Védrine (2019), this Conference should involve randomly selected citizens' panels, experts, and EU leaders, and result in a *refounding act* to propose all necessary changes for a renewed European political project, including if needed a revision of the Treaties (Macron 2019). The idea was taken up by the newly appointed President of the European Commission, Ursula von der Leyen, who called in her opening statement in July 2019 for a "new push for democracy". The three pillars of this "push" were the improvement of the *Spitzenkandidaten*-system, the right of initiative for the European Parliament, and the launch of the CoFoE.

From then on, the three major EU Institutions shaped an exercise that was absolutely unique in its scope and format, in particular with the use of a multilingual digital platform and the creation of transnational citizens' panels. Building on its previous experiences of deliberative democracy and national specificities, the French government seized the opportunity of the Conference to deploy a national panel equally unique in its design, which could be complementary to the EU level exercise and enrich its results. The CoFoE, both in its national and European versions, was also the central piece of the third pillar of the French Presidency of the Council of the European Union's motto: *Relance, Puissance, Appartenance*. The third concept, "*Appartenance*", or "*Sense of Belonging*", reflects the need to build and develop a shared European horizon. With regard to this dual ambition, this paper will examine *to what extent the Conference on the Future of Europe allowed to overcome binary debates on the European Union in France, and highlighted the existence of a common European political awareness?*

2. Specificity and commitments of the French government for the regional panels on the Future of Europe

The government made the choice of a two-fold consultation combined with an ambitious territorial approach. The French national exercise took the form of 18 regional conferences in the thirteen metropolitan regions and the five French overseas regions, held over three weekends in September and October 2021, and each involving between 30 and 50 randomly selected citizens (746 in total).

Fig. 1:   18 regional conferences, 13 in metropolitan France and 5 in overseas regions

A regional synthesis report of these 18 regional panels was then produced during a national panel held on 15 to 17 October 2021 at the French Economic, Social and Environmental Council (CESE) in Paris, involving 98 volunteers randomly selected amongst the citizens who had participated in the 18 regional conferences. The participants in the consultation were asked one single open question: "*As French citizens, what changes do you want for Europe?*".

Additionally, the government wished to highlight specifically the views of the young French people ahead of the European Year of Youth 2022. An online consultation entitled "*Parole aux Jeunes*" ("Young People Have Their Say") was thus organised by the Ministry of European and Foreign Affairs in collaboration with Make.org. More than 50.000 young people aged 15 to 35 shared their ideas and priorities for Europe in 2035.

The results of these two consultations were gathered in a final report prioritizing 14 changes that French citizens wanted to see happen for the future of Europe. This report was handed over to the French government in November. A follow-up committee of 15 French citizens was then created: 14 citizens (7 women and 7 men) who had participated in the regional conferences and one representative of the "*Parole aux Jeunes*" consultation were entrusted with the task of carrying and defending the French proposals at EU level. For six months, they participated in the working groups and plenary assemblies of the CoFoE in Strasbourg, negotiating to ensure that the French proposals were taken into account in the final European recommendations. During the closing ceremony of the Conference on 9 May 2022, they helped to present the proposals of European citizens to the presidents of the three main EU institutions. This citizen follow-up committee was the central element of the government's duty to follow up, as well as a means to articulate the French national exercise with EU deliberations.

The French national panel of the CoFoE is underpinned by the commitments that the government has signed up to on participatory democracy, which are based on three principles: *transparency*, *neutrality* and the *duty to follow up*. The methodology was established with the constant objective of ensuring transparency for citizens, with a specific will to make all the information relating to the consultation publicly available. The commitment to neutrality was pursued at all preparatory stages of the consultation, for instance by ensuring absence of bias in selecting participants, a total freedom of expression during discussions, neutrality of expertise provided, and the expression of citizens' input free of influence from the government or any other stakeholder. During debates at the regional and national level, experts were present during the discussion times to answer citizens' questions and provide clarification, while making sure to maintain a neutral stance. The French government also set an ambitious and innovative scheme to ensure that citizens would have a concrete right to follow up.

In order to ensure that the consultation's methodology respected these three commitments from its inception, a *college of three independent guarantors* was created. The three guarantors – Mrs Elisabeth Guigou, Mr Bernard Poignant and Mr Patrick Bernasconi – were respectively appointed by the President of the European Parliament, the President of the French National Assembly, and the Minister for European affairs. Their missions were to check the sincerity of the citizens' selection and the application of the representativeness criteria in the composition of panels for the regional conferences, to make recommendations on the conduct of the panels and the selection of experts, to attend the regional conferences and the national synthesis conference as observers, and to write a public and independent report at the end of the national exercise of the CoFoE.

The three principles mentioned above were reflected in the consultation in the form of six strong methodological choices:

- *Territorialisation and proximity to citizens*: The aim of organising these 18 panels at regional level was to be as close to citizens as possible to gather their views. This approach also enriched the consultation by revealing the lines of consensus and disagreement among the regions on different issue;

- *Diversity of citizen profiles and random selection*: A recruitment target of 50 citizens per regional conference was set ahead of the process, with the exception of the overseas conferences of Martinique, Mayotte, Guadeloupe, and Guyana, for which the target was 30 to 40 citizens, and the conference of the Grand Est region, at which five German citizens from the three bordering *Länder* were also present. The citizens invited to participate in the regional conferences were drawn by lot through random selection of telephone numbers. In order to be eligible, the selected citizens had to be over 18 years old and either be French or permanent legal residents in France. Each regional citizens' panel needed to be representative of the diversity of the regional population and to bring together a variety of views on Europe;

- *Transparency of the process*: The guarantors of the consultation published an independent final report on the process at its end, and all documents from the consultations – the syntheses of all 18 regional conference, the synthesis of the national conference, the final report and the report from the citizen follow-up committee – are all publicly available on the digital platform of the government dedicated to participatory democracy[1];

- *An open discussion with no fixed agenda*: The citizens participating in the national consultation were asked one single question: "*As French citizens, what changes do you want for Europe?*". The aim was to allow the citizens to enjoy total freedom in regard to the subjects they wished to discuss. The French national exercise was in this respect different but complementary to the European exercise, which structured its discussions and propositions around nine topics: climate change and the environment, health; a stronger economy, social justice and jobs, EU in the world, values and rights, rule of law, security, digital transformation, European democracy, migration; education, culture, youth and sport;

- *Reverse expertise*: According to the chosen methodological approach, collective reflection takes place on the basis of the experiences and opinions of citizens, who then question experts in order to support their discussions and consolidate their working hypotheses. To achieve this objective and ensure the highest possible level

---

1   See Participation-citoyenne.gouv.fr 2021: Participer à la construction des politiques publiques. https://www.participation-citoyenne.gouv.fr/ (12.07.2022).

of neutrality, experts were mobilised in the various regions, including from academia and local Europe Direct Information Centres. During the national conference in Paris, 19 high-level experts from academia, think-tanks and the diplomatic corps were present as well as fact-checkers;

- *Duty to follow up and articulation with the EU-level exercise*, including the setup of a French follow-up citizen committee who took part in all plenary assemblies of the CoFoE.

Since 2017, the French government launched several large-scale deliberative exercises, with the underlying belief that citizen participation should be at the centre of national debates and public policy-making. However, the elaboration of a fully-fledged theory and an operational methodology of participatory democracy remains incremental. In this context, we must learn from previous experiences and determine how they influenced the setup of the French national panel for the Conference.

During the *Citizens' Climate Convention* (CCC), citizens were asked to formulate concrete solutions to answer one very specific question: "*How to reduce greenhouse gas emissions by 40% by 2030 in a spirit of social justice?*" To achieve this mission, the 150 randomly selected citizens heard more than 140 experts to help them draft concrete proposals. These experts were scientists, associations, trade unionists, administrators, entrepreneurs, as well as politicians - the President of the Republic, the Prime Minister and the Minister of Ecological and Solidarity Transition were auditioned. While it is fair to say that no expert is inherently neutral in their approach or knowledge of a subject, concerns were raised by many that their interventions could have oriented the debates and led citizens to formulate one proposal more than others. With time, their role became even more difficult when citizens became themselves experts of the subject and formulated very precise and detailed propositions that could be implemented in national law. The CCC therefore forced the government to question the added value of external expertise and to rethink its modalities especially as to when this expertise would be the most needed by the citizens. First of all, we must guard against the idea that the result of deliberative process should be a pure emanation of citizens' ideas, mostly because their political consciousness is in any case fuelled by social interactions that they have in their daily environments. The starting point should be to aim at a co-construction between citizens and experts, which ultimately leads to the emergence of proposals or new subjects that the citizens will consider as the most urgent or of the highest priority. To establish these priorities, citizens must be provided with the most neutral and objective expertise possible, based almost exclusively on facts. For the national exercise of the CoFoE, in order to minimise influence on participants in the process of identifying their aspirations for Europe, the decision was made not to provide any information or expertise in advance, but to take questions raised by the citizens themselves as the starting point ("*reverse expertise*").

Another lesson can be drawn from the *Grand Débat National* in 2018. The main objective of this consultation was to listen to the French citizens in order to draw the fault lines in French society and to gather their demands with the help of several tools including panels, digital contributions, and *cahiers de doléances* placed in local entities. The debate was therefore inherently open and had no predetermined limits. As underlined by the Prime

Minister Edouard Philippe, "the general idea of the [Grand Débat National] [was] to make it an English garden rather than a jardin à la française, it ha[d] to be abundant". In order to provide a framework for the debate nonetheless, questions were directly asked to the participants on four major issues: the ecological transition, taxation, democracy, and citizenship, and finally the organisation of the State and public services. For the CoFoE, considering that nine subjects were already pointed out at EU level, the French government decided to implement an approach that would allow citizens to decide for themselves on tabling the desired changes by responding to one single open question, without being constrained by any specific subject or a predetermined normative framework. This choice enables citizens to determine by themselves the angle through which they decide to approach a specific topic, without putting themselves in the shoes of other actors, may they be public policy makers or legislators.

In this respect, experience has shown that citizens understand the specificity of their role very well where it is explained clearly in advance by the organisers. During the CCC, the formulation of the initial question led the citizens to act partly in their deliberations as regulators who had to come up with concrete solutions answering a specific problem. This situation was with no doubt accentuated by the promise made by President Macron at the beginning of the Convention to submit every proposition that would come out of it to a vote in Parliament, to a referendum or to direct regulatory implementation, "without filter", if they were sufficiently precise and detailed. This statement was later qualified by the President who reminded that the government, the assemblies, and the administration would still have to amend the final propositions. For the French panellists the situation was different in that the results of the national exercise would in any case not constitute the end of the Conference's work. It was clear from the beginning that the French propositions would constitute one of the national contributions and as such fuel the work of the plenary assembly at EU level. French citizens involved in the Conference therefore had a clear view of the exit point and of their role in the overall process, including the subsequent responsibilities of the different institutions in the follow-up phase. In this context, the role of the French government – as well as other French members of the plenary assembly of the Conference – was to accompany the French citizens and to make sure that national results were taken into account.

The national exercise for the CoFoE had a specificity in its necessary articulation with the EU-level exercise. This, as well as the ambivalent media coverage of political debates on Europe at national level, could have led to fears that the consultation would not attract interest from the randomly selected citizens. However, on the contrary, we have observed a particularly high interest for the consultation. The response rate of citizens contacted who said that they were interested in participating in one of the 18 regional conferences was between 40% and 60%, depending on the region. This response rate is equivalent to the one observed for the CCC, but is also much higher than the one for the *Grand Débat National*, despite very low media coverage. This was the first indication that this Conference could be an important milestone to overcome the presupposed lack of interest and linked caricatured debates on Europe in France.

3. The results of the French panel of CoFoE: between originality of proposals and real convergence vis-à-vis the institutions and other European panels

At the end of the French exercise of the CoFoE, the French citizens managed to define priority changes for the Europe of 2035: (1) developing energy sobriety; (2) strengthening defense and common security; (3) fostering collective economic performance; (4) establishing citizen power; (5) moving towards a federation of European states; (6) proposing exchange programs; (7) sharing European cultures through federating events; (8) harmonizing health; (9) developing strategic sectors at the European level; (10) improving the protection of environments and ecosystems. These changes, which are each associated with concrete proposals and detailed success criteria, demonstrate the particularly constructive and operational nature of the French panel. Most of the proposals are realistic, and while many of them are in line with the policies currently being pursued by the European institutions, some are original and potentially promising. It is important to note that the citizens formulated proposals to respond to concrete problems occurring in their daily lives.

Above all, far from the image of a country divided between EU supporters and Eurosceptics, the French panel reveals that citizens are particularly ambitious towards European integration, with critics being mainly concerned with the lack of efficiency or the absence of competence of the Union on a given subject. In fact, the French final report explicitly expresses the desire to move towards a form of European federalism (proposal 5), while the measure considered as the most necessary is a quite disruptive one: the promotion of "energy sobriety" in daily life (proposal 1, see Ministère de l'Europe et des Affaires Étrangères 2021).

It should be noted that the absence of proposals aimed at opposing the European construction cannot be simply considered a consequence of the formulation of the initial question (*"As French citizens, what changes do you want for Europe?"*), given that Eurosceptic citizens were able to express their point of view just as much as citizens in favour of the European project. It seems that the debate itself fostered a real awareness of the need for policies on a continental scale as well as a strategic approach to rely on existing supranational institutions instead of trying to challenge them.

The second striking element that emerges from the French panel is the convergence of national proposals with the final results of the Conference. In their proposals, French and European citizens alike have expressed the wish for a Europe that is more ecological, social, and democratic and thus intervenes more directly in their daily lives and in national political frameworks. In concrete terms, the vast majority of French and European proposals correspond to a desire to deepen existing policies – in the areas of ecology, defense, social justice, etc. – in order to accentuate their scope or accelerate their effects. But what is remarkable is that French and Europeans citizens alike recommend deepening EU integration in areas identified as important in order to face current crises or to strengthen the feeling of belonging to Europe. This is particularly the case of topics such as health, environment, education, and foreign policy. This wish for deeper integration would be reflected either by an expansion of the European Union's competences or by a strengthening of its institutions and agencies.

For instance, on the health-related subjects, the French panel wanted to "harmonize health and make it accessible to all Europeans through a common health policy" (ibid.), while the European report similarly calls for the inclusion of "health and healthcare" among the competences shared between the European Union and its Member States, "in order to achieve the necessary coordinated, long-term action at Union level" (proposal 8.3, Conference on the Future of Europe 2022). Second example: on education, the French panel wants "Europe to be more present, even interventionist, in the areas of education and research", while the European report proposes the establishment of new shared competences in the field of education – which is currently only a supporting competence –, in order to allow the creation of "an inclusive European Education Area within which all citizens have equal access to quality education and life-long learning" (ibid.). In the same sense, the French and the Europeans also agree on the expansion of the European Union's competences. Among the most important proposals they share, they both call for the right for the European Parliament to exercise legislative initiative, or the reform towards qualified majority voting in the Council.

The convergence is visible in the demand for regulation, which could be surprising given the criticisms traditionally levelled at the European Union. The final report of the Conference points out the will of citizens to see the Union "promote a plant-based diet on the grounds of climate protection and the preservation of the environment" (proposal 6.8), "develop at EU level a standard educational programme on healthy lifestyles" (proposal 9.2, ibid.), while the French report pleads for the Union to "oblige [companies] to be more transparent about their production methods, in particular by means of ecological scores", or to make "citizen participation compulsory" (Ministère de l'Europe et des Affaires Étrangères 2021).

Thirdly, it appears that the measures proposed are, for the most part, in line with the priorities already expressed or implemented by the European Union, notably during Ursula von der Leyen's last State of the Union speech, but with greater ambition, especially on ecological and social issues. For example, both the French and European reports make extremely concrete recommendations on energy and food developments, which are in accordance with the *European Green Deal* and the *Fit for 55* Strategy. Citizens confirm the importance of European intervention on these issues and emphasize the urgency of addressing the problem of European public action not only from the point of view of agricultural or energy production, but also from the point of view of uses and social consequences for citizens. In so doing, citizens support the recent *Farm to Fork* strategy, which was conceived precisely as a policy on the scale of the food system as a whole beyond the mandate of the Common Agricultural Policy which focuses mainly on production.

Thus, both national and European dimensions of the Conference revealed a real political proximity amongst European citizens. In their diversity, they all showed a shared awareness of the challenges of ecological transition, digital transition, but also of strategic autonomy and defense, economic recovery, or social justice.

4. Towards the emergence of a hybrid EU model between representative and participatory democracy?

The Conference on the Future of Europe is an unprecedented exercise in its scope and ambition: it aims at allowing European citizens to directly express their wishes for the Europe of the future and thus participate in the construction of the European Union of tomorrow. No citizen participatory exercise had ever been carried out on this double scale, i.e. national and continental. The Conference has enabled clear guidelines to be drawn up for the years to come, and it is now up to the European institutions to take them on board and to orient their future policies on the basis of these results.

However, there are certainly ways to improve this type of exercise. These improvements concern, first of all, the methodology of selecting citizens by lot, which should allow a greater representativeness of the diversity of society. The challenge will be to reach those who rarely engage with politics or have not voted in previous European elections. In this respect, the creation of a citizen status, specially designed for this type of participatory exercise, could facilitate the inclusion of more diverse profiles. But more generally, a reflection deserves to be conducted to facilitate both, for citizens, the fact of participating in such an exercise, and for European institutions, the modalities of recourse to citizen panels. In particular, it would be necessary to consider the best time to resort to this type of participatory exercise in order to maximize their usefulness. For example, at the European scale, it could be considered that citizens should be approached at the beginning of a new legislature when the Commission and the Council define the priorities for the coming years, or in the context of a treaty change (Den Dooven 2022). In a recent communication, the European Commission itself proposed ways of making citizen participation at European level more permanent (European Commission 2022).

If citizens' panels will not, on their own, solve the feeling of disconnect between citizens and European institutions, they have nevertheless the potential to show the interest of the public in European integration. Indeed, the French experience of the Conference appeared as a particularly effective remedy to address the lack of intelligibility of the European Union. The appropriation, by the French citizens who experienced it – and *a fortiori* by the French follow-up committee which was able to follow the Conference throughout its entire duration –, of the European stakes and of the functioning of the European institutions, highlights the importance of this type of participatory exercise to fight against the lack of understanding of the European democratic deficit and, more generally, of the EU as a whole. Indeed, participation as such appears to be a very effective means for combating not only the lack of interest in European democratic life, but also – if necessary – for legitimizing, or on the contrary for questioning, the relevance of major political orientations and decisions taken by the European institutions.

Above all, the observed proximity of the proposals put forward by French and European citizens to the general roadmap of the European institutions points out the fact that the rejection of the European project by some Europeans is less of a result of a disagreement towards the European policies that are being implemented, and instead originates in a criticism of the inefficiency, slowness and, above all, lack of ambition of the European institutions. Consequently, this type of participatory exercise appears to be a particularly valuable instrument for encouraging the development of a constructive and positive relationship between citizens and the European Union. It can encourage the development of a debate that goes beyond the Manichean pro- or anti-EU postures and be the place for fruitful discussions on how to transform the Union in accordance with the expectations of its citizens. More generally, these exercises of participatory democracy, accompanied by better media coverage, could certainly contribute, to a certain extent, to meet the citizens' demand for a holistic educational approach towards the EU (Conference on the Future of Europe 2022).

That being said, with the fragmentation of national political spaces being particularly strong and the democratic deficit so deep, it remains a particularly complex endeavour to bring citizens closer to the European institutions. In fact, the resonance of the Conference in the French and European political space remains very limited, overshadowed by electoral debates or international news. Thus, even if we should not overestimate the weight that this type of exercise can play in the evolution of the relationship of citizens towards Europe, it is nevertheless certain that the EU would benefit from the perpetuation of this type of exercise and its tools – in particular the digital platform and the citizens' panels – in a way that remains to be defined.

As Bernard Manin (1985) points out, collective deliberation has not only an epistemic value – in the sense that it allows to discover the best decisions to be made – but also an ethical value because it leads citizens to open themselves up to the general interest. In this perspective, we can consider that the deliberations that take place during citizens' panels enable to both rationalize and moralize individual choices: by exposing themselves to the proposals and objections formulated by others, citizens become more informed, more coherent, and more oriented towards the public good. Hélène Landemore (2017) even argues that the cognitive diversity associated with the inclusion of many individuals from different backgrounds improves the epistemic quality of decisions. In other words, the more diverse the individuals are, the more different views are expressed and the better are the decisions taken.

Therefore, we could consider that encouraging the development of this type of exercise within the European Union, as complementary to representative democracy, could have virtues from a perspective of equity – i.e. equal opportunities to influence the decisions taken –, but also according to rational considerations – given that the support of citizens would favour the taking of good decisions –, and participate in a democratic hybridization that would help addressing the democratic deficit of the EU.

While the French exercise of the CoFoE was a 100% citizen-driven panel, the creation of the plenary assembly of the Conference opened a new chapter in the history of deliberation, where citizen participation and deliberative democracy go hand in hand with traditional representative democracy. Despite the institutional obstacles, the Conference has thus contributed to creating a unique and innovative democratic space where citizens' opinions could fuel the definition process of the European political agenda, and this in real co-construction with EU institutions, national parliamentarians, and representatives of civil society.

What if this hybrid model could become the basis for a renewed and truly political EU citizenship? Until now, EU citizenship has merely been a legal status, unable to address the democratic deficit and legitimacy issues that the EU is still facing. As Justine Lacroix (2009) puts it, a political Union can emerge without the existence of a European *demos*, if the EU invents a new form of citizenship based on rights but also on the ever-greater openness of the political debate on European issues. During the Conference, we have seen that citizens, both at the national and European level, have grasped the complexity of European issues and defended their opinions through open debates with various stakeholders from all 27 Member States, thus refusing to give in to the ease of binary debates. In this respect, the CoFoE made it possible to move, in Jürgen Habermas' (1981) words, from a "logic of arguing" to an "argumentative rationality" which could lead to the emergence of a European public sphere. Despite many institutional obstacles that arose during the Conference and that one shall not ignore, it is fair to say that it contributed to turn the concept of EU citizenship into a dynamic reality corresponding to the advent of a genuinely European political culture consistent with the *sui generis* nature of the Union.

5. Conclusion

At its genesis, the purpose of the Conference on the Future of Europe was to review our common policies and institutions to define key priorities and necessary changes for the future of the EU. Its result was intended to bring up a new collective agenda on which common action could be based to overcome traditional hurdles and reluctance. Now that this first part of the Conference has come to an end, its outcome demonstrates a strong proximity of citizens' concerns at national and supranational levels with priorities that were already put forward by the EU institutions. More precisely, it appears that the gap between citizens' expectations and the decisions taken by European institutions lies less in the content of their policies than in the method used to achieve them. In reality, most citizens criticize the Union for its lack of efficiency, ambition, or political courage. Thus, the criticisms reflect less a rejection of the European Union as such and rather a desire for a Union that is capable of addressing concrete issues that citizens encounter in their daily lives.

While this convergence may lead some commentators to express doubts about the overall usefulness and novelty of the exercise, we, on the contrary, believe that the expression of similar priorities amongst citizens, stakeholders and institutions reveals a *de facto* convergence of European political cultures. As such, it makes the concept of "*sense of belonging*" tangible and could provide for an increased legitimacy of EU action in the highlighted policy areas. This "*European political awareness*" revealed by the CoFoE may not constitute a revolution in EU politics in itself, but it questions the method and oppositions that existed for decades on our continent. As such, it should be considered as a milestone for the emergence of a European public sphere.

In the coming years, we will need to think collectively about how to build on the results of the Conference on the Future of Europe, may it be by implementing sustainable tools of deliberative democracy – for instance through an institutionalisation of participatory exercises at EU level – or by reinforcing representative democracy – through transnational lists or by creating a new right of initiative for the European Parliament. The Conference gives the European Union a unique opportunity to define its own political model between representative and participative democracy, as well as its priorities – even if some in the Community choose to move at different speeds to achieve it.

6. References

Chopin, Thierry/Gressani, Gilles/Valla, Natacha/Damon, Julien/Varma, Tara 2021: Une Europe pour aujourd'hui et pour demain : Souveraineté, solidarités, identité commune, Paris.

Conference on the Future of Europe 2022: Report on the final outcome, 09.05.2022. https://futureu.europa.eu/pages/reporting?locale=en (12.07.2022).

Den Dooven, Ward 2022: Conference on the Future of Europe: a glimpse into the future of participatory democracy?, in: European Policy Brief No. 75. https://www.egmontinstitute.be/content/uploads/2022/02/epb-75-CoFoE-Ward-den-Dooven.pdf?type=pdf (12.07.2022).

European Commission 2022: Communication from the Commission to the European Parliament, the European Council, the Council, the European Economic and Social Committee and The Committee of the Regions. Conference on the Future of Europe Report. Putting Vision into Concrete Action, COM(2022) 404 final, Brussels. 17.06.2022. https://eur-lex.europa.eu/legal-content/EN/TXT/?uri=CELEX%3A52022DC0404&qid=1655899763798 (12.07.2022).

Habermas, Jürgen 1981: Theorie des kommunikativen Handelns, Berlin.

Lacroix, Justine 2009: Une citoyenneté européenne est-elle possible?, in: La Vie des Idées, 03.06.2009. https://bit.ly/3PTpiNc (12.07.2022).

Landemore, Hélène 2017: Democratic Reason: Politics, Collective Intelligence, and the Rule of the Many, Princeton.

Macron, Emmanuel 2019: Dear Europe, Brexit is a lesson for all of us: it's time for renewal, in: The Guardian, 04.03.2019. https://www.theguardian.com/commentisfree/2019/mar/04/europe-brexit-uk (12.07.2022).

Manin, Bernard 1985: Volonté générale ou deliberation? Esquisse d'une théorie de la délibération politique, in: Le Débat 33(1), pp. 72–94.

Ministère de l'Europe et des Affaires Étrangères 2021: Rapport - Contribution citoyenne à la Conférence sur l'avenir de l'Europe. https://www.diplomatie.gouv.fr/IMG/pdf/2021 1126_-_cofe_-_rapport_final_cle42c536.pdf (12.07.2022).

Védrine, Hubert 2019: Face au chaos, sauver l'Europe!, Paris.

The Belgian experiments of deliberative democracy –
An analysis of the institutionalisation of deliberative citizen participation in multi-level Belgium

Ann-Mireille Sautter/Min Reuchamps[1]

1. Introduction

In recent years, a 'wave' of deliberative democracy has swept through an ever growing number of states (OECD 2021: 3). The mushrooming of deliberative democracy appears to mark an unseen trend in democratic innovation (Bächtiger et al. 2018). This trend has now reached the very heart of Europe, the European Union. With the launch of the *Conference on the Future of Europe (CoFoE)* a new era appears to have begun: one, in which deliberation is no longer limited to the scope of the municipality, the region or the nation-state. With an ambitious project the EU has created various forms of citizen participation via its Multilingual digital platform and the four European Citizens' panels that debated some of the greatest challenges posed to society today. The sheer scale of the European deliberative project raises hopes that the road of deliberation within the framework of the European Union does not stop here. In Belgium, the initiative was met with open arms. The government officially reported 26 events, organised independently from one another, that were held in the CoFoE's context and brought together citizens, elected representatives (MPs), and representatives of civil society (FPS Foreign Affairs 2022). The topics addressed throughout these three weeks were related to two subjects, namely climate change by debating matters of mobility, energy and sustainability, and democracy, debating citizen participation and communication. Not only do these initiatives show the willingness of Belgian citizens to participate, if we look closely many of the events produced recommendations that demand more inclusion of citizens into public decision-making.

The large variety of events held in the context of the CoFoE throughout Belgium showcases the country's general experience with deliberative democracy. Citizen participation has been a tool that has persistently marked the last 22 years (Vrydagh et al. 2020). Even more so, a growing number of parliaments have permanently introduced participatory mechanisms since 2019, namely the Permanent Citizen Dialogue of the German-speaking community as well as the deliberative commissions of the different parliaments in the Walloon and the Brussels-Capital-region.

---

1   The authors would like to declare that they have been directly involved in designing the processes that are described in this article. Min Reuchamps was part of the group of experts asked by the bureau of the Parliament of the German-speaking Community to elaborate the model of the Permanent Citizen Dialogue for which he observed and evaluated the implementation of a team composed of Christoph Niessen, Rebecca Gebauer and Ann-Mireille Sautter who attended several meetings in parliament. Min Reuchamps was also involved in the design of the deliberative commissions in Brussels at the request of the combined bureau of the Brussels Regional Parliament and the French-speaking Brussels Parliament. Finally, for a period of two years, he was appointed by the Walloon Parliament as a member of the accompanying scientific committee for the deliberative commissions organised by the region of Wallonia.

The implementation of deliberative citizen participation is often justified on epistemic grounds or proposed as a remedy for citizens' dissatisfaction with representative democracy, as it is supposed to restore the proximity between citizens and their MPs. However, political leaders do not only integrate the public and thereby enrich the political debate around certain policy matters, they also cede autonomy to citizens as they find themselves publicly constraint by recommendations. So, why would elected representatives implement and, even more so, institutionalise deliberative mechanisms on such a broad scale? The answer to the question in the Belgian case might provide an exploration that could be tested in the wider context of the CoFoE and the supranational and national initiatives it has triggered.

2. A *'Three I's approach'* to elected representatives and deliberative democracy

The question of the democratic preferences of elected representatives has long been overlooked by studies on participatory and deliberative democracy. Elected representatives were seen as guardians of representative democracy, a perspective that assumed a hostility towards the deployment of these mechanisms. The implementation of theoretical ideals drew most academic attention to their deliberative dimensions in which elected officials were no longer central actors. However, the mushrooming of deliberative mechanisms has encouraged recent works to take a closer look at the role of MPs within the process. Recently, a *'Three I's approach'* has been put forward to analyse the emergence of democratic innovations within the political arena (Edelenbos/Van Meerkerk 2015; Hall/Taylor 1997; Palier/Surel 2005), with which variables are regrouped into *interests, ideas and institutions*. It provides a paradigm through which interactions of single variables can be understood within a broader scope of consideration. Explanatory variables that have been already associated with citizen participation would thus be reorganised into these three concepts (Caluwaerts et al. 2020; Junius et al. 2020; Lowndes et al. 2001).

Interest-driven or strategic justifications are some of the most publicised considerations. Deliberative mechanisms are often presented as a means to increase the legitimacy or effectiveness of political decisions, given that the substance of the decision-making process is enriched by the life experience of citizens (Blondiaux 2008; Edelenbos 2005; Zurn 2007). Moreover, the stance of MPs can also arise from a strategic consideration towards their position within the representative system to reorient the relationship between citizens and politics (Ryan 2014). Deliberation moves towards a form of networked governance in which citizens and MPs interact on an equal basis to shape policy decisions, which implies a change in power dynamic. This change inevitably faces resistance (de Sousa Santos 1998). Especially the 'winners' of the electoral system, i.e. the governing majority, are assumed to be more reluctant towards far-reaching participatory reforms, whereas opposition MPs perceive it as a possibility of political distinction and influence (Bowler et al. 2006: 437; Junius et al. 2020).

At the same time, the perception of deliberative democracy can depend on an ideational vision, in which democracy is not a mere decision-making mechanism, but a social ideal (Mayer et al. 2005). As it increases the inclusion of citizens into decision-making, citizen participation becomes an end in itself. This vision can depend on personal conviction

68

(Lefebvre et al. 2020); some representatives might seek to revitalise democracy, whereas others are more sceptical, fearing a political deadlock. Literature has also highlighted the role of ideology of MPs. Traditionally, it was argued that more left-winged or environmentalist MPs tend to favour citizen participation, which emerged from new social movements and sought to empower citizens (Cohen/Fung 2011; Fung/Wright 2003; Geissel/Hess 2017; Heinelt 2013). However, this argument tends to overgeneralise apparently shared priorities between left-winged parties while glossing over significant differences (Galais/Font 2011). Furthermore, democratic innovations have gained broad popularity also within the right and far-right (Jacquet et al. 2015; Rangoni et al. 2021; Schiffino et al. 2019). Yet, while the left-right continuum might not determine whether MPs support citizen participation, their ideology still influences which models MPs prefer (direct/deliberative) and whether they believe it to be a cure for the 'democratic disconnect' (Junius et al. 2020).

The structure of *institutions* and underlying formal and informal rules can also influence whether or not political actors are willing to implement deliberative democracy (Palier/Surel 2005). Within this *institutional* vision, a double dimension must be considered. On the one hand, the general experience within the institution plays a crucial role. The degree of political professionalisation and thus the institutional socialisation of an MP can significantly impact how they perceive the need for participatory reform, where newcomers might be tempted to change established rules (Niessen 2019). On the other hand, the institutional choices made by the respective institutions have to be considered. The results of a study on the attitude of Swedish local politicians towards unconventional participation show that the more experience elected representatives have, the greater the acceptance towards democratic innovation (Gilljam et al. 2012: 260).

3. Belgian experiments

In Belgium, deliberative democracy has a relatively long tradition. Within the scholarship, the experimentation with deliberative democracy has increased after the G1000, a citizens' summit organised by public figures, civil society activists and scholars in 2011 and 2012. In a context of national crisis[2], the G1000 assembled 704 citizens to discuss on political subjects. However, despite more than 20 years of experience of deliberation on the local level and the G1000, deliberative democracy has reached the federal level only this year (Vrydagh et al. 2020). Since 2011, citizen participation has been limited to the regional and community level[3] due to a historic experience, the *Royal Question* on the return of King Leopold III. from exile.

---

2   At this time, Belgium had been unable to form a government for more than 500 days.
3   The Belgium system, consociational federalism, regroups two models of institutional design within one system, namely federalism and consociationalism to accommodate the tensions between the Dutch-speaking and the French-speaking population (Caluwaerts/Reuchamps 2015). Consociational elements of power-sharing can be found in, e.g., the formation of coalition governments. Belgium's federal structure accommodates the division through a dual system, in which multiple entities coexist, namely language communities and regions (Deschouwer 2012). Three language communities (the Dutch-, the French- and the German-speaking Community) are tasked with cultural matters among other matters. Three regions

This historic example is often presented as illustration of the divisions between Dutch- and French-speakers. In its light, some authors argue that citizen participation has become more common on community and regional level as the population is much more homogeneous (Van Crombrugge 2021). By jurisdiction of the State Council, citizen participation is also limited to consultative, i.e. non-binding, models and can only cover matters in which the respective entity is competent thus limiting its thematic scope (see Fn. 3).

Formalisation of citizen participation has picked up speed since 2019. The question that arises is to what extent *interests, ideas* and *institutions* have played a role in the way MPs justify the implementation and institutionalisation of deliberative democracy on the regional level. So far, no systematic comparison has been conducted on the Belgian case. The qualitative comparison allows us to better understand the interdependence of different factors and the attitudes towards deliberative democracy.[4] Below, we present the Ostbelgien Modell, the Permanent Citizen Dialogue of the German-speaking Community, then the deliberative commissions, in the Brussels-Capital-Region and Wallonia.

3.1 The Ostbelgien Modell

On 25 February 2019, the Parliament of the German-speaking Community unanimously adopted a decree establishing a model for permanent citizen deliberation ('*Permanenter Bürgerdialog*'; see Niessen/Reuchamps 2019; 2022). It consists of a Citizens' Council ('*Bürgerrat*') composed of 24 randomly selected members meeting monthly. The Council is mandated to initiate, set the budget and to select the topics of Citizens' Assemblies ('*Bürgerversammlungen*'). These are composed of a varying number of randomly select-ed citizens drawn from the population of the German-speaking community aged 16 and older. The objectif is to deliberate and make recommendations. The whole process is accompanied by the Permanent secretariat ('*Permanentes Sekretariat*'), a civil servant mandated by the Citizens' Council. The deliberations are followed by a three-stage con-trol process during which the recommendations are presented by the Citizens' Assembly to Parliament and then followed up by the Citizens' Council. Unless the competent parlia-mentary committee and/or ministers give a justified opinion to the contrary, the recom-menddations are supposed to be respected by parliamentary or governmental action, with an official report one year later.

This process – internationally known as the 'Ostbelgien Modell' – is embedded in a particular political and institutional context. The German-speaking Community, also known as East Belgium ('Ostbelgien'), is, with 77.000 inhabitants, the smallest federate entity in

---

(the Flemish Region, the Walloon Region, and the Brussels-Capital-Region) are tasked with matters related to territory. These layers do not perfectly overlap. As the Brussels-Capital-Region is officially bilingual, both the French-speaking and Dutch-speaking community exercise, e.g. cultural, education and health related competences within Brussels. The French-speakers of Brussels have their own parliament (the Assembly of the French-speaking Community Commission [COCOF]).

4 To do so, we have analysed the preparatory documents, on which the final decisions to institutionalise deliberative citizen participation were based. Furthermore, we have conducted interviews with some twenty parliamentarians and, more generally, have been able to participate in numerous preparatory and follow-up meetings.

the country. MPs are only 'part-time politicians' and usually exercise another professional occupation. It is argued that they thus maintain regular contact with the German-speaking population and are more open to its participation (Niessen 2021). Despite the Community's size, Ostbelgien has extensive legislative power (Bouhon et al. 2015), allowing it to put an ambitious citizen deliberation scheme at the heart of existing institutions. The very idea of institutionalisation came from its political leaders, namely the minister-president of the government and successive presidents of parliament. They commissioned a group of experts, organised by the G1000 umbrella organisation (Caluwaerts/Reuchamps 2018), with the task to develop a deliberative model. The proposal was then debated and refined by the leaders of each parliamentary political group. The final proposal was adopted by a unanimous vote.

Macq and Jacquet (2021) identify three reasons behind this institutionalisation. First, the MPs wished to integrate the viewpoint of randomly selected citizens into the decision-making process in order to benefit from diverse types of experience and expertise, a classic *interest*-driven consideration. To MPs, this 'life experience' was not necessarily present in traditional decision-making processes despite their openness and double function as both citizens and elected officials. Second, MPs employed it as a *strategy* to reduce mistrust towards political institutions through deliberation. In their eyes, it would show that citizens' opinions mattered, but would also provide an occasion to acquaint citizens with the complexity of public decision-making. Their hope was that deliberation would restore the legitimacy of traditional party families. Third, the MPs were encouraged by the fact that the model's permanent character would be a 'world's first', allowing the Community to give itself a brand image and reference point. From an *ideational* and *interest*-driven point of view, it would allow to put it on the world map of scholars and practitioners.

Interestingly, initial fears that the proposal would go too far and cede too much political control to the citizens within the Assembly, most prominently voiced by the largest opposition party, the Christian-democrats, were ultimately dismissed (Niessen/ Reuchamps 2022: 139) firstly, based on *institutional* consideration, namely the constraints imposed by the Belgian constitution, which would not allow for binding decision-making by citizens and therefore leave a sufficient margin of appreciation to politicians. Secondly, both the Christian-democrats, as well as the radical democratic Vivant believed in the *idea* that any form of integrating citizen into decision-making would be better than none and therefore ultimately supported the Ostbelgien Modell.

3.2 The Deliberative Commissions

While much international attention has been drawn to the Ostbelgien Modell, other regions started to experiment with deliberative democracy as well. In December 2019, the Parliament of the Brussels-Capital Region[5] and the French-speaking Brussels Parliament of the COCOF adopted an amendment to their procedural rules. The elected representatives officially introduced deliberative commissions composed of both elected representatives and

---

5   To be precise, the Parliament includes the General Assembly of Common Community Commission (COCOM) that deals with person-related matters that cannot be attributed to a language group. The Assembly of the COCOM has thus also introduced deliberative commissions.

randomly selected citizens to jointly develop recommendations on political issues. Inspired by the Brussels model, the Parliament of Wallonia followed in October 2020[6]. In concrete terms, each parliament can call upon a parliamentary committee composed of both citizens and parliamentarians[7] to draft recommendations on a given issue. Any resident in Brussels aged 16 and above can be drawn by lot and participate. In contrast, Walloon citizens can only be drawn if they have acquired voting rights for the Walloon Parliament, meaning that only Belgian citizens residing in Wallonia over the age of 18 are entitled to participate. The difference is explained by the distinct demographic realities. Brussels has a much younger and larger non-Belgian population (who are therefore not entitled to vote in regional elections).

This commission works in three stages: After the public gathering of information, participants deliberate behind closed doors. Then the recommendations are presented to the public, which is followed by a vote. While the power of citizens in this deliberative process is important, their vote is not binding due to the institutional constraints in Belgium. Therefore, the recommendations are voted on separately for each of the proposed recommendations: a secret, consultative vote for the citizens and a public, binding vote by an absolute majority of MPs in the commission. Recommendations approved by both groups are incorporated into a report that is submitted to the competent standing committee, which is composed of the MPs of the deliberative commission. Within six months, this standing committee must provide and present a follow-up report on what has been done with the recommendations at a public meeting to which the participating citizens are invited.[8]

The deliberative commissions realise an ambition that was voiced during the regional election campaigns by the green opposition parties in spring 2019 (Vrydagh et al. 2021). Due to the electoral success of the Dutch-speaking Groen and the French-speaking Ecolo, both parties joined the regional governments in Brussels and Wallonia after the general elections. The commissions were subsequently included in the coalition agreements and mirror the Ostbelgien experience. Shared characteristics are the institutionalisation, the use of drawing participants by lot, and a clear vision of deliberation as an adjunct to democratic decision-making. Yet, the deliberative commissions differ in two respects: by the integration of deliberative commissions into the very functioning of parliament, allowing the commissions to take advantage of the entire administrative body instead of a Permanent secretary, and, above all, by their mixed nature.

However, here too Wallonia differs from Brussels, as both an adapted Ostbelgien Modell[9] and the Brussels-inspired deliberative commissions were proposed within a short

---

6   Until today no deliberative commission has been organised within the Walloon Parliament. The COVID-19 pandemic certainly plays a role, but it probably also reflects area lack of political ambition.

7   The ratio in the Brussels regional parliament is 45 citizens to 15 parliamentarians, in the COCOF the ratio is 12-36 and in Wallonia the ratio is two-thirds/one-third. The parliamentarians are precisely those who sit on the standing committee under whose competence the subject falls (Reuchamps 2020).

8   To date, three deliberative commissions have been held and have produced 43 recommendations on the implementation of 5G (organised by Parliament of Brussels-Capital region), 97 for homeless and poorly housed people in the Brussels Region (principally organised by the COCOM), 22 on citizen involvement in times of crisis (organised by COCOF).

9   The proposal foresaw an additional popular consultation on the recommendations.

period. The former was supported by the opposition and the later by the governing majority. The opposition perceived the organisation of an independent and randomly selected Citizens' assembly as the *philosophically* most appropriate model due to fears that a mixed model risked generating a power imbalance. Furthermore, they criticised a lack of posterior control of the citizens, which could further damage the credibility of politics. Thus, the opposition explicitly preferred the three-stage control mechanism of the Ostbelgien Modell. Nevertheless, the opposition voted in favour of the majority proposal out of *ideational conviction*, as they believed any improvement would be better than none. The majority, on the other hand, argued that the Ostbelgien Modell would not be feasible due to the much larger Walloon population and the high risk of drop-outs due to long travel distances for participants. Furthermore, having *experienced* multiple less successful citizens' assemblies, some MPs argued that argued that thanks to the socialising between MPs and citizens, MPs would have higher levels of commitment towards the implementation of the final recommendations.

Thus, in both regional parliaments the majority favoured deliberative commissions. The reasoning was three-fold. Firstly, the introduction of a mixed deliberative model aligns with an *ideational* and ideological vision of democratic renewal proposed by the green parties. Inspiration was drawn from the Irish 'constitutional convention' set up in 2013 to solve contentious societal issues and which was composed of 33 MPs and 66 randomly selected citizens (Suiter et al. 2016). Ecolo and Groen retained the principle of a partnership between two groups that usually do not debate one another. The parties consider the mixed formula as a key factor in the success of the Irish experience. In Wallonia, MPs explicitly believe that deliberative commissions are more likely to produce feasible and socially acceptable outcome due to an internal control mechanism via the expertise of MPs and an external control mechanism due to electoral accountability. For these arguments, a majority emerged in favour of directly involving a randomly selected group of citizens *alongside* MPs in parliamentary committee work. Secondly, similar to the Permanent Citizens Dialogue, the deliberative commissions institutionalise a novel formula, both in Belgium and in other parts of the world, which motivated decision-makers to experiment with the mixed deliberative model in Brussels. The MPs behind the project realised that, if it were to come to fruition quickly, their institutionalised system of bringing together MPs and citizens would be a 'world's first'. Finally, two *institutional* elements should be noted, namely the arrival of a significant number of new MPs after the 2019 regional elections and the rejuvenation of the average age of MPs. These are decisive factors for the success of the process. First-time MPs are often more positive about the implementation of citizen participation mechanisms, as they aim to bridge the existing "gap" between citizens and the political level (Rangoni et al. 2021), for which mixed deliberative commissions are proposed as a solution.

4.   The Belgian laboratory of deliberative democracy

During the last twenty years, Belgium has become a laboratory for democratic innovations. Despite its constitutional framework, which does not allow for binding involvement of citizens in formal public decision-making processes, several Belgian parliaments have taken a crucial step by experimenting with the institutionalisation of citizen participation and by creating innovative, deliberative mechanisms. The introduction of specific mechanisms and models was justified on various grounds and this chapter does not claim to be exhaustive regarding the motivation. Multiple justifications emerged such as the hope that deliberative democracy could decrease the divide between citizens and politicians (Macq/Jacquet 2021). Similarly, the *interest*-driven consideration of bringing citizens' experience and expertise into decision-making as an element of enrichment has been broadly discussed (among others Blondiaux 2008).

Tab. 1: Non-exhaustive summary of justifications presented by MPs

	Interests	Ideas	Institutions
German-speaking Community	Citizens' experience Restore legitimacy *World's First*	*World's First*	Margin of appreciation Constraints
Brussels Parliaments	*World' First*	Decrease divide citizen-politician *World' First*	New MPs Rejuvenation
Parliament of Wallonia	Citizens' experience Efficacy	Decrease divide citizen-politician Mixed as more legitimate	Save electoral model Previous inefficiency New MPs Constraints

Source: compiled by the authors.

Some of the above-identified elements deserve discussion. Some factors that emerge in the discourse of politicians can be attributed to at least two categories. The motivation to be a 'world's first' could serve both a strategic purpose of putting a region on the map of practitioners and scholars and an ideational one of igniting an innovation by learning from flaws and errors of previous experiences on a path to improved citizen participation. Another element is the effect of electoral turnover and rejuvenation of the regional parliaments of Brussels and Wallonia. As Niessen (2019) expected, this effect appeared to have allowed to help question the parliamentary functioning and break with a strict separation between citizens and politicians. Additionally, it appears that the presence of institutional constraints can ease the way of permanently institutionalising deliberation. In the case of Ostbelgien, MPs retain a margin of appreciation once the recommendations are presented. In the Walloon case, MPs believed that a mixed model without binding citizens' vote would help control the content of the recommendations while providing a basis for accountability through the binding vote of the participating MPs.

The experimentations that we can observe in Belgium today are crucial for two reasons. Firstly, because they open a research agenda towards a wider cross-country comparison. Many of the chapters in this book have highlighted the diversity of citizen participation that has taken place in the framework of the CoFoE. Some of the initiatives break with institutional constraints possibly out of philosophical convictions, other might have been implemented due to strategic considerations. The CoFoE has thus generated somewhat of an experimental setting that provides the opportunity to test and further investigate the diversity of reasons why deliberative democracy is used in the first place. The CoFoE raises similar questions in itself. What factors drove its implementation? How do *interests, ideas* and *institutions* shape diverse formats that emerged on the EU-level?

Secondly, Belgium showcases how institutionalisation of deliberative democracy can succeed despite what some authors identify as a permanent cessation of political autonomy. The Ostbelgien Modell and the deliberative commissions have, through careful design and contextual factors, grown into permanent aspects of the Belgian political life. Despite the restraining constitutional framework and reluctance of some parties towards specific models, it is clear that MPs are willing to rethink democracy as they recognise the need for democratic renewal. For practitioners, the reasoning behind the 'why' MPs implement deliberative mechanisms might not be as salient as to ask 'why they do not' or what strategies are implemented to cope with constraints of deliberative models or reluctance voiced by opposing MPs. The investigation of MPs' reasoning thus remains crucial independently of the level of analysis.

5. References

Bächtiger, Andreas/Dryzek, John S./Mansbridge, Jane/Warren, Mark E. (eds.) 2018: The Oxford Handbook of Deliberative Democracy, Oxford.

Blondiaux, Loïc 2008: Le nouvel esprit de la démocratie: Actualité de la démocratie participative, Paris.

Bouhon, Frédéric/Niessen, Christoph/Reuchamps, Min 2015: La Communauté germanophone après la sixième réforme de l'État : état des lieux, débats et perspectives, in: Courrier hebdomadaire du CRISP (CRISP) 2266-2267, pp. 5–71.

Bowler, Shaun/Donovan, Todd/Karp, Jeffrey A. 2006: Why Politicians Like Electoral Institutions: Self-Interest, Values, or Ideology?, in: The Journal of Politics 68(2), pp. 434–446.

Caluwaerts, Didier/Reuchamps, Min 2013: Combining Federalism with Consociationalism: Is Belgian Consociational Federalism Digging its Own Grave?, in: Ethnopolitics 14(3), pp. 277–295.

Caluwaerts, Didier/Reuchamps, Min 2018: The Legitimacy of Citizen-led Deliberative Democracy: The G1000 in Belgium, Abingdon.

Caluwaerts, Didier/Kern, Anna/Reuchamps, Min/Valcke, Tony 2020: Between Party Democracy and Citizen Democracy: Explaining Attitudes of Flemish Local Chairs Towards Democratic Innovations, in: Politics of the Low Countries 2(2), pp. 192–213.

Cohen, Joshua/Fung, Archon 2011: Le projet de la démocratie radicale, in: Raisons politiques 42(2), pp. 115–130.

Deschouwer, Kris 2012: The Politics of Belgium, New York.

de Sousa Santos, Boaventura 1998: Participatory Budgeting in Porto Alegre: Toward a Redistributive Democracy, in: Politics & Society 26(4), pp. 461–510.

Edelenbos, Jurian 2005: Institutional Implications of Interactive Governance: Insights from Dutch Practice, in: Governance. An International Journal of Policy, Administration and Institutions 18(1), pp. 111–134.

Edelenbos, Jurian/van Meerkerk, Ingmar 2015: Connective capacity in water governance practices: The meaning of trust and boundary spanning for integrated performance. Current Opinion in Environmental Sustainability 12, pp. 25–29.

Federal Public Service Foreign Affairs, Foreign Trade and Development Cooperation (FPS Foreign Affairs) (ed.) 2022: Belgium in the Conference on the Future of Europe, Brussels. https://futureu.europa.eu/pages/belgium (25.08.2022).

Fung, Archon/Wright, Erik O. (eds.) 2003: Deepening Democracy: Institutional Innovations in Empowered Participatory Governance, New York.

Galais, Carol/Font, Joan 2011: Bringing them in: Explanatory factors of successful mobilization in participatory processes. Paper presented at the EHSS conference, Paris.

Geissel, Brigitte/Hess, Pamela 2017: Explaining Political Efficacy in Deliberative Procedures - A Novel Methodological Approach, in: Journal of Public Deliberation 13(2). https://doi.org/10.16997/jdd.280.

Gilljam, Mikael/Persson, Mikael/Karlsson, David 2012: Representatives' Attitudes Toward Citizen Protests in Sweden: The Impact of Ideology, Parliamentary Position, and Experiences, in: Legislative Studies Quarterly 37(2), pp. 251–268.

Hall, Peter A./Taylor, Rosemary R. C. 1997: La science politique et les trois néo-institutionnalismes, in: Revue française de science politique (RFSP) 47(3–4), pp. 469–496.

Heinelt, Hubert 2013: Councillors' Notions of Democracy, and their Role Perception and Behaviour in the Changing Context of Local Democracy, in: Local Government Studies 39(5), pp. 640–660.

Jacquet, Vincent/Schiffino, Nathalie/Reuchamps, Min/Latinis, Delphine 2015: Union sacrée ou union forcée? Les parlementaires belges face à l'impératif délibératif, in: Participations 13(3), pp. 171–203.

Junius, Nino/Matthieu, Joke/Caluwaerts, Didier/Erzeel, Silvia 2020: Is It Interests, Ideas or Institutions? Explaining Elected Representatives' Positions Toward Democratic Innovations in 15 European Countries, in: Frontiers in Political Science, 12.11.2020. https://doi.org/10.3389/fpos.2020.584439.

Lefebvre, Rémi/Talpin, Julien/Petit, Guillaume 2020: Les adjoint·es à la démocratie participative. Une catégorie d'élu·es entre spécialisation fonctionnelle et misère positionnelle, in: Participations 26-27(1), pp. 41–75.

Lowndes, Vivien/Pratchett, Lawrence/Stoker, Gerry 2001: Trends in Public Participation: Part 2 – Citizens' Perspectives, in: Public Administration 79(2), pp. 445–455.

Macq, Hadrien/Jacquet, Vincent 2021: Institutionalising participatory and deliberative procedures: The origins of the first permanent citizens' assembly, in: European Journal of Political Research online, 27.11.2021. https://doi.org/10.1111/1475-6765.12499.

Mayer, Igor/Edelenbos, Jurian/Monnikhof, René 2005: Interactive Policy Development: Undermining or Sustaining Democracy?, in: Public Administration 83(1), pp. 179–199.

Niessen, Christoph 2019: When citizen deliberation enters real politics: how politicians and stakeholders envision the place of a deliberative mini-public in political decision-making, in: Policy Sciences 52(3), pp. 481–503.

Niessen, Christoph/Reuchamps, Min 2019: Le dialogue citoyen permanent en Communauté Germanophone, in: Courrier hebdomadaire du CRISP (CRISP) 2426, pp. 5–38.

Niessen, Christoph 2021: Federalization in the slipstream: How the German-speaking Community of Belgium became one of the smallest federal entities in the world, in: Nations and Nationalism 27(4), pp. 1026–1046.

Niessen, Christoph/Reuchamps, Min 2022: Institutionalising Citizen Deliberation in Parliament: The Permanent Citizens' Dialogue in the German-speaking Community of Belgium, in: Parliamentary Affairs 75(1), pp. 135–153.

Organisation for Economic Co-operation and Development (OECD) (ed.) 2021: Innovative Citizen Participation and New Democratic Institutions. Catching the deliberative wave. https://bit.ly/3YiNTR2 (25.08.2022).

Palier, Bruno/Surel, Yves 2005: Les " trois I" et l'analy0073e de l'État en action, in: Revue française de science politique (RFSP) 55(1), pp. 7–32.

Rangoni, Sacha/Bedock, Camille/Talukder, David 2021: More competent thus more legitimate? MPs' discourses on deliberative mini-publics, in: Acta Politica online, 22.06.2021. https://doi.org/10.1057/s41269-021-00209-4.

Reuchamps, Min 2020: Belgium's experiment in permanent forms of deliberative democracy. ConstitutionNet, 17.01.2020. http://constitutionnet.org/news/belgiums-experiment-permanent-forms-deliberative-democracy (30.05.2022).

Ryan, Matt 2014: Advancing comparison of democratic innovations: A medium-N fuzzy-set qualitative comparative analysis of participatory budgeting (Doctoral Thesis), Southampton.

Schiffino, Nathalie/Jacquet, Vincent/Cogels, Maximilien/Reuchamps, Min 2019: Les gouvernants face aux transformations de la démocratie. Le point de vue des ministres et des présidents de parti, in: Gouvernement et action publique 2(2), pp. 57–80.

Suiter, Jane/Harris, Clodagh/Farrell, David M./O'Malley, Eoin 2016: The Irish Constitutional Convention: a case of 'high legitimacy'?, in: *Reuchamps, Min/Suiter, Jane (eds.)*: Constitutional deliberative democracy in Europe, Colchester, pp. 33–51.

Van Crommbrugge, Roland 2021: Laboratories for democracy Democratic renewal in the Belgian federation, in: *Deseure, Brecht/Geenens, Raf/Sottiaux Stefan (eds.)*: Sovereignty, Civic Participation and Constitutional Law. The People versus the Nation in Belgium, London, pp. 217–235.

Vrydagh, Julien/Bottin, Jehan/Reuchamps, Min/Bouhon, Frédéric/Devillers, Sophie 2021: Les commissions délibératives entre parlementaires et citoyens tirés au sort au sein des assemblées bruxelloises, in: Courrier hebdomadaire du CRISP (CRISP) 2492, pp. 5–68.

Vrydagh, Julien/Devillers, Sophie/Talukder, David/Jacquet, Vincent/Bottin, Jehan 2020: Les mini-publics en Belgique (2001-2018): expériences de panels citoyens délibératifs, in: Courrier hebdomadaire du CRISP (CRISP) 2477-2478, pp. 5–72.

Zurn, Christopher F. 2007: Deliberative democracy and the institutions of judicial review, New York.

The Conference on the Future of Europe in Germany: Activities at federal and *Länder* level

Gabriele Abels

1. Introduction

In the context of the Conference on the Future of Europe (CoFoE) a total of about 350 events took place in Germany, plus about 1,500 ideas and 4,650 comments from Germany made it into the official Multilingual Digital Platform. Climate change, environment protection and strengthening democracy were the core issues (Bundesregierung 2022). This is the official record. However, a closer look is necessary. Activities were organized mainly by civil society organizations (about 300), while the *Länder* organized about 50 events and the Federal government about 14 citizens' dialogues, only one of them being an official national citizens' forum (ibid.).

Despite these considerable numbers, Germany's official position towards and involvement in CoFoE can be characterized as ambiguous. Several factors help to explain this ambivalence: One the one hand, the population is pro-European. In 2022, 73% of Germans consider EU membership as "a good thing", i.e., 11 percentage points above the EU27 average (European Parliament 2022: 16). A "pro-European basic consensus" (Niedermayer 2021: 195; translation by the author) exists also in the party system, even if this is slightly changing with positions becoming more differentiated, particularly at the fringes of the party system. Overall, this speaks in favour of strong participation.

On the other hand, there are also some external and domestic factors which need to be considered. Franco-German relations, which have come under stress, are a major external factor. The renewal of the old "friendship treaty" (i.e., the Elysée Treaty of 1963) in 2019 via the Treaty of Aachen could not make up for the many ups and downs, especially since 2012. In this sense, CoFoE provided a window of opportunity for Franco-German leadership.

Furthermore, several structural characteristics have influenced the approach towards the Conference and the corresponding activities. Firstly, over the course of CoFoE's development and implementation national elections took place, leading to a change in government. Secondly, Germany is a federal country. The 16 *Länder* enjoy strong participation rights in EU affairs granted in Article 23 of the constitution (*Grundgesetz,* GG); their main channel of participation is the *Bundesrat*. In the past, the *Länder* have responded to different degrees and in different ways to EU affairs. Thirdly, representative democracy has a strong tradition, whereas participatory and deliberative formats are almost completely absent at national level and, moreover, unevenly implemented in the *Länder*. All these factors have an impact on whether, how, and in which ways national and regional actors have responded to and participated in CoFoE.

This contribution will investigate the German activities in relation to CoFoE. It does not claim to be an exhaustive analysis. Yet, I will sketch out the participation of the core institutions at the federal as well as the *Länder* level. Moreover, I consider the governmental as well as the parliamentary dimension. In comparison to Austria (see Meyer et al. in this volume) some striking differences and similarities come up.

The paper proceeds as follows[1]: In section 2 I will investigate the position of the federal government – against the background of Franco-German relations –, as well as the activities at federal level in the *Bundestag* and the *Bundesrat*. Section 3 will focus on the level of the *Länder*. Finally, section 4 will draw some conclusions.

2. The federal level and CoFoE

2.1 Situating CoFoE in the light of Franco-German relations

We cannot understand the activities at national level without considering Franco-German relations and their function for the European integration process. For Germany, France is clearly an "indispensable ally in European policy-making" (Krotz/Schild 2018). These relations have come under stress – or even to a standstill – during the "EU polycrisis", ever since the "Euro crisis" (see Lequesne/Schild 2018; Mourlon-Druol 2017; Schild 2020). During the 16 years of her chancellorship Angela Merkel has dealt with four different French Presidents and relationships have seen many "ups and downs" (Pistorius 2021). In addition, the potential leadership of the tandem itself has become much more complex in an enlarged Union (Schild 2010). CoFoE was initiated against this challenging background.

While the idea for the CoFoE-format originated in the Elysée, i.e. the palace of the French President in Paris, in spring 2019 (see introduction to this volume; see also Metzger and Torres-Ader), it quickly made it to the German *Bundeskanzleramt*, the Chancellery, in Berlin. The question was how then-Chancellor Angela Merkel would respond to the reform impetus by her ambitious French colleague, Emmanuel Macron, after having remained silent to Macron's proposals for the previous two years.

In 2017, Macron has campaigned for Presidency on a very Europhile agenda. Ever since in office he has presented ambitious ideas for reforming the EU, for instance in his famous Sorbonne speech "Initiative for Europe" as of 26 September 2017. Germany was intended to be a key ally. Macron proclaims:

"So first of all I am making the proposal to Germany for a new partnership. We will not agree on everything, or straightaway, but we will discuss everything … On all the issues I have talked about, France and Germany can inject decisive, practical momentum." (Macron 2017)

For the hesitant German Chancellor the reform visions were way too aspiring. One commentator wrote that "the sheer magnitude of his plan [in the Sorbonne speech] runs the risk of creating shock and awe in Berlin" (Briançon 2017). In the months to come, Macron became increasingly frustrated by the lack of response. Merkel's approach to EU politics is characterized as "conservational pragmatic" (Heermann et al. 2022: 477; translation by the author). Her focus was instead on holding the Union together in times of crisis; pushing for ambitious reforms risked triggering further disputes among the already estranged member states.

---

1   Methodologically, this contribution is mainly based on official documents, i.e. parliamentary debates and resolutions, governmental information. Informal background talks with some actors were conducted. I am grateful to my research assistant Cem Yildirim for his support in data collection and analysis.

The French President voiced his discontent and frustration over German reluctance for reforms fairly open in his speech on the occasion of receiving the prestigious Charlemagne Prize on 10 May 2018 (Macron 2018). In March 2019, with European Parliament elections on the horizon, Macron published his open letter to the "Citizens of Europe" (Macron 2019), issued in many national newspapers. He invited the citizens to "set up, with the representatives of the European institutions and the Member States, *a Conference for Europe in order to propose all the changes our political project needs,* with an open mind, even to amending the treaties" (Macron 2019; emphasis in original).

Finally, a sign of life came from the German Chancellor. The result was a Franco-German non-paper issued in November 2019. It asserts the claim for intergovernmental leadership and, moreover, Franco-German leadership. Even though it was only a two-pager, it became the "blueprint" for CoFoE. In this non-paper both governments called for a future conference which "needs to involve all three EU institutions" (Franco-German non-paper 2019: 1). It shall be "chaired by a senior European personality", who "shall be advised by a small Steering Group" (ibid.). A two-step process was proposed: In the first phase the focus shall be on "issues related to EU democratic functioning", especially issues like transnational lists for European elections, the "lead candidate system" (*Spitzenkandidaten*), or "issues related to citizens' participation" (ibid.). The second phase shall be devoted to policy priorities. The conference shall "identify, by blocks of policies, the main reforms to implement as a matter of priority, setting out the types of changes to be made (legal – incl. possible treaty change, financial, organizational etc.)" (ibid.). While the non-paper neither specified the topics nor the governance structure, it did set the path for the next European Council (EUCO) summit in 2019.

Some observers argue that CoFoE actually became an opportunity to overcome some of the previous tensions in Franco-German relations and to demonstrate unity (Momatz/ Herszenhorn 2019). Certainly, a response to French initiatives was long overdue. Europe was – formally – high on the agenda of the *Merkel IV* government. Coalition building was extremely difficult after the September 2017 federal elections. After months of negotiations, yet another "grand coalition" with the social democrats was installed. The coalition agreement prioritized the need for "a new awakening for Europe" (*Ein neuer Aufbruch für Europa*) and proclaims that

"we want Germany to take an active part in the debate over the future of the EU and we aim at strengthening European integration, we also want that citizens can participate in national public dialogues on European reform debates. Thereby, we want Europe to be closer to the citizens and more transparent and renew trust" (Koalitionsvertrag 2018: 6; translation by the author).

Nevertheless, the actual policy by the Chancellor herself, as well as by the Foreign Ministry, was less ambitious. While the coalition agreement – at least rhetorically – paved the way for stronger German engagement in CoFoE, the behaviour can be classified as an "ambivalent approach" (von Ondarza/Ålander 2021: 20). In their assessment of the German expectations von Ondarza and Ålander (ibid.) attest that Germany was "on board but lacking vision". They also affirm that "[a]lthough it [Germany] originally brought forward a non-paper with France in November 2019 on how to shape and use the Conference, the Conference was not a priority for Germany during its presidency of the EU Council in the second half of 2020" (ibid.). Over the course of 2021, when inter-institutional compromises were finalized under the Portuguese Council Presidency, "Germany has begun to develop ideas for the Conference. Nevertheless, there is still no clear vision with regard to its priorities" (ibid.). Pertaining to the vital question of treaty changes as a potential outcome, the Merkel government pursued a "cautious approach" (ibid.). However, the government was more committed on citizen participation. Indeed, some citizens' dialogues on the EU were already conducted in 2018, hence prior to CoFoE.

In sum, von Ondarza and Ålander conclude: "While Germany was not particularly enthusiastic about the Conference in the earlier stages and during its Council presidency, it is now committed to making the best of the opportunity to involve citizens" (ibid.). Simultaneously, upcoming national elections only allowed the Merkel government to take the role of a "passive participant" (ibid.) in CoFoE, especially since it was likely that a new coalition government would come into power in autumn 2021. Furthermore, in the whole electoral campaign and also in the major media events (e.g. the nationwide broadcasted discussion of the three lead candidates of the CDU, SPD, and – for the first time – the Greens) European affairs were hardly discussed; CoFoE was not mentioned.

Based on the election results, a three-party "traffic light coalition"[2] was formed consisting of the social democrats (SPD), the Greens and the liberal FDP. Coalition-building was indeed faster than initially feared: the new government came into office on 8 December 2021. It presents itself as a progressive reform coalition after 16 years of conservative leadership under Chancellor Merkel. Again, European integration is a prominent issue in the coalition agreement. In the chapter on "Germany's responsibility for Europe and the world" the coalition partners confirm their commitment to "a democratically strengthened, capable of acting, and strategically sovereign European Union" (Koalitionsvertrag 2021: 131; translation by the author) – a wording that reflects Macron's motto. CoFoE is now explicitly mentioned and even linked to the need for a follow-up convention on institutional reforms deemed necessary.

"We use the Conference on the Future of Europe for reforms. We support the necessary treaty changes. The Conference should lead to a constitutional convention and to the further development of a federal European state, which is organised in a decentral manner according to the principles of subsidiarity and proportionality and based on the Charter of Fundamental Rights. We want to strengthen the European Parliament (EP), e.g. with regard to the right of initiative – preferably in the Treaties, otherwise inter-institutionally. We will give priority to the Community method again, but go ahead with individual member states where necessary. We support a uniform European electoral law with partly transnational lists and a binding system of lead candidates" (ibid.).

Given this strong commitment it is not surprising that – in the current follow-up process to CoFoE – the government formed a coalition with five other member states (Belgium, Italy, Luxembourg, the Netherlands, and Spain). Recently, this sextet issued a non-paper in which it declared to "remain in principle open to necessary treaty changes that are jointly defined" (Non-paper 2022). This paper stands in contrast to another non-paper by 13 member states who strongly oppose a convention and treaty change (Permanent Representation of Sweden

---

2 Because of the parties' emblematic colours: red for the SPD, yellow for the FDP, and green for Bündnis90/Die Grünen.

to the European Union 2022). France supports a convention, but remained neutral in this dispute in May 2022, since it was still holding the rotating Council Presidency.

2.2 Activities of the Federal Government

Besides the strong rhetorical commitment, many of the actual national activities of the federal government were last minute – even though some experience with citizens' dialogues on the future of Europe, dating back to 2018, already existed (see BT-Drucksache 19/5752).[3] A website was set-up early[4], which was accompanied by social media activities on Facebook, Twitter, and Instagram. Yet, on substantial issues, the Merkel government was fairly reluctant. The government declared that it did not intent to issue an official position before the upcoming elections in September 2021. There was some coordination among the Chancellery, the Foreign Ministry, and the Federal Press Office. At the start of CoFoE, the SPD Foreign Minister, Heiko Maas, posted a video and his State Minister for European Affairs, Michael Roth, published a podcast to mobilize citizens (BT-Drucksache 19/31895). The Foreign Ministry was most active in conducting some transborder dialogues (with France, Italy, Luxembourg, Czech Republic). Further citizens' dialogues were conducted by individual ministries based on the principle of ministerial responsibility (Ressortprinzip).

The government did not plan an official national dialogue before the September 2021 election (ibid.: 5). Yet, State Minister Roth developed "plans to organise citizen participation in innovative formats" (von Ondarza/Ålander 2021: 20). Hence, the new government could follow up on these preparations when it took office in December 2021. A singular national event was organized last minute in January 2022 (Auswärtiges Amt 2022). It focused on five topics – reflecting the official CoFoE topics – ideas and contributions from German citizens on the Multilingual Digital Platform. Deliberation took place in a two-step, digital-only event involving about 100 randomly selected citizens. After a weekend of deliberation in the citizens' panels (five groups with 20 citizens each, plus additional experts) in early January 2022, the concluding conference was organized mid-January, resulting in a list with ten recommendations. All of them were voted on by the citizens, requiring a super-majority of 70 %. The recommendations were handed over to the new green Minister for Foreign Affairs, Annalena Baerbock, and they were discussed at this concluding conference by official German delegates to CoFoE, including the citizens who participated in the CoFoE supranational events. The recommendations were then uploaded on the CoFoE Digital Platform, and they were also induced into the CoFoE at the third Conference Plenary, which was devoted to the presentation of the results from national citizens' dialogues. The presentation was made by the official delegate of the German dialogues, Stephanie Hartung, who is one of the founders of the pro-European movement Pulse of Europe and well connected to other civil society organizations (BT-Drucksache 19/31575: 19).

In sum, firstly, the upcoming national election and the change in government influenced the intensity and direction of governmental activities. Secondly, we can observe a strong streamlining of the national event with supranational activities in terms of timing (even if

---

3   References to documents by the Bundestag and Bundesrat only by the official document number.
4   See www.bundesregierung.de/konferenz-zur-zukunft-europas (16.08.2022).

last minute), themes, and rules of conduct. Thirdly, the way CoFoE was dealt with fits into the general patterns of how European Affairs are organized in the government with some degree of leadership and coordination of the Chancellery on the one hand and the principle of ministerial responsibility on the other.

2.3 *German delegates in the CoFoE structure*

The number of Germans in the various bodies of the Conference is quite high. Besides the randomly selected citizens, this includes several high-level politicians. This pertains to the Executive Board but even more so to the Conference Plenary. For instance, the Prime Minister (Winfried Kretschmann) and the Minister of Justice (Guido Wolf) from Baden-Württemberg plus the Chair of the *Bundestag*'s European Affairs Committee (Gunther Krichbaum) participated as observers for the COSAC[5] Troika in some meetings of the Executive Board. In addition, three of the seven MEPs delegated as members respectively observers to the Executive Board were from Germany (Daniel Freund, Greens; Manfred Weber, EPP (CDU/CSU); Helmut Scholz, Linke).

The Conference Plenary had a total of 38 participants from Germany; this is about 8.5% of all 449 Plenary members.[6] Also, several Germans were sitting on the Executive Board.

- The Federal Government was represented by the State Minister for European Affairs as part of the Council delegates (Michael Roth, later Anna Lührmann) and a State Secretary from the Ministry of Economics.

- The *Bundestag* and *Bundesrat* shared the four positions for national parliamentary delegates. The *Bundestag* delegated two members of its European Affairs Committee, the two delegates elected by the *Bundesrat* both held the rank of State Ministers for federal and European affairs (from Lower Saxony and Hessia).

- The delegation of the European Parliament to the Conference Plenary had 13 German MEPs out of a total of 108 delegates, which is proportional to the number of German seats. As mentioned, three of the seven political groups delegate German MEPs as observers to the Executive Board.

- Also, there were four Germans among the Social Partners and among the delegates from the European Economic and Social Committee.

- The delegation from the European Committee of the Regions (CoR) had three high-ranking German members: two presidents of German state parliaments (from Bavaria and from Baden-Württemberg) plus a State Secretary for European Affairs (from North Rhine-Westphalia).

- Finally, eleven citizens from Germany were in the group representing the "European citizens' panels, National citizens' panels and events, European Youth Forum".

---

5   COSAC is the Conference of European Affairs Committees of the national parliaments of the member states. The abbreviation comes from the French *Conférence des Organes spécialisées dans les affaires communautaires*.

6   Own calculation based on list for second plenary session in October 2021; see list on https://futureu.europa. eu/pages/plenary?locale=en (15.08.2022).

The Foreign Ministry set up some virtual events among the official German delegates from the federal and the *Länder* level to allow for networking and ensuring exchange of information (see Aras in this volume).

2.4 Parliamentary activities in the Bundestag and Bundesrat

CoFoE was accompanied by parliamentary discussions from the very beginning – both in the *Bundestag* as well as in the *Bundesrat*. It received information directly from the European Commission, but also from the national government. The constitutional provision laid out in Art. 23 GG are the basis for their strong domestic participation rights. Accordingly, the government has to inform both parliamentary chambers as early as possible, and – depending on the issue – it has to consider their position when developing a national position for negotiations in the Council. Overall, the *Bundestag* has been and still is more reluctant to make use of its rights in EU affairs (see also Abels 2021; Beichelt 2012), while the *Bundesrat* has advocated for stronger participation rights early on to compensate for *Länder* competences being hollowed out due to their transfer to the EU level (see Hrbek 2021).

2.4.1 Bundestag

It would be beyond the scope of this contribution to include all debates and activities in the *Bundestag* in detail. The way CoFoE was dealt with reflects the overall approach and practices of the *Bundestag* in general as well as in EU affairs in particular. This pertains to the structures of a "working parliament" with a strong involvement of committees, the parliamentary logic of government vs. opposition dynamics and party politics respectively, and the "watchdog", i.e. control function, plus "policy-shaper" ambitions of the *Bundestag* (see Höing 2015). CoFoE was on the agenda of the *Bundestag* plenum several times. It was also discussed in the European Affairs Committee (EAC) as the responsible committee dealing with general issues of European integration. Furthermore, the EAC chair, Gunter Krichbaum, and the committee member Axel Schäfer became the official two delegates of the *Bundestag* to CoFoE's Conference Plenary.

Overall, CoFoE as an innovative method and its outcome was welcomed by most political parties, reflecting the still broad pro-European consensus in the German party system (Niedermayer 2021). The only exception is the right-wing populist *Alternative für Deutschland* (AfD; see Böttger/Tekin 2021), which even favours a German EU Exit (*Dexit*).[7] It used various interpellation rights and took a strong stance against CoFoE throughout the process and in the aftermath – in the EAC as well as in the plenum (resembling the Austrian FPÖ approach, see Meyer et al. in this volume).

For instance, when Krichbaum and Schäfer were elected by the plenum on 11 June 2021 as representatives of the German *Bundestag*. This offered the AfD an opportunity for substantial critique, since both delegates came from the, at that time, two biggest parliamentary parties – the CDU and the SPD –, which were part of the then-government coalition. This was contested among all opposition parties – above all the AfD. It criticized this as

---

7   In the 19th Bundestag (2017–2021) initially 94 out of 705 MPs came from the AfD, in the current 20th Bundestag (since 2021) the number decreased to 83 out of 736 MPs.

"undemocratic" and voted against the two delegates, while the FDP and the Greens abstained (BT/Plenarprotokoll 19/234). Both MPs remained to represent the German *Bundestag* even after the change in government in December 2021.

Especially opposition parties used their interpellation rights to receive information from the government about the development of CoFoE at EU level and about its national implementation. The Greens, for instance, already issued a "*Kleine Anfrage*" (small enquiry)[8] in 2018 about the predecessor, the citizens' dialogues, and their evaluation (BT-Drucksache 19/5312). On CoFoE Green MPs wanted to know in written questions (*schriftliche Frage*)[9] why the government had not signed a letter issued by five ministers for Foreign Affairs in support of initiating the Conference (BT-Drucksache 19/19021: 19) and how information of the official German civil society delegate is safeguarded (BT-Drucksache 19/31575: 19). Questions about the delayed start, issues of transparency and citizen participation were tabled in an enquiry as of 9 March 2021 by the party *Die Linke* (BT-Drucksache 19/27448). The government, in its swift written response as of 23 March 2021, outlines the state of play at EU level and its own position (BT-Drucksache 19/27769). The liberal FDP put forward three such enquiries: On 25 November 2020 it forwarded a list of 16 questions, focussing exclusively on the role of the Committee of the Regions in CoFoE (BT-Drucksache 19/24697), to which the government responded on 22 December 2020 (BT-Drucksache 19/25604). On 13 April 2021 it issued a list of 14 questions about the governmental position, where it sees the need to reform the EU and the current implementation of CoFoE (BT-Drucksache 19/28392), to which the government responded within three weeks (BT-Drucksache 19/29252). Another set of questions was issued on 9 July 2021 about governmental activities in Germany and accompanying (social) media activities (BT-Drucksache 19/31457). Also, to this enquiry the response as of 5 August 2021 was swift and detailed (BT- Drucksache 19/31895). Finally, the AfD posed a written question about the cost for CoFoE at EU (BT-Drucksache 20/534: 40) and at national level (BT-Drucksache 20/602: 51).

CoFoE was discussed several times in the plenary. It was also included in the regular government statements in plenary and de-briefings to parliament by both chancellors since 2020. For instance, there was an "agreed debate" on 27 January 2022 (Deutscher Bundestag 2022a). This debate, firstly, provided an opportunity for the new government – in office since 8 December 2021 – to position itself. The new State Minister for European Affairs, Anna Lührmann, called CoFoE a "booster for European democracy" and applauded the enthusiasm of the participating citizens. Secondly, the debate already focused on the follow-up process. All political parties welcomed CoFoE and praised its innovative nature. Especially the parties in government committed themselves to respecting the recommend-dations and to a sincere discussion of the numerous ideas – including institutional reforms. They emphasized the possibility of a formal convention in line with the coalition agreement. While cross-partisan agreement existed in this debate, the only exception was, again, the AfD which condemned CoFoE as a federalist undertaking and a betrayal of citizens. Typical

---

8   The government responds to this type of enquiry by political groups in written form. The response is not discussed in the plenary but feeds into future opposition strategies.

9   In contrast to "Kleine Anfragen" (see footnote 8) these questions can be issued by individual MPs.

is the comment by the vice-chair of the political group and EAC member Norbert Klein-wächter: "Europe's future will only be prosperous if this European Union has no future" (Ibid.: 899; translation by the author). The left-wing fringe party *Die Linke*, a "soft", policy-based Eurosceptic party, emphasized the need for social Europe and a role for the accession countries from the Western Balkan in CoFoE.

The positions and sentiments in this debate were reflected in the, thus far, final debate focusing on the follow-up (Deutscher Bundestag 2022b). In his report on the extraordinary European Council Summit, Chancellor Scholz briefly mentioned CoFoE. This debate was becoming quite heated when point 18 on the agendas was discussed, i.e. a formal request (*Antrag*) by the AfD under the heading "saving democracy – distancing from the future conference" (BT-Drucksache 20/1868; translation by the author). In their request the populist party questions the democratic legitimacy of the CoFoE process and its outcome. The party argues that the selection of citizens was far from random and that there was a bias towards left-leaning, pro-European citizens instead. In the end, the request was transferred to the EAC for further discussion, where it will certainly be outvoted.

In sum, in the *Bundestag* we can observe the normal path of partisan and parliamentary politics alongside the still broad pro-integrationist consensus.

2.4.2 Bundesrat and executive federalism

CoFoE was also discussed within the structures of German executive federalism and in the framework of the "responsibility for integration" imposed on the *Länder* by the German Constitutional Court. Besides the *Bundesrat* – as de facto second chamber[10] – the Conference of European Affairs Ministers (*Europaminister-Konferenz*, EMK) from the 16 *Länder* is key. CoFoE was discussed in both settings.

Already in the early days of CoFoE in January 2020, the 82nd EMK issued a resolution in which the ministers welcome CoFoE as a citizens-based impulse for European democracy (EMK 2020). They highlight their claim that the German *Länder* as regions with legislative competences[11] must be able to participate in this process and in discussions over the future of the EU. They ask the European Commission for up-to-date information and the federal government for participation in line with constitutional requirements. At the 87th EMK in September 2021 CoFoE was mentioned in relation to strengthening European democracy and Union citizenship (EMK 2021). Finally, at its 89th meeting in Brussels in June 2022, the EMK (2022) adopted a resolution to the proposals of the future conference. They emphasize the value of citizens' participation in the future debate. Even if the recommendations can only be consultative, they assure that these should have a "significant weight" in the discussion. They praise the contribution by the *Länder* and call for a better public campaigning in the follow-up process. They also announce that they will investigate some proposals made in more detail and that their assessment is not yet final. Unsurprisingly, they emphasize some aspects related to the competences and power of regions. In this line, they underscore the

---

10 In constitutional terms it is not a second chamber. It consists of delegates from the state governments. Its key task is territorial representation in federal legislation.

11 These regions are organized in CALRE, i.e. the Conference of European Regional Legislative Assemblies (see https://www.calrenet.eu/).

principle of subsidiarity, the need to strengthen the role of national parliaments as guardians of subsidiarity, and their rights to have a say on all recommendations which affect the constitutional competences of the *Länder*. This could, in principle, also affect the *passerelle* clause for a move from unanimity to majority voting in the Council. Interestingly, 11 of the 16 *Länder* (mainly centre-left governments or governments with left-leaning parties as coalition partners) declare in an annex to the official protocol their openness to a convention and their participation therein.

The *Bundesrat* discussed CoFoE at its 986th, 1009th, 1023rd and 1028th plenary sessions (see also Peters and Ziegenbalg in this volume). Prepared by its Chamber for European Affairs (CEA; *Europakammer*) the *Bundesrat* has responded to the various Communications issued by the European Commission on CoFoE. It has adopted several resolutions which were handed over the federal government and directly to the Commission.[12] The first such response was a resolution adopted on 13 March 2020 on the Commission's initial Communication on CoFoE (986th session, BR-Drucksache 37/20). The *Bundesrat* welcomes CoFoE as an impulse to European democracy as well as the direct participation of citizens. It emphasized the rich experiences in several German *Länder* with such dialogues. It calls for decentral events as well as for a clear objective and idea for the follow-up. It also demands to put the topic of a stronger role for national parliaments in relation to the system of subsidiarity control on the agenda. Finally, it demands a strong participation of national parliaments in CoFoE itself, including delegates from second chambers such as the *Bundesrat*. The resolution adopted in its session on 6 November 2020 takes a broader perspective and reflects the challenges by the Covid-19 pandemic. The *Bundesrat* also asks the government to become more active in the Council with the aim to issue as concrete roadmap for CoFoE (BR-Drucksache 591/20). In its 1009th session on 8 October 2021 (BR-Drucksache 738/21) adopts a resolution in which it welcomes the participation of its delegates to the Conference Plenary. It renews its earlier calls for the need to include discussions over institutional reforms on the CoFoE agenda especially with a special focus on the role of national governments and the need for changes to the current system of subsidiarity control. It also calls for having a stronger say in forming the position of the national government on EU reforms.

The follow-up and the Commission's Communication outlining the plans "from vision to concrete action" were discussed in the 1023rd session on 8 July 2022 (BR-Plenarprotokoll 1023). In this debate, the Russian invasion of Ukraine had an impact on the debate and the call for action. Again, both delegates to the Conference Plenary – the minister from Saxony and the federal State Minister for European Affairs – welcome CoFoE and call for a serious response to the recommendations, avoiding disenchantment among citizens and increasing the strategic sovereignty of the EU. In the end, the *Bundesrat* adopted a decision (BR-Drucksache 283/22) which focuses on the issue of subsidiarity and calls for a stronger role for national parliaments. It welcomes the CoFoE recommendations which go in this direction (including options for a "green card"). It emphasized it constitutional right to participate and have an impact on EU affairs in the domestic arena.

---

12 For the list of documents see https://www.bundesrat.de/bv.html?id=0037-20 (28.11.2022).

On 25 November 2022, the Bundesrat adopted another decision in relation to the Commission's Communication on the CoFoE follow-up (BR-Drucksache 282/22). Given the Commission's position on the follow-up of many policies resp. in relation to numerous treaty provisions, the *Bundesrat's* decision emphasizes its constitutionally guaranteed domestic participation rights. In areas where the *Länder* have (co-)legislation rights it demands that the federal government must coordinate its negotiating position with the *Länder* and take the positions of the *Bundesrat* into account, especially in case of competence transfer due to the *passerelle* clause or treaty change. The (non-conclusive) list of policy issues mentioned in the decision includes taxation, electoral law, civil rights (i.e., freedom of establishment or issuance of identity documents), criminal law, public prosecution, and policy cooperation, budget monitoring, environmental policy, trade policy in the field of media and culture, expending the European Court of Justice mandate in relation to intellectual property rights. Finally, changes in the composition of the Committee of the Regions are an issue of particular interest for the *Bundesrat*.

In sum, the *Länder* governments were quite active and channelled their activities via the normal routes of the *Bundesrat* and the EMK. Their focus was on policy fields and specific issues that are of relevance for the *Länder*, but they also take responsibility for the process at large and welcome CoFoE. Unlike in the *Bundestag*, the discussion is much more consensual. The AfD, an advocate of "hard" Eurosceptic positions, is not a member of any state government – thus, it is neither represented in the EMK nor in the *Bundesrat*.

3. CoFoE activities in the German *Länder*

In the EU, the German *Länder* belong to the group of "regions with legislative competences". Based on this provision, they claim a more active role in European affairs for themselves – not only in the domestic arena, but also in EU level policy-making. Subsidiarity concerns are a key issue, which is already prominent in the various resolutions adopted by the *Bundesrat*. [13] While there is some executive dominance, in the last decade regional parliaments such as the German *Landtage* have become more active in EU affairs, yet to different degrees (Abels 2013).

This is also the case regarding CoFoE: Some *Länder* – governments and/or parliaments – were more active than others. According to the official record, about 50 events were organized by the states (Bundesregierung 2022). Furthermore, as a result of lobbying via the European Committee of the Regions (CoR), a higher share of regional delegates was admitted to the Conference Plenary (see also Petzold in this volume). Three delegates came from the German *Länder*: Ilse Aigner, President of the Bavarian State Parliament and CoR delegate on behalf of the Regional Parliaments of Germany; Muhterem Aras, President of the State Parliament of Baden-Württemberg (see also her contribution to this volume); Mark Speich, State Secretary for Federal, European and International Affairs of North Rhine-Westphalia and Chair of the CoR's CIVEX Commission for Citizenship, Governance, Institutional and External Affairs. Hence, delegates from the state level were, for the first

---

13   We see a similar reasoning in other member states with such type of regions; see Kölling in this volume.

time, *directly* involved in an institutionalized and potentially "constitutional process" at EU level.

The following analysis is not exhaustive, but it will point out first findings. Examples of activities from some states will be outlined in more detail.

- We can observe differences between the 16 *Länder* regarding the level of CoFoE-related activities. Only few states remained fairly inactive in terms of government and parliamentary activities; they restricted their activities to raise awareness for CoFoE and to mobilize its citizens to participate (e.g. Hamburg, Saxony-Anhalt). Others were highly active, adopted parliamentary resolutions and governments set up citizens' dialogues – often jointly with other regions across borders.

- Furthermore, we find an executive bias in so far as most CoFoE activities, i.e., actual citizens' dialogues were mainly organized by state governments, sometimes jointly with parliaments. In most *Landtage*, CoFoE was on the agenda at some point in time – especially before it started or in the early days and towards the end; often resolutions were adopted. Some of the more active states are also, in general, more active in EU affairs. However, there is neither a clear pattern regarding the general level of activity in EU affairs and on CoFoE nor regarding parties in government.

- Especially those *Länder* with national borders often organized dialogue events with border regions, i.e., with Austria, Belgium, the Czech Republic, France, and Poland. Already existing Euroregions, Interreg projects, and other formats of regional (or even municipal, i.e. twin cities) cooperation were often used to organize these transborder events. Some dialogues were organized with member state which are not direct neighbours (i.e., Croatia). Experiences with digital formats helped to set them up.

- Digital formats were used in many states, especially, but not only for transborder events. Some state conducted virtual deliberations only (e.g. North Rhine-Westphalia). Yet, often also in-person events took place, if Covid-19 regulations allowed to do so.

- In addition, many dialogues were particularly directed to young people (sometimes combined with the framework of the European Year of Youth 2022). Sometimes this involved more creative formats such as poetry slams and comic events (Schleswig-Holstein), or direct exchange between citizens and MEPs during a Ferris wheel ride labelled the "Europa*Rad" (Bavaria).

- Often the events were accompanied by systematic documentation, reporting and evaluation. Usually, the results of dialogue events were fed into the official CoFoE Multilingual Digital Platform.

- Finally, the support offered by the CoR in terms of developing a toolbox and providing financial resources for translation services was important for several *Länder*, such as for Baden-Württemberg, Bavaria, North Rhine-Westphalia, Rhineland-Palatine, and Saxony.

Baden-Württemberg was the most active among the *Länder* organizing many events – including transborder dialogues. Its strong record in citizens' dialogues, which has mainly been promoted by the government under green party leadership in the past decade, has been a supportive factor. This is further discussed in other contributions to this volume in more detail (see Aras as well as Peters and Ziegenbalg in this volume).

Bavaria was very active as well – including the state parliament.[14] Overall, Bavaria is very active in EU affairs. Regarding CoFoE the high level of activity is also due to the fact that its President, Ilse Aigner, was also the official CoR delegate of regional parliaments with legislative powers in the CoFoE Conference Plenary. Hence, Aigner frequently reported back to her own parliament and fostered discussion. The EAC of the Bavarian *Landtag*, for instance, set up an exchange meeting with the President of the European Economic and Social Committee before the official start of CoFoE, in which they focused on the opportunities provided for citizens' participation. An exchange with Commission representatives was on the agenda of the EAC in May 2022 to discuss the follow-up process. In Bavaria, where party politics is characterized by clear conservative dominance: firstly, the strong position of the conservative CSU (as a regional party) plus, secondly, the party of "Freie Wähler". They currently form the government coalition and are both strong supporters of subsidiarity, federalism, regional diversity, and a strong role for regions. Along these lines, in February 2021 the government coalition issued a proposal for stronger regional parliamentary involvement in CoFoE (Bayerischer Landtag, Drs. 18/13772).

North Rhine-Westphalia concentrated on online deliberation #NRWgestaltetEuropa only. While the state had been active in initiating citizens dialogues already in 2019 as part of its "Beneluxjahr.NRW" in order to discuss opportunities for stronger regional cooperation with the bordering Benelux countries, no cross-border dialogue with these states took place as part of CoFoE. Instead, dialogues were set up with France, Poland, and also Croatia.

Among the East German states Saxony was quite active. Governed by a three-party coalition with a conservative Prime Minister the Minister for Democracy, Europe, and Equality, Katja Meier, comes from the green party. Saxony was involved in the 6-region-dialogue organized by Baden-Württemberg and set up transborder dialogues with neighbouring regions in Poland and the Czech Republic.

Brandenburg also organized several events, some of them cross-border with Poland. Moreover, Brandenburg joined the pilot project "Input from political debates in regional parliaments" early on – a project jointly set up by the CoR and CALRE that indirectly linked to CoFoE. Its aim is to strengthen the impact of regional parliaments with legislative competences on pre-legislative discussions in the EU. This is – as previously mentioned – a core focus of regional activities by the German states, but also by the CoR, in CoFoE.

A number of parliamentary debates in the *Länder* revolved around CoFoE and several corresponding resolutions were adopted. In these state parliament debates the pattern observed in the *Bundestag* is also present, i.e. the broad pro-integrationist consensus – even if there is dissent – in the sense of "soft Euroscepticism" on particular policies and projects (e.g. social or health union, climate policy). For instance, the Landtag of Baden-Württemberg adopted a resolution on 18 January 2022 in which it calls for "regions as co-shapers

---

14 See on this also the report by Barón et al. 2022.

and mediators of a democratic, sustainable Europe in diversity" to which CoFoE can give an impulse. The resolution was proposed and adopted by the government coalition plus all opposition parties, except for the AfD (Landtag von Baden-Württemberg, Drucksache 17/1664). Similarly in Bavaria, where the government coalition proposed a joint resolution calling for the continuation of the Conference in February 2022 (Bayerischer Landtag, Drs. 18/21819). It was adopted by a broad cross-partisan consensus in the EAC and in the plenary – with only the AfD opposing it.

In all debates the only deviant case in terms of the principled nature of its "hard Euroscepticism" is the AfD.[15] The party is currently represented in 15 state parliaments (no longer in Schleswig-Holstein); yet, the share of mandates strongly diverges. For instance, in Saxony the AfD is the second strongest party (31% of seats in the state parliament), similar in Brandenburg (26% of the seats), whereas in Hamburg it is a clear minority (5% of the seats). During the debate on CoFoE in the *Landtag* of Brandenburg in November 2021 its EAC member, Felix Teichner, advocated the AfD's vision of a Europe of nation-states.

"Dear EU fanatics! Your EU policies are divisive, they are wrong, and they are damaging. Your EU policies counteract the original European idea of sovereign and thus strong partner states. Your EU policy stands for paternalism, moral arrogance and is driven by globalist fanaticism" (Landtag Brandenburg, Plenarprotokoll 7/54: 38; translation by the author).

In Thuringia – known for its especially extremist AfD – its parliamentary political group in the *Landtag* issued a resolution on 2 February 2022 which questions the legitimacy of CoFoE. The AfD claims that discussion in the citizens' panels "is a matter of supervised and monitored discussions and, accordingly, of a guided discourse" and thus "staged legitimacy" (Thüringer Landtag, Drucksache 7/4615: 3; translation by the author). They demand a "Dexit" if radical reforms of the EU should fail (ibid.: point 8).

With the end of CoFoE, parliamentary debate is becoming intense again once more. Since I cannot go into the details for all state parliaments, the discussion in and response of the so-called *Landtagspräsidentenkonferenz* (LPK) is taken as a proxy, even if this includes also non-German state parliaments.[16] Exchange on EU affairs, developments in federalisms, and subsidiarity are regular topics on the LPK agenda; fostering the role of regional parliaments in EU policy-making is a key concern. The LPK adopted three declarations on CoFoE: before the official start on 1 February 2021, on an interim evaluation on 24 January 2022, and recently on the final report on 21 June 2022. The main message is that it welcomes CoFoE and citizens' participation as part of a process for democratizing EU politics. It also emphasizes the important contribution of regions and the need for stronger involvement – especially for those regions with legislative powers. The key point in the declaration as of June 2022 is the following:

"The Presidents welcome the fact that, as stated in the final report [of CoFoE], the Conference Plenary emphasises the indispensable role of the regional parliaments in the subsidiarity early warning system and calls for a

---

15 The differentiation between soft, i.e. as opposition to certain policies, vs. hard, i.e. "outright rejection of the entire project", Euroscepticism goes back to Taggart/Szczerbiak 2001.

16 The LPK, i.e. a regular meeting of the presidents of the parliaments of German-speaking regions, already exists for a number of years. While initially membership consisted of the presidents of the German and Austrian state parliaments, it was extended to also include the German-speaking Community of Belgium and the South Tyrolean Parliament.

review of this mechanism. They endorse the demand in the final report that in future the national and also the regional parliaments with legislative powers should be able to propose legislative initiatives at European level. Without prejudice to the increased need for formalised direct dialogue between regional parliaments and the EU institutions, the Presidents support the proposal to further strengthen the role of the European Committee of the Regions (CoR) in matters with territorial implications" (LPK 2022: point 6; translation by the author).

"The Presidents expressly welcome the fact that the final report takes up the demand of regional parliaments to improve the decision-making process of the European Union in the sense of greater transparency for the citizens and to involve, in particular, regional and local representatives more closely." (Ibid.: point 8; translation by the author)

Finally, they support the call to set up a convention based on Article 48 TEU to discuss the need for treaty changes and overtly request to be actively involved in the follow-up process, including in a convention (ibid.: point 12f.). Hence, again we find the motive identified in the *Bundesrat* response, i.e., strengthening the various channels of territiorial interest representation via direct involvement of regions as well as via the CoR.

4. Conclusions

Given that this is a preliminary analysis, the conclusions cannot be final. Obviously, actors from and in Germany were actively involved in CoFoE. This pertains to federal as well as *Länder* level actors, to governments as well as parliaments. Originally, CoFoE offered the Merkel IV government an opportunity to ease some of the tensions in Franco-German relations. At the same time the government was fairly reluctant to become active, since – due to the delay of CoFoE's start – general elections were on the horizon. The new government since December 2021 has adopted a more pro-active stance; it openly supports a follow-up convention and discussion about treaty change. Recently, it linked the prospect of enlargement to the need for institutional reforms: "No EU-reform, no enlargement" (Noyan 2022). This is meant to put pressure on the coalition of 13 member states (see Permanent Representation of Sweden to the European Union 2022) which support enlargement but oppose treaty reforms, especially the switch to majority voting on issues which so far require unanimity in the Council.

As for the various actors at federal and state level, it is obvious that CoFoE offers a "window of opportunity" to revive claims which have been on the agenda already in the past such as a stronger role for parliaments and for regions in EU affairs. Hence, the kind of activities, the nature of debates, and the demands follow the path set in the past. Yet, given the diversity and varying degree of participation in CoFoE, it is not so clear if and how the level of these activities correlates to overall activities in EU affairs, to resources or to other factors. This would require more in-depth research.

What has changed in the German landscape is the kind of Euroscepticism in the party system, which impacts upon the debates around CoFoE. Overall, we still find a broad cross-partisan consensus that European integration is positive and essential for Germany. Yet, when it comes to particular policy issues, position become more differentiated and politicized. Apparent in parties at the fringes, this can be classified as "soft Euroscepticism", which is related to specific issues and projects. CoFoE is overall widely hailed for its innovative nature of citizens' participation.

Yet, with the AfD being represented in the *Bundestag* and currently in 15 state parliaments, a "hard", principled Eurosceptic discourse has found its way into the German discourse. Interestingly, while supportive of direct democracy (referenda) – in order to give citizens a voice against "corrupt elites" – deliberative democracy and its instruments are not supported but denounced as "guided" and abusive forms of participation. This narrative is also present in the FPÖ discourse in Austria (see Meyer et al. in this volume). If this framing is prominent throughout the extreme right in Europe would need to be studied.

When it comes to the *Länder*, the supportive role of the CoR is evident. The CoR has been able to plan a long-term strategy in relation to CoFoE and link it to its overall goals of strengthening its role in EU policy-making and empowering the regions. Even if CoFoE was in the end about citizens' participation and deliberating policy ideas among and with citizens, it was also a welcome opportunity to emphasize institutional reform issues that have been on the agenda of regional and parliamentary actors for a longer period of time. Against this background we have to evaluate, for instance, the joint CoR-CALRE pilot project to increase pre-legislative impact of regional parliaments at EU level. The fact that of the 28 participating state parliaments from six member states five come from Germany (Baden-Württemberg, Bavaria, Brandenburg, Saxony, and Thuringia) is telling.

In sum, there is still a need for further research which would dig deeper into intra-state comparison among the German *Länder* and actors as well as inter-state comparison with other EU member states. Finally, the debate on CoFoE in Germany clearly illustrates that the EU is still a dynamic polity. Far from being obsolete, the debates over the role of regions and their involvement in European affairs – in the domestic as well as in the supranational decision-making arena – will continue.

5. References

Abels, Gabriele 2013: Adapting to Lisbon: Reforming the role of German Landesparlamente in EU Affairs, in: German Politics 22(4), pp. 353–378.

Abels, Gabriele 2021: Die Rolle des Bundestags in der deutschen Europapolitik aus politologischer Perspektive, in: *Böttger, Kathrin/Jopp, Mathias (eds.)*: Handbuch zur deutschen Europapolitik, 2nd revised edition, Baden-Baden, pp. 129–146.

Barón, Cosima/Deckarm, Renke/Vorbach, Johannes 2022: Der Bayerische Beitrag zur Zukunftskonferenz, in: Politische Studien Nr. 501. https://www.hss.de/download/publications/PS_501_EUROPAS_ZUKUNFT_06_neu.pdf (15.08.2022).

Beichelt, Timm 2012: Recovering Space Lost? The German Bundestag's New Potential in European Politics, in: German Politics 21(2), pp. 143–160.

Böttger, Katrin/Tekin, Funda 2021: Germany: Eurosceptics and the Illusion of an Alternative, in: *Kaeding, Michael/Pollak, Johannes/Schmidt, Paul (eds.)*: Euroscepticism and the Future of Europe, Cham, pp. 51–54.

Briançon, Pierre 2017: 5 takeaways from Macron's big speech on Europe's future, in: Politico, 26.09.2017. https://www.politico.eu/article/5-takeaways-from-macrons-big-speech-on-europes-future/ (30.07.2022).

European Parliament 2022: Germany: Socio-demographic trendlines – EP Eurobarometer (2007–2022). https://bit.ly/3KnV4B0 (15.08.2022).

Heermann, Max/Leuffen, Dirk/Tigges, Fabian/Mounchid, Pascal 2022: Nur wer sich ändert, bleibt sich treu? Die Europapolitik der Regierung Merkel IV, in: *Zohlnhöfer, Reimut/ Engler, Fabian (eds.)*: Das Ende der Merkel-Jahre: Eine Bilanz der Regierung Merkel 2018–2021, Wiesbaden, pp. 475–500.

Höing, Oliver 2015: With a Little Help of the Constitutional Court: The Bundestag on Its Way to an Active Policy Shaper, in: *Hefftler, Claudia/Neuhold, Christine/Rozenberg, Olivier/Smith, Julie (eds.)*: The Palgrave Handbook of National Parliaments and the European Union, Basingstoke, pp. 191–208.

Hrbek, Rudolf 2021: Die Rolle der Länder und des Bundesrates in der deutschen Europapolitik, in: *Böttger, Kathrin/Jopp, Mathias (eds.)*: Handbuch zur deutschen Europapolitik, 2nd revised edition, Baden-Baden, pp. 147–168.

Krotz, Ulrich/Schild, Joachim 2018: France: Germany's Indispensable Ally in European Policy-Making, German European Policy Series No. 1, Berlin. http://archiv.iep-berlin.de/ en/publications/geps-01-18/ (15.08.2022).

Lequesne, Christian/Schild, Joachim 2018: La relation franco-allemande et la relance de l'Union européenne, in: Allemagne d'aujourd'hui 226(4), pp. 33–47.

Momatz, Rym/Herszenhorn, David M. 2019: Berlin and Paris outline plan for EU makeover: Two-page document aims to show Franco-German partnership overcoming recent tensions, in: Politico, 26.11.2019. https://www.politico.eu/article/berlin-and-paris-outline-plan-for-eu-makeover/ (30.07.2022).

Mourlon-Druol, Emmanuel 2017: Rethinking Franco-German relations: a historical perspective, Bruegel Policy Contribution No. 29. https://www.bruegel.org/policy-brief/ rethinking-franco-german-relations-historical-perspective (30.07.2022).

Niedermayer, Oskar 2021: Deutsche Parteien und Europa, in: Böttger, *Kathrin/Jopp, Mathias (eds.)*: Handbuch zur deutschen Europapolitik, 2nd revised edition, Baden-Baden, pp. 195–210.

Noyan, Oliver 2022: German top aide: No EU-reform, no enlargement, EurActiv, 28.11. 2022. https://www.euractiv.com/section/politics/news/german-top-aide-no-eu-reform-no-enlargement/ (28.11.2022).

Pistorius, Magdalena 2021: From Chirac to Macron: The four Franco-German duos of the Merkel era, in: EurActiv, 20.09.2021. https://www.euractiv.com/section/politics/news/ from-chirac-to-macron-the-four-franco-german-duos-of-the-merkel-era/ (15.08.2021).

Schild, Joachim 2010: Mission Impossible? The Potential for Franco-German Leadership in the Enlarged EU, in: Journal of Common Market Studies 48(5), pp. 1367–1390.

Schild, Joachim 2020: EMU's Asymmetries and Asymmetries in German and French Influence on EMU Governance Reforms, in: Journal of European Integration 42(3), pp. 447–462.

Taggart, Paul/Szczerbiak, Aleks 2001: Parties, positions and Europe: Euroscepticism in the EU candidate states of Central and Eastern Europe, Working Paper No. 46, Sussex European Institute.

von Ondarza, Nicolai/Ålander, Minna 2021: Germany: on board but lacking vision, in: *Ålander, Minna/von Ondarza, Nicolai/Russack, Sophia (eds.)*: Managed Expectations: EU Member States Views on the Conference on the Future of Europe, EPIN Report, Berlin, p. 20.

6. Primary sources (if not referenced in text with official document number)

Auswärtiges Amt 2022: National Citizens' Panel on the Future of Europe – final report. February 2022, Berlin. https://bit.ly/3QDVDbI (30.07.2022).

Bundesregierung 2022: Beiträge Deutschlands zur Konferenz zur Zukunft Europas: 1.500 Ideen und 350 Veranstaltungen. https://www.bundesregierung.de/breg-de/themen/europa/eu-zukunftskonferenz-2030938 (31.07.2022).

Deutscher Bundestag 2022a: Stenographischer Bericht, 14. Sitzung vom 27.01.2022, Berlin. https://dserver.bundestag.de/btp/20/20014.pdf (15.08.2022).

Deutscher Bundestag 2022b: Stenographischer Bericht, 37. Sitzung vom 19.05.2022, Berlin. https://dserver.bundestag.de/btp/20/20037.pdf#P.3642 (15.08.2022).

EMK 2020: Beschluss der 82. Europaministerkonferenz vom 29./30. Januar 2020, Brüssel. https://bit.ly/3c0SeVE (15.08.2022).

EMK 2021: Beschluss der 87. Europaministerkonferenz vom 8./9. September 2021, Chemnitz. https://bit.ly/3K03Tkd (15.08.2022).

EMK 2022: Stellungnahme zu den Vorschlägen der Konferenz zur Zukunft Europas, Beschluss der 89. Europaministerkonferenz vom 13./14. Juni 2022, Brüssel. https://bit.ly/3AvDKGU (15.08.2022).

Franco-German non-paper 2019: Conference on the Future of Europe: Franco-German non-paper on key questions and guidelines. https://www.politico.eu/wp-content/uploads/2019/11/Conference-on-the-Future-of-Europe.pdf (30.04.2022).

Koalitionsvertrag 2018: Ein neuer Aufbruch für Europa. Eine neue Dynamik für Deutschland. Ein neuer Zusammenhalt für unser Land. Koalitionsvertrag zwischen CDU, CSU und SPD.

Koalitionsvertrag 2021: Mehr Fortschritt wagen: Bündnis für Freiheit, Gerechtigkeit und Nachhaltigkeit. Koalitionsvertrag zwischen SPD, Bündnis90/Die Grünen und FDP.

LPK 2022: Erklärung der Präsidentinnen und Präsidenten der deutschen und österreichischen Landesparlamente und des Südtiroler Landtags unter Beteiligung des Parlaments der Deutschsprachigen Gemeinschaft Belgiens zum Abschlussbericht der Konferenz zur Zukunft Europas vom Mai 2022. Beschlossen für die deutschen Landesparlamente in Bremen am 21. Juni 2022. https://bit.ly/3wcHt9Q (15.08.2022).

Macron, Emmanuel 2017: Initiative for Europe. Sorbonne speech of Emmanuel Marcon, 26.09.2017. https://bit.ly/2Ef4tYI (30.07.2022).

Macron, Emmanuel 2018: Speech by M. Emmanuel Macron, President of the Republic, on receiving the Charlemagne Prize, 10.05.2018. https://www.elysee.fr/en/emmanuel-macron/2018/05/10/speech-by-m-emmanuel-macron-president-of-the-republic-on-receiving-the-charlemagne-prize-1 (30.07.2022).

Macron, Emmanuel 2019: For European renewal, 04.03.2019. https://www.elysee.fr/en/emmanuel-macron/2019/03/04/for-european-renewal (30.07.2022).

Non-paper 2022: Non-paper submitted by Germany, Belgium, Italy, Luxembourg, the Netherlands, and Spain on implementing the proposals of the Plenary of the "Conference on the Future of Europe" 2022, 13.05.2022. https://twitter.com/alemannoEU/status/1526922932970262528 (15.08.2022).

Permanent Representation of Sweden to the European Union 2022: Non-paper by Bulgaria, Croatia, the Czech Republic, Denmark, Estonia, Finland, Latvia, Lithuania, Malta, Poland, Romania, Slovenia, and Sweden on the outcome of and follow-up to the Conference on the Future of Europe, 09.05.2022. https://twitter.com/swedenineu/status/1523637827686531072 (07.07.2022).

The Conference on the Future of Europe – Personal experiences and expectations from the perspective of state parliaments

Muhterem Aras

European integration has led to a shift of competences not only from the national level, but also from the *Länder* – respectively regions – to the European Union. This shift was necessary as well as politically desired. However, European integration poses great challenges for the *Länder* and their parliaments. The reason for this is the repercussions of integration on the structure of competences within the Federal Republic of Germany.

According to Article 23 of the German Basic Law (*Grundgesetz*, GG), the participation of the *Länder* in European decision-making takes place via the *Bundesrat*, in which only the *Länder* governments are represented. Since the parliaments of the 16 German *Länder* (*Landtage*) have no rights of participation in the *Bundesrat* as a federal body according to Article 51 GG, this alone would exclude them from participation in European integration. However, a democratic Europe also requires the state parliaments as directly elected representatives of the people at regional level. This is also necessary because of their mediating role, which they play due to the fact that they are closer to the people. Today, the state parliaments are highly committed to safeguarding their democratic rights to shape and control EU multi-level democracy. This happens, firstly, through their participation in the state's internal decision-making process on EU projects and, secondly, at the European level via participation in the European Committee of the Regions (CoR).

The participation of the *Landtag* of Baden-Württemberg in EU affairs has a long tradition. Since 1989, participation had been based on an agreement with the state government. In 1995, the *Landtag* of Baden-Württemberg was the first German state parliament to anchor its participation in European decision-making constitutionally by introducing Article 34a of the Constitution of Baden-Württemberg. Due to the further expansion of EU competences with the 2009 Treaty of Lisbon, the *Landtag* sharpened the constitutional article in 2011. For the first time, it introduced the possibility of binding the state Government to resolutions of the *Landtag* on EU projects.

Regarding participation in the CoR, the *Landtag* of Baden-Württemberg has been represented by at least one alternate member in consultation with the state government since the CoR was founded. This is similar in other state parliaments. In the current term of office, Baden-Württemberg is even entitled to two full CoR seats, which Florian Hassler, State Secretary for Political Coordination and Europe, holds for the state government and I hold for the *Landtag*.

Through the CoR, I actively participated in the plenary session of the Conference on the Future of Europe (CoFoE) between June 2021 and April 2022, as well as in meetings of the Conference Plenary Working Group on Climate Change and Environment (both digitally and on the ground in Strasbourg). CoFoE was the culmination of an unprecedented EU-wide project of citizen participation: on Monday, 9 May 2022, the CoFoE delegates in Strasbourg handed over the final report to the President of the European Parliament, Roberta Metsola, the President of the Commission, Ursula von der Leyen, and the President of France, Emmanuel Macron, as acting President of the Council Presidency. This final event was preceded by a courageous, innovative and participatory process. Baden-Württemberg has participated in this process with strong commitment on the part of the state parliament and government. In addition, many municipalities and citizens participated in CoFoE (see also Peters and Ziegenbalg in this volume).

1. From idea to implementation - the future conference starts with a delay

The idea of a "Conference on the Future of Europe" goes back to an initiative by Emmanuel Macron in his famous Sorbonne speech, held at the university in Paris in 2017 (Macron 2017). Picking up on these preliminary ideas, Ursula von der Leyen announced in her speech as candidate for the office of President of the European Commission on 16 July 2019 (European Commission 2019) before the European Parliament in Strasbourg that she would launch an EU-wide discussion process, scheduled to last two years. All Europeans were to express their opinion there on the future of Europe and contribute to better preparing the EU for the current and future challenges.

The list of important topics ranged from building a healthy, sustainable continent, fighting climate change, strengthening social justice, accelerating digital transformation, the EU's role in the world and strengthening the rule of law and democratic processes. In addition, there were cross-cutting issues for discussion such as better regulation, the application of the principles of subsidiarity and proportionality, the implementation and enforcement of the acquis and transparency. At that time, no one had any idea that the Covid-19 pandemic and the Russian war on Ukraine were to dominate the conference agenda.

In the early days, it was anything but clear that CoFoE would actually achieve good results. This was especially true in view of the disagreement among the member states in the Council, for example on issues such as migration and the rule of law. After the announcement of this hitherto unique EU-wide reflection process by Commission President von der Leyen, it actually took months before all questions concerning the division of competences between the European Parliament, the Council and the European Commission on the organisation and conduct of CoFoE were clarified. Due to the pandemic and these conflicts alike, the start of the conference, which was originally planned for 9 May 2020, was considerably delayed. For instance, for a long time there was no agreement in sight on the question of who should chair the conference. It was the compromise proposal of the Portuguese EU Council Presidency – proposing to entrust the leadership to a tripartite body consisting of the President of the Commission, the President of the European Parliament and the Presidency of the current EU Council Presidency – that a breakthrough in the negotiations finally occured in early March 2021. In the end, the launch event could take place in the European Parliament in Strasbourg on 9 May 2021.

Despite the late start, the duration of the process was limited to one year. Hence, the original end date of mid-2022, i.e. the end of the 2022 French Council Presidency, was retained. From my point of view as CoR's delegate in the Conference Plenary to CoFoE, it would have made more sense to maintain a two-year process in order to have sufficient time for elaboration and discussion. Given the tight schedule, there was a certain time pressure to quickly achieve results within one year.

2. The importance of citizen participation in the future conference

The conference was the first of its kind with citizen-driven proposals and debates in the framework of an EU-wide reform conference. EU-wide participation was made possible by four so-called European Citizens' Panels, which formed the core of CoFoE. Each panel assembled 200 randomly selected people from all 27 member states, one third of whom were young people between the ages of 16 and 25. The following themes were set for the four panels:

- A stronger economy, social justice and employment/education, culture, youth and sport/digital transformation;
- Democracy in Europe/Values and Rights, Rule of Law, Security;
- Climate Change and Environment/Health;
- The EU in the world/Migration

All four citizen panels met for sessions over three weekends and developed recommenddations.

Beyond the four EU citizens' panels, all actors at local, regional and national levels of the member states were called upon to participate in CoFoE by organizing citizens' panels and thematic, also cross-border, events. At the federal level in Germany, a national citizens' panel drew up recommendations on the future of Europe (see Abels in this volume on the German case). Numerous local authorities and federal states also participated in this process. In addition, all EU citizens were called upon to contribute their ideas and suggestions on the future of Europe and to discuss them with the other actors on a multilingual digital platform[1] set up especially for this purpose. The contributions from national, regional, and local as well as cross-border events could also be posted there and thus flow into the further discussions. The *Landtag* of Baden-Württemberg also actively participated in the process.

3. Participation of the State Parliament of Baden-Württemberg in CoFoE

3.1 Citizen's Panels on the future of Europe

State parliaments are close to the citizens. In public discourse, the members of parliament can bring European concerns closer to the citizens and take up their concerns. Therefore, in my view, the state parliament was also called upon in a special to have an effect on the citizens and to become visible in the CoFoE process.

---

1 See https://futureu.europa.eu/.

For this reason I, as President of the *Landtag* of Baden-Württemberg, initiated a citizens' forum in the *Landtag*. It started on 28 October 2021 with 40 young random citizens between the ages of 16 and 30 from all over the state. After the kick-off event, the young citizens worked out their demands regarding the future of Europe via online formats. They brought in a high level of expertise and strong commitment on the following three topics:

- Climate change as a global challenge;

- Democracy, rule of law, EU values, populism;

- Migration and the causes of flight.

I was very impressed by the good and concrete ideas as well as the focused discussions, for example on the common values of the EU, climate change and migration as a challenge. The young people were very eager to debate, they were committed and passionate, but also stubborn and sometimes controversial about the issues. However, they all agreed on one point: "The fundamental values and human rights in the Member States are non-negotiable" – this was one of the paramount results of this citizens' forum. This statement is particularly important to me. It shows that young people are very aware of the importance of the achievements of our European democracies.

The *Landtag* fed the concerns and demands of the participants into the multilingual platform of the conference in December 2021. I took key demands to the meetings of my Conference Plenary's Working Group on climate change and the environment. Some of the proposals from the *Landtag's* Citizens' Forum are also reflected in the conference report, such as a "right to repair electronic devices".

3.2 Decisions on CoFoE

On 23 November 2021, the European Affairs Committee of our *Landtag* discussed CoFoE in a public hearing with experts. The results of this hearing, to which I also contributed my experiences from the CoFoE Process, were the foundation for the *Landtag's* resolution as of 2 February 2022 (Landtag of Baden-Württemberg 2022). Of particular importance to the *Landtag* was the demand that citizen participation – in different formats – should be used more intensively at the various levels of the EU consultation and decision-making processes also beyond CoFoE. In the resolution, the state government is requested to evaluate the formats of citizens' forums developed as a contribution to CoFoE in Baden-Württemberg and in the border region with neighbouring countries, and to communicate the results transparently and widely. Furthermore, the state government is requested to continue regional and cross-border citizens' dialogues on European policy issues, as initiated and carried out by the state government and the state parliament in the form of a citizens' dialogue, in future on an ad hoc basis, with special consideration of the target group of young people.

In addition, regions and regional parliaments, as legislators and mediators of European policy, must play a central role in the EU multi-level system, according to the *Landtag* resolution. They must use and further expand their scope for action in accordance with the principle of subsidiarity. In particular, border regions like Baden-Württemberg should be strengthened as laboratories of European integration.

4. Positions of the state parliaments on CoFoE

Once a year, the so-called *Landtagspräsidenten-Konferenz* (in short LPK) meets. This is a meeting of the Presidents of the German and Austrian regional parliaments, of the South Tyrolean regional parliament, of the German *Bundestag*, of the German *Bundesrat* under participation of the Parliament of the German-speaking Community of Belgium. The intention is to exchange views and positions on current European policy issues. What these parliaments have in common is the federal structure of the respective nation states they belong to. The state parliaments are part of the group of regional parliaments with legislative powers.

As legislators who, among other things, implement European legislation on the ground, the LPK contributed two Declarations as of 1 February 2021 and of 24 January 2022 to CoFoE. We welcomed the Future Process and supported the further development of the European Union. Addressing the European Union, we expressed our conviction that it can only credibly represent its values of democracy, the rule of law and fundamental rights to the outside world, if it lives up to these principles itself. Hence, we called for effective measures against their violation in member states. In addition, we stressed the importance of closely involving citizens in order to make their concerns and proposals for the future direction of EU policies more heard.

Furthermore, it was an absolute novelty of CoFoE that regional politicians could directly participate in a European institutionalised conference process for the first time. Against this background, we also considered CoFoE to be an opportunity to call for the active role of regional parliaments with legislative powers in the European multi-level system. We argue that their role needs to be further strengthened in general and for them to be better integrated into European policy-making and the decision-making processes.

With regard to follow-up measures, such as legislative proposals to implement the conference results, we urged that the distribution of competences among the different levels in the EU system and the principles of subsidiarity and proportionality enshrined in the Treaties must be respected. Our main institutional demands are

- an extension of the 8-week period for subsidiarity review to 12 weeks;

- a lowering of the so-called "yellow card" quorum under the subsidiarity early warning system. This allows national parliaments to argue that the objectives of an EU legislative proposal proposed by the European Commission can be effectively achieved at member state level itself (Article 5(3) TEU in conjunction with Protocol No. 2 on the application of the principles of subsidiarity and proportionality);

- the introduction of a so-called "green card" for national parliaments, in particular to enable them to submit proposals for European legislative initiatives; and finally,

- we reiterated our demand to strengthen the tasks of the CoR and its opportunities for participation.

5.   Work in the Conference Plenary and in the working groups of CoFoE

While the Executive Committee made the central decisions on the procedures and organisation of CoFoE, the work in and the results from the four European Citizens' panels provided the substantive basis for the work in the Conference Plenary and in the working groups of the conference. The task of the Conference Plenary, consisting of 449 members, was to ensure that the recommendations of the European Citizens' Panels were discussed according to topics in the respective working groups and in an open-ended manner. They were complemented by the concerns from the national and regional citizens' panels and the content of the multilingual digital platform.

Citizens from all over the EU accounted for 108 delegates in the Conference Plenary. Of these, 80 representatives came from the European Citizens' Panels, 27 from national citizens' Panels or conference events (one per Member State) and one seat went to the President of the European Youth Forum. This shows the great importance attached to the perspective of civil society. The number of regional and local representatives was also very high: Of the 30 representatives in this group, 18 members came from the CoR, including myself, plus six local and six regional politicians from important European territorial associations. They were able to bring local and regional perspectives to CoFoE, thus contributing to the democratic strengthening of the Conference Plenary. The plenary sessions were prepared by nine thematic working groups on the main topics of CoFoE. The working group members represented the political and institutional balance of the Conference Plenary. I myself was an active member of the working group "Climate Change and Environment". From October 2021 to the end of April 2022 we held a total of eight meetings to discuss – in depth and in divergent ways – all aspects of our field of activity. In the end, we came up with a set of recommendations.

It was very positive that the citizens from the European Citizens' Panel had a large share of speaking time in my working group. They were the first to speak and were thus able to push the discussions. I was deeply impressed by the commitment and the enthusiasm of the citizens for the future of Europe. I participated in all meetings. In so doing, I was able to contribute my experience from parliamentary work for and in Baden-Württemberg in a goal-oriented way. Thereby, I was able to actively shape the contents of the recommendations of our working group on the final report of the future conference.

5.1   Networking on different levels

The lack of structures and ambiguities in the procedures caused great difficulties for all participants, especially in the initial stage of CoFoE. In addition, there was strong time pressure. The meeting documents and accompanying documents were always sent at very short notice. All this provided an immense challenge for us as delegates – despite the valuable support we received from the Committee of the Regions (CoR). These challenges could only be mastered with a lot of commitment from all participants.

The good cooperation at all levels was helpful. For example, we exchanged information about the work in the working groups and Conference Plenary assembly at irregular intervals, mostly virtually, in the circle of German representatives from the federal government and the *Länder*. Thereby, we could keep each other directly informed about important developments.

In addition, the CoR delegation also met regularly before the Conference Plenary sessions in Strasbourg. The focus of these meetings was on the CoR's priorities and the work of individual delegates. These meetings enabled us to coordinate regional policy positions. They were a prerequisite for the then-acting CoR President Apostolos Tzitzikostas to be a committed advocate regarding the institutional concerns and interests of the CoR and of local and regional authorities.

6. The CoFoE on the home straight – key results

After six months of intensive work from September 2021 to February 2022, the four European Citizens' Panels presented their recommendations. These were the basis of the final CoFoE report of May 2022, which was prepared by the Executive Committee on the basis of the discussions in the working groups and taking into account the results of the discussions in the Conference Plenary. This final report contains 49 proposals and more than 300 actions to be pursued by the EU institutions and by the Member States in nine thematic areas (Conference on the Future of Europe 2022). They overall aim is to better prepare the European Union for current and future challenges, such as bringing about the green transition as quickly as possible through investment in renewable energy and advancing the ecological transformation for more energy independence, and granting the EU a more active role in health protection as a lesson from the Corona crisis.

Working out the decisive demands for the future of Europe from the many recommendations by the European citizens was a great challenge. For me personally, it was important to strengthen the visibility of regional parliaments with legislative powers and to bring their concerns, as well as those of regional and local authorities, to the conference agenda.

The European Union is facing tremendous challenges with the destruction of our natural resources, the deepening of social and societal divisions and, last but not least, Russia's war against Ukraine in 2022. It is therefore all the more important that citizens actively campaign for a strong, value-oriented EU. In my view, the EU must also increase its speed in order to accelerate the transition to renewable energies. In addition, the EU must lose no time in sustaining the rule of law, it must finally take effective measures against violations of the European values which are laid down in the EU Treaty. That is why, for example, I have campaigned for the distribution of EU funds to be linked to the rule of law situation in the EU member states. I strongly believe that only through effective sanctions will the EU also gain the respect of those who attack or despise it. Such a change in the general conditionality regulation for financial sanctions for violations of the rule of law (and not only for violations affecting the EU budget) was also demanded by EU citizens in their Citizens' panel. This was also taken up in the final CoFoE report.

Other important demands of an institutional nature, which were raised by the citizens (and which I personally advocated) and which were also taken up in the final report, are: A European Constitution that protects democracy and fundamental rights; consideration of the abolition of unanimity in Council voting; a right of legislative initiative for the European Parliament and common electoral lists which allows citizens to vote directly for European party lists with candidates from all member countries.

6.1 Key results from the perspective of German state parliaments

In the LPK's Declaration on Europe of 21 June 2022 (LPK 2022) we as Presidents of the German-speaking regional parliaments expressed our views on the outcome of the Future Conference. We strongly welcomed the intensively conducted dialogue process together with the citizens. We also welcomed in the final CoFoE report the fact that active subsidiarity and the multi-level nature of the EU are recognised as key principles for the functioning of the European Union. The fact that the report emphasises the indispensable role of regional parliaments in the subsidiarity early warning system and that it also calls for a review of this mechanism is very positive in our view. The same applies to the demand that in the future national as well as regional parliaments with legislative powers should be able to actively propose legislative initiatives at European level (so-called "green card").

Consequently, the final report took up the demand of regional parliaments to further develop the EU decision-making process in the sense of greater transparency for citizens and, in particular, to involve regional and local representatives to a greater extent. According to the regional parliaments' presidents, the proposed continuation of citizens' assemblies at European level should be seen as a complement to representative democracy, but can and must not replace it. The debate on the practical design of European citizens' participation formats must include and not bypass the regional parliaments. It is particularly important to call for the active involvement of the regional parliaments with legislative powers in the follow-up phase that will now follow to implement the recommendations in the final report.

In their declaration, the Presidents also support the call of the Conference Plenary to the EU institutions, as listed in the final report, to consider the initiation of a convention in accordance with Article 48 TEU. This should include an open-ended debate on possible treaty changes in order to implement the recommendations (Conference on the Future of Europe 2022: 84). In such convention the regional parliaments with legislative competences must be involved.

Finally, it is a great success that the report calls for a reform of the CoR in the proposal on subsidiarity. It demands a CoR reform "to encompass adequate channels of dialogue for regions as well as cities and municipalities, giving it an enhanced role in the institutional architecture, if matters with a territorial impact are concerned" (ibid.: 84, proposal 40, measure 3).

I am also extremely pleased that the LPK Declaration on CoFoE also supports the proposal that all legal means should be considered to address violations of the rule of law.

7. Follow-up and outlook

With the participation of a wide variety of people and institutions, the Conference on the Future of Europe has made history. Local and regional authorities, especially we as representatives of regional parliaments with legislative powers, have also achieved important accomplishments as far as participation in EU decision-making is concerned. However, there is no obligation to implement the ideas and reform proposals presented by the conference. Amendments to EU Treaties have to be approved unanimously by the Member States, which is a high hurdle.

Since the ending of the future conference, the European Parliament, the Council and the European Commission are now considering, within their respective spheres of competence and in agreement with the European treaties, how to effectively follow up on the final report and which of the 49 recommendations they want to launch.

- In a resolution of 9 June 2022 (European Parliament 2022), the European Parliament calls on the European Council to launch a Convention to revise the EU Treaties. The majority of MEPs are in favour of treaty changes under the ordinary amendment procedure. They favour the abolition of veto right in most areas in the Council, as well as stronger integration in the areas of health, energy, defence, and in social and economic policy. They also call for better protection of EU fundamental values and a full and direct right of initiative for the European Parliament, as currently only the Commission has the right to take legislative initiatives.

- The Commission takes stock of CoFoE in its Communication of 17 June 2022 (European Commission 2022). Presenting a brief assessment of the individual measures it comes to the conclusion that many demands are already included in the legislative process. Building on the success of CoFoE, the Commission intends to set up Europe-wide citizens' panels on certain important projects. In these panels, which will have a recommendatory character, one-third of participants should be made up of young people. The first of these new citizens' panels are to be set up in 2023 and will now become a regular feature of our democratic life as Commission President Ursula von der Leyen announced in her yearly State of the Union address on 14 September 2022. According to the European Commissions's work program for 2023, these citizens' panels will take place on initiatives on food waste, learning mobility and virtual worlds. .

- Finally, the General Secretariat of the Council of the EU presented a detailed preliminary technical assessment, according to which Treaty changes would only be necessary for the implementation of 18 individual measures. The use of flexibility clauses can be considered for the implementation of some individual measures. However, since the hurdles for the application of these clauses are very high, this also means that the implementation of far more than 18 individual measures will be difficult. By the end of its six-month presidency on 30 June 2022, the French Council Presidency was unable to reach an agreement among the member states in the Council on how to deal with the proposed far-reaching amendments. There is currently no majority among the heads of state and government in the European Council for the establishment of a convention. Yet, the European Council would have to discuss and unanimously decide on possible treaty changes in the aftermath of the future conference. Hence, the room for manoeuvre is limited. The now acting Czech and the subsequent Swedish EU presidencies in 2023 have also spoken out against treaty reforms and a convention in so-called non-papers.

In a feedback event with all 800 random citizens from the four European Citizens' Panels, the three EU institutions intend to follow up on their activities and take stock of the progress made. This event will take place on 2 December 2022.

8. Conclusion

The Europe-wide reform process within the CoFoE framework has generated a spirit of optimism and enthusiasm at many levels: European citizens, representatives of the European Parliament, the Council and the European Commission, from national parliaments, from the CoR, the European Economic and Social Committee (EESC) and civil society made an impressive commitment in Strasbourg: it is a commitment to democracy, the rule of law and peace – it is a commitment to the European Union.

The proposals in the final report pursue the common goal of stronger integration. This is particularly important in times of historical upheaval, which the Russian Federation's war of aggression on Ukraine, which violates international law, has brought about: supposed convictions can no longer be taken for granted. Peace and freedom, democracy and the rule of law cannot be taken for granted. Our liberal way of life and our values are in danger and must be defended.

In my view there cannot and must not be a return to the agenda of 2019. This would gamble away confidence in the EU's ability to act and reform in the long term. CoFoE made clear that coherence is needed for development at the European, national, regional and local levels. Because this is about the central challenges of our time: Climate change, sustainability, responsible transformation of our economy and society, democracy and the rule of law. In short, it is about a profound change that affects the lives of all of us.

We need to take everyone with us on this journey. Above all, the change must be supported by the grassroots of our society in order to be truly accepted by all. In order for this to succeed, we need to make citizen participation a permanent feature. We must maintain this new approach and apply it to all levels of decision-making in the EU, without weakening representative democracy.

For the future, it will be crucial not to disappoint the trust of citizens. The responsibility for seriously addressing the results of CoFoE now lies with the EU institutions. They have to deal with it in a serious manner and to communicate transparently which recommendations will be implemented, when and how. And they must communicate just as transparently which recommendations cannot be implemented and why this is the case.

I consider it a positive sign that in the political sphere, the exchange on what should make the EU sustainable, resilient and capable of action has become even more intense after the official closing of the conference on 9 May 2022.

As a member of the CoR, I will be able to build on precisely this as rapporteur for the European Commission's communication on the "Single Market Emergency Instrument (SMEI)". It is about ensuring the functioning of the internal market in crisis situations. As a lesson from the national measures and border closures during the Covid-19 pandemic, we must regulate how we can maintain the free movement of goods and people in the future, and to produce and distribute goods essential to crisis management in the short term. In the CoR, I will in particular bring in the perspective of local and regional authorities and insist on the protection of their interests.

As President of the *Landtag* of Baden-Württemberg, I will continue to work to ensure that the position of the German *Länder* parliaments as federal actors is heard in the context of the emerging new structure of EU multi-level democracy.

9. References

Conference on the Future of Europe 2022: Report on the final outcome, May 2022. https://futureu.europa.eu/pages/reporting (03.09.2022).

European Commission 2019: Opening Statement in the European Parliament Plenary Session by Ursula von der Leyen, Candidate for President of the European Commission, Strasbourg, 16.07.2019. https://ec.europa.eu/commission/presscorner/detail/en/SPEECH_19_4230 (03.09.2022).

European Commission 2022: Conference on the Future of Europe. Putting Vision into Concrete Action, COM/2022/404 final, Brussels, 17.06.2022. https://ec.europa.eu/info/sites/default/files/communication_1.pdf (03.09.2022).

European Parliament 2022: Resolution of 9 June 2022 on the call for a Convention for the revision of the Treaties. https://www.europarl.europa.eu/doceo/document/TA-9-2022-0244_EN.html (03.09.2022).

Macron, Emmanuel 2017: Initiative for Europe. Sorbonne speech, 26.09.2017. http://international.blogs.ouest-france.fr/archive/2017/09/29/macron-sorbonne-verbatim-europe-18583.html (03.09.2022).

Landtag von Baden-Württemberg 2022: Impulse zur Zukunftskonferenz der Europäischen Union – Regionen als Mitgestalter und Vermittler eines demokratischen, nachhaltigen Europas in Vielfalt, 02.02.2022, Drs. 17/1756.

LPK 2022: Erklärung der Präsidentinnen und Präsidenten der deutschen und österreichischen Landesparlamente und des Südtiroler Landtags unter Beteiligung des Parlaments der Deutschsprachigen Gemeinschaft Belgiens zum Abschlussbericht der Konferenz zur Zukunft Europas vom Mai 2022, Bremen, 21.06.2022. https://www.bremische-buergerschaft.de/uploads/media/LPK_Erklaerung_zum_Abschlussbericht_zur_Konferenz_zur_Zukunft_Europas_01.pdf (12.08.2022).

The contribution of Baden-Württemberg to the Conference on the Future of Europe – Taking the conversation to the people

Timo Peters/Florian Ziegenbalg[1]

On 9 May 2022 the report on the final outcome of the Conference on the Future of Europe (CoFoE) was handed over to the Presidents of the European Commission, the European Parliament and the President of the French Republic; the then President of the Council. This represented another step within the long-lasting debate on the future of Europe and at the same time the provisional completion of a novel process, which opened up new possibilities for citizens' participation and the involvement of European regions. Baden-Württemberg has seized this novel opportunity by involving citizens via regional citizens' dialogues and promoting proposals for the future of the EU, which incorporated the results of these dialogues. However, these CoFoE-related activities were only a small part in a larger history of the State of Baden-Württemberg engaging in dialogues with citizens on the future of European integration and other crucial EU issues. This contribution will first give an overview of previous developments and activities regarding citizen participation before then elaborating on the various citizens' dialogues organized as part of the CoFoE. As we will illustrate, the regional experiences with citizens' participation can be effectively used as lessons for current developments at the EU level. These deliberative processes in Europe's regions are important for developing a democratic future for the EU.

1. The debate on the future of Europe in Baden-Württemberg

The Baden-Württemberg State Government is closely monitoring and participating in the debate on the development of the EU since the late 1980s. During the Constitutional Convention in 2002/2003 the then-Minister President Erwin Teufel played an active role as representative of the German *Bundesrat*. Following the British referendum on Brexit, the debate on the future of the EU has entered a new phase throughout the Union. This is also reflected in the discussions and positioning of the Baden-Württemberg State Government. In his government declaration on 1 June 2016, Minister President Winfried Kretschmann stated: "The centrifugal forces that can be observed everywhere in Europe at the moment fill us with great concern for this reason. But we are convinced that we can master this challenge" (Landtag Baden-Württemberg, 2016: 33). In this sense, the State Government of Baden-Württemberg welcomed with great interest the White Paper on the Future of Europe published by the European Commission on 1 March 2017 (European Commission 2017). In its report to the State Parliament (*Landtag*) on the White Paper (Landtag Baden-Württemberg 2017), the State Government stressed that it welcomes the Commission starting the process of reflection in a multifaceted and open-ended manner, by merely

---

1 This article reflects the personal opinion of the authors and is not an official statement of the State Ministry of Baden-Württemberg.

pointing out various paths the EU could take. The State Government welcomed that the Commission had not simply imposed a scenario from above, but had created space for a debate on the EU's future that was first and foremost taking place at the grass roots level, especially in the parliaments and with citizens, rather than in Brussels or Strasbourg. Baden-Württemberg therefore committed itself to accompany the reflection process on all levels, including the debate inside the *Land*.

On 11 July 2017, the State Government of Baden-Württemberg adopted a draft paper from the Ministry of Justice and Europe on the subject of the White paper process. In this submission, the State Government committed itself to a Europe that leaves room for decisions taken in the regions, counties, cities, and municipalities. It also reaffirmed that in the State Government's view regional development should remain at the EU level, because support from the Structural Funds continues to be of great importance for the state. The Ministry of Justice and Europe was commissioned to continue monitoring the process in close cooperation with the ministries, evaluate the European Commission's reflection papers on the White Paper, agree on a position for the State Government and inform the *Landtag* at every step.

2.   The "Dialogue on Europe" in Baden-Württemberg

Independently of this, the State Ministry and the Ministry of Justice and Europe were tasked to conduct a broad-based "Dialogue on Europe", which took place from October 2017 to the end of 2018. Especially in rural areas, this "Dialogue on Europe" should engage with citizens in a conversation on Europe through formats of citizens' participation that take on board the wishes and suggestions of the citizens of Baden-Württemberg.

The State Government launched this dialogue in order to take an active role in the debate on the future of the EU. The aim was to initiate a dialogue with citizens, as well as with experts from politics, science, business, and society. Various deliberative formats were developed for the State Government's "Dialogue on Europe", which were centered on three "Cornerstones":

1st Cornerstone – Expert Forum and Specialist Forums: The Expert Forum was chaired by the Minister of Justice and European Affairs, Guido Wolf, and State Secretary Volker Ratzmann from the State Ministry as deputy chair. It included 19 representatives from academia and the business community, trade unions, the church, the cultural sector, and the media. Members of the State Parliament of Baden-Württemberg as well as Members of the European Parliament (MEPs) from Baden-Württemberg were also part of the forum. The work of the expert forum was complemented by five specialist forums with speakers on the topics of innovation, youth, local authorities, safety, and the environment.

2nd Cornerstone – Citizens' Dialogue: The State Councillor for Citizens' Participation and Civil Society, Gisela Erler, chaired six "Citizens' Dialogues" that took place in Bad Mergentheim, Rastatt, Ravensburg, Tuttlingen, Freiburg and Stuttgart. Randomly selected citizens had the opportunity to formulate their ideas for Europe and to discuss them with representatives of the State Government, the President of the European Commission, Jean-Claude Juncker, and EU Commissioner Günther Oettinger. A special feature of the "Dialogue on Europe" were prior interviews with citizens selected at random: With the help of the residents' registration database, citizens were picked at random and personally invited to the local citizens' dialogues. As a result, a wide variety of different perspectives on EU issues were highlighted during the State's dialogue process.

3rd Cornerstone – Public events: The "Dialogue on Europe" was accompanied by numerous public events. These started with a discussion with Minister President Winfried Kretschmann; the Minister of Justice and European Affairs, Guido Wolf; the President of the Federal Constitutional Court, Andreas Voßkuhle; and the former German Foreign Minister, Joschka Fischer. Panel discussions were held in Aalen, Vellberg and Stuttgart on the topics of EU finances, cross-border labour markets, Europe, and rural areas. In Pforzheim, Tuttlingen and Stuttgart discussion groups and school events were organised on the topics of town twinning and regional development. To conclude the series of events, the Federal President of the Republic of Austria, Alexander Van der Bellen, delivered a keynote address in the series "Stuttgart Speeches on Europe".

The contributions from the dialogue process were collated and formed the basis for the State Government's "Guiding Principles on Europe" (State Government of Baden-Württemberg 2019b). The paper was adopted on 17 January 2019 and handed over to Commission President Jean-Claude Juncker in Brussels on 21 January 2019. The Guiding Principles' ten visions for the future of the EU illustrate the direction the State Government wishes the Union to take in the years ahead. Ten compelling headings outline what the State Government expects not only from the EU, but also from itself to contribute to the process. These Guiding Principles include a forward-looking declaration by the State Government regarding its own self-conception and its basic tenets on European integration. Internally, it provides orientation and thus guides as well as motivates government action. Externally, it explicates the State Government's position with regard to European policy. In this sense, with its Guiding Principles the state actively contributed to the debate on the future of the EU.

3. Baden-Württemberg's activities and involvement in the Conference on the Future of Europe

3.1 Launch of the Conference on the Future of Europe

The State Government welcomed the announcement of incoming Commission President Ursula von der Leyen to launch a Conference on the Future of Europe, made in her speech before the European Parliament on 16 July 2019. On 3 December 2019 the State Government adopted a position paper outlining its concerns regarding the EU to the new Commission in order to influence the work programme for the next four years (State Government of Baden-Württemberg 2019a). The key point of reference were the Guiding Principles of January 2019. In this position paper the State Government expressed its hope that the Conference on the Future of Europe would also involve the regions. The German *Länder* should be included in the deliberations with representatives that are entitled to vote. As a successful example of fruitful cooperation, the State Government recalled the European

Convention, in which Baden-Württemberg participated with numerous initiatives on behalf of the *Länder* as representative of the *Bundesrat* (upper house of the German parliament). Another demand was that citizens should also be involved in the Conference. In the paper, the state recalled its positive experiences with the "Dialogue on Europe", the method of randomly selecting participants, and the particular combination of participation formats (exchange in expert rounds and citizens' dialogues). The State Government offered to support the Commission with its experience in organising citizens' dialogues.

On 13 March 2020, Baden-Württemberg initiated as a co-sponsor a resolution in the EU Committee of the *Bundesrat* regarding the Commission's Communication on the CoFoE (Bundesrat 2020). Therein, the German *Länder* called for an inclusion of regional actors and an early involvement of national parliaments. The future conference should also discuss the possibilities for strengthening the participation rights of national parliaments. The *Bundesrat* reiterated its call for an extension of the deadline for submitting reasoned opinions ("subsidiarity complaints") in order to allow national parliaments to exercise a more efficient scrutiny. It suggested that the selection of participants in citizens' dialogues should ensure that the broadest possible range of different viewpoints are included. The *Bundesrat* also referred to its experience with the "Dialogue on Europe" in Baden-Württemberg and to other successful citizens' dialogues, which included a random selection of citizens as well as the valuable combination of citizen forums and expert forums. These features have been successfully tested in several regions.

Due to the Covid-19 pandemic the start of the CoFoE had to be postponed. On 11 March 2021, the Presidents of the European Parliament, the Council, and the Commission signed the Joint Declaration, which sets out the scope, structure, objectives, and principles of the CoFoE. This enabled the Conference to start its work with an official kick-off event on 9 May 2021. The German *Länder* were represented in the Conference Plenary with two delegates of the *Bundesrat* as part of the group of 108 representatives from national parliaments. Among the 18 regional and local delegates proposed by the European Committee of the Regions (CoR) in the Conference Plenary was the President of the State Parliament of Baden-Württemberg (*Landtag*), Muhterem Aras. In the Executive Board a permanent observer represented the COSAC Troika from the past, current and upcoming presidencies. Until 30 June 2021, the Minister for Justice and Europe, Guido Wolf, and Minister President Winfried Kretschmann represented the *Bundesrat* holding the rotating presidency of the *Conference of Parliamentary Committees for Union Affairs of Parliaments of the European Union* (COSAC). Minister Wolf and Minister President Kretschmann successfully advocated for the equal representation of national parliaments and the European Parliament (each 108 delegates) as well as an improved representation of the regions via the CoR (18 delegates) in the Conference Plenary.

On 8 October 2021, the *Bundesrat* adopted a resolution regarding the Conference (Bundesrat 2021), which deals with the participation of national parliaments. The resolution was prepared and introduced by the state of Baden-Württemberg and a group of German *Länder* governments. Among other things, the *Länder* were concerned with improving the opportunities of national parliaments to contribute to the EU legislative process, i.e. with the ability to present own proposals ("green card") as part of the so-called subsidiarity control system.

3.2 Citizens' Dialogues

Between July 2021 and December 2021, the State Ministry of Baden-Württemberg organized citizens' dialogues and events, to get actively involved in the CoFoE. These events and dialogues were supposed to give young people and ordinary citizens a place to express their ideas and visions for a shared European future. The State Ministry has not only organized dialogues in Baden-Württemberg, but also conducted joint dialogues with regions in France, Poland, the Czech Republic, Italy, Spain and in the Danube river region. Therefore, the results not only represent ideas originating in Baden-Württemberg, but also pan-European visions on the future of Europe.

The core element of Baden-Württemberg's involvement in the CoFoE were the citizens' dialogues with randomly selected citizens. Several dialogue events were organized in Baden-Württemberg and together with international partners. All events were organized and moderated with the help of a professional team of moderators.

The State Ministry furthermore conducted a digital citizens' dialogue with six medium-sized municipalities in Baden-Württemberg (Tauberbischofsheim, Bad Waldsee, Hechingen, Philippsburg, Donaueschingen and Künzelsau). From those municipalities five hundred citizens were randomly selected from the official register of residents and invited to participate. During the selection process special attention was given to gender parity and the inclusion of citizens with a wide variety of migratory backgrounds and from different age cohorts. This is important to ensure that a variety of citizen groups are represented and that the results portray views from different parts of society. A total of 65 people participated in the citizens' dialogue on 22-23 October 2021 and 12-13 November 2021. On the first weekend, citizens identified the main issues for the future of the EU that were important to them; in five working groups they outlined their ideas and recommendations for taking action. On the second weekend, participants further developed their initial ideas and proposals within the different working groups with the support of external experts. These discussion results were then consolidated by the whole group of citizens.

As part of the cross-border dialogue between Baden-Württemberg and the French region Grand Est on 19-20 November 2021, citizens from three medium-sized municipalities in Baden-Württemberg (Iffezheim, Müllheim, Gundelfingen) and three municipalities in the Grand Est region (Sarreguemines, Marckolsheim, Buschwiller) were asked how they view Europe's future and the future of cross-border cooperation between the two regions. In working groups, they formulated a range of specific ideas and proposals on various topics, which were subsequently consolidated with input from all participants. The municipalities of Baden-Württemberg each invited 500 citizens that were randomly selected from the register of residents; from the Grand Est region, people were recruited from the electoral roll of the three municipalities. In total, 35 people took part. The event was translated simultaneously into German and French.

In cooperation with the CoR and the Bertelsmann Foundation, the State Ministry of Baden-Württemberg and the Ministry of Justice and for Democracy, Europe and Equality of Saxony held a six-region dialogue with the partner regions of Grand Est (France), Dolnośląskie (Poland) as well as Karlovasy Kraj and Ústecký Kraj (Czech Republic) on 10-11 December 2021. This citizens' dialogue was attended by 65 citizens from the above-mentioned regions. The event was translated simultaneously into German, French, Polish and Czech. The topics of "Climate protection and the environment", "Strengthening cooperation in cross-border collaboration" and "Democracy and European values" were raised in two previously held cross-border citizens' dialogues between the regions of Baden-Württemberg and Grand Est as well as between Saxony, Lower Silesia, Ústí and Karlovy Vary. These topics were further explored in the six-region dialogue. After a review of the previous two citizens' dialogues, a discussion between political represent-tatives from the individual regions and experts took place. On the second day, participants working in six small multilingual groups developed specific ideas and recommendations for action in three thematic areas.

Working together with local Europe Direct Information Centres (EDIC) the State Ministry organised a series of discussions for young adults from the "Four Motors for Europe" regions (Baden-Württemberg, Catalonia, Auvergne Rhône-Alpes, Lombardy). A kick-off meeting was held in June 2021 to identify the topics for the youth panels. During a workshop on 10 October 2021, young people from the four partner regions prepared their contributions on the topics of digitalisation and mental health.

The "Youth.Danube.Salon" took place from 27 to 29 September 2021 and on 15 October 2021. The aim of this series of events was to encourage the participation of young people from the Danube countries and to hear their ideas and aspirations for the future of Europe. Young people from non-EU countries such as Serbia and Ukraine also got in-volved. At the conference, the focus was on the perspectives of young people from non-EU countries in the Danube region and particularly the opportunities they have for partici-pating and cooperating at the European level. In addition, they discussed increasing East-West migration and engaged in an intergenerational dialogue on topics such as climate change, digitalisation, interregional civil society cooperation, and cultural heritage. Finally, on 15 October 2021, a selection of young people presented the core aspects covered by the previous conferences in a panel discussion in Berlin. In total, some 260 people from all 14 Danube countries took part in the online conferences and about 50 people from nine countries attended the hybrid event at the State Representation in Berlin.

The dialogues and events generated a multitude of ideas for shaping Europe's future. Because the participants were given plenty of space and time to debate, the recommenda-tions were thoroughly deliberated and evaluated. Across all events, the topics of European values, climate change, and the EU in the world were the most pressing topics. After the events, all results were posted on the official Future of Europe Multilingual Digital Plat-form[2] to make sure that they influence the European debate.

The whole process was evaluated by the University of Hohenheim, which concluded that the events, process and results as a whole were judged (very) positively by the citi-zens. The participants declared that they would take part in a similar process again and

---

2 See https://futureu.europa.eu/ (27.07.2022).

they believed that a dialogue on the future of Europe is necessary and valuable. Especially young people were attracted to the format and topic. But also many elderly people found it necessary. In sum, it was a very positive experience and shows that people value the opportunity of being heard and are willing to participate.

3.3 Impulses for the debates of the Conference Plenary

With an online debriefing series on the CoFoE's Plenary sessions State Secretary for European Affairs, Florian Hassler, evaluated the debates with different members of the Plenary. This debriefing series also aimed at informing a wider public about the Conference. At the different debriefings State Secretary Hassler welcomed the CoR representative and president of the State Parliament of Baden-Württemberg, Muhterem Aras; representative of the European Parliament, MEP Daniel Freund; representative of civil society and Secretary General of the Union of European Federalists, Anna Echterhoff; representative of the German *Bundestag* MP Gunter Krichbaum; representative of the European Parliament, MEP Sven Simon; and representative of the German government, Minister of State Anna Lührmann.

At the 148th plenary session of the CoR, State Secretary Hassler reported on the positive experiences gained with the instrument of citizens' dialogues during the debate with members of the Working Group on European Democracy of the Conference. He stressed that the feedback by citizens has to be seriously considered and reflected in the final report. It would be necessary to clarify in due time what the CoFoE follow-up process will look like and how the citizens' recommendations will be implemented in practice. The CoR adopted a resolution on the CoFoE (Committee of the Regions 2022). Here, State Secretary Hassler was able to push for an amendment that calls for the institutionalisation of new forms of citizen participation at the EU level, in the form of citizens' dialogues with randomly selected citizens on specific issues.

3.4 Positioning in the final phase of the Conference

In early 2022, the State Ministry evaluated the findings of the Citizens' Dialogues and summarised them in the brochure "Contributions from the State of Baden-Württemberg to the Conference on the Future of Europe" (State Government of Baden-Württemberg 2022). The results of the Citizens' Dialogues have been incorporated into a State Government position paper on the Conference adopted on 15 February 2022. The position paper, in addition to the regional government's vision for Europe, contains key positions on institutional issues in concise form and is part of the brochure. The key points in the position paper are the following:

- Different formats of citizen participation, as successfully implemented in Baden-Württemberg, should be established at the EU level with randomly selected citizens and on specific questions. For the State Government, these formats offer an opportunity to foster greater transparency and acceptance for EU politics, as well as bridge the gap between citizens and the EU level, which for them oftentimes seems abstract and its decision-making process remote.

- The State Government supports an institutional reform of the EU. Among other things it advocates for an extension of qualified majority voting in the Council, especially in the field of foreign and security policy. It also calls for the strengthening of democratic principles through a legislative right of initiative for the European Parliament and the linking of European elections with the selection of the Commission President. In addition, there is a desire that the next EU reform should also address the division of competences on the basis of the subsidiarity principle.

- The *Land* is committed to ensuring that parliaments in the Member States have greater opportunities to participate in the legislative process. The current 8-week deadline for submitting subsidiarity concerns or complaints is not feasible in practice and should be extended to 12 weeks.

- Strengthening the rule of law is an important concern that Baden-Württemberg has been pursuing for a long time. If the existing EU instruments to monitor compliance with the rule of law prove to be ineffective in the long run, new and more effective instruments must be considered in the form of treaty changes.

- The State Government sees the need to improve the framework for cross-border cooperation in order to remove hurdles for employees, service providers and students in border areas.

The brochure was sent to members of the Conference Plenary and personally handed over to the representative of the French Council Presidency, State Secretary Clément Beaune, as co-chair of the Conference and to the representative of the German Federal Government, Minister of State for Europe Anna Lührmann.

3.5 *CoFoE Outcome*

During a formal meeting in Strasbourg on 9 May 2022 the final report of the Conference on the Future of Europe was handed over to the joint leadership, i.e. the President of the European Commission, President of the European Parliament, and the President of the French Republic holding the Council presidency.

The State Government welcomed that nearly all its proposals were reflected in the recommendations of the final report. These are *inter alia*:

- Introduction of citizens' dialogues at the EU level;

- improving the influence of national parliaments, e.g. via a right to propose legislation (so-called green card);

- extension of qualified majority voting in the Council, in particular in foreign and security policy;

- strengthening the instruments of compliance with the rule of law;

- strengthening democratic principles through the right of initiative and the linking of European elections with the selection of the Commission President.

On 17 June the Commission adopted its Communication on the follow-up process on the CoFoE (European Commission 2022), which offers an assessment on the proposals made by the CoFoE and the next steps. In its briefing to the *Landtag*, the State Government welcomed that the Commission had closely scrutinised the proposals of the CoFoE and has carried out an evaluation regarding their implementation (Landtag Baden-Württemberg 2022). The State Government especially supported the Commission's intention to permanently establish the instrument of citizens' dialogues with randomly selected citizens at EU level. The aim is to obtain at obtaining feedback on selected thematically limited and controversial issues, especially in the run-up to legislative initiatives. In addition to the dialogue formats at EU level, local, regional and cross-border dialogues could also be organised, the results of which are to be included in the process.

On the institutional reform the Statement Government gave its support on the European Parliament's call for a Convention for the revision of the Treatises (European Parliament 2022), but also acknowledged that further discussions among the member states will be needed in order to find a common ground.

4. Conclusions

The experiences of Baden-Württemberg from the previous "Dialogue on Europe" indirectly served as a blueprint for the organisation of the CoFoE. Thus, the citizens' dialogue instrument was used for the first time at the EU level in the context of the CoFoE. Furthermore, the general direction for the future of the EU that was formulated in the 2019 State Government's "Guiding Principles on Europe" is also reflected in the final CoFoE report. In this respect, the Guiding Principles have also proven to be a guiding principle for the debate at the EU level. The final CoFoE report also confirmed the results of the citizens' dialogues conducted in Baden-Württemberg and the resulting demands of the State Government for the Conference.

For Europe and for Baden-Württemberg the CoFoE was a great success. It offered various opportunities to get involved. The State Government of Baden-Württemberg has used these possibilities successfully and showed how European politics can be brought closer to the people and what role a regional body can play in a dialogue process at the EU level.

However, the dialogue also produced some take-aways and lessons that should be reflected moving forward. First, the Conference was an incubator for a modern form of democratic participation at the European, regional, and local level. The random selection was successful in including a diverse group of participants. Since most events were online conferences, this allowed people from "all walks of life" and regions to easily come together and interact with each other. Together with the opportunity of digital simultaneous translation, it was a unique experience of being part of a trans-European public. After this experience, many have learned a lot about public participation and about the *do*'s and *don't*'s. These experiences and the gained expertise on all levels of government are a valuable basis for more public dialogue on European issues in the future. This know-how and motivation should be used for future processes.

Second, it was helpful that the CoR and the Bertelsmann Foundation rolled out a program to facilitate the participation of municipalities and regions in the process. But many cities and regions could not participate because of the lack of financial resources. Hence, in the future it would be necessary to find ways to support more regions and cities to get involved in the process.

A final point is that broad public awareness for the CoFoE was missing. The European Commission did a good job in supporting a shared CoFoE identity via logos, texts, and social media posts. But it would require a cross-European media campaign to make the process and the possibility for all European citizens to participate more publicly known.

European democracy was enriched by the Conference. Now it is time to build on this experience, go one step further and to implement public participation in European policy-making for a more democratic European future.

5. References

Bundesrat 2020: Beschluss des Bundesrates zur Mitteilung der Kommission an das Europäische Parlament und den Rat: Gestaltung der Konferenz zur Zukunft Europas, COM(2020) 27 final, 13.03.2020, BR-Drs. 37/20(B).

Bundesrat 2021: Beschluss des Bundesrates: Mitteilung der Kommission an das Europäische Parlament und den Rat: Gestaltung der Konferenz zur Zukunft Europas, COM(2020) 27 final, 08.10.2021, BR-Drs. 738/21(B).

Committee of the Regions 2022: Resolution on the contribution of the local and regional authorities to the Conference on the Future of Europe, 148th plenary session, 26-27 January 2022, RESOL-VII/019.

European Commission 2017: White paper on the future of Europe, 01.03.2017. https://ec.europa.eu/info/publications/white-paper-future-europe_en (29.05.2022).

European Commission 2022: Communication from the Commission to the European Parliament, the European Council, the Council, the European Economic and Social Committee and the Committee of the Regions: Conference on the Future of Europe – Putting Vision into Concrete Action, COM (2022) 404 final, 17.6.2022.

European Parliament 2022: Resolution of 9 June 2022 on the call for a Convention for the revision of the Treaties (2022/2705 (RSP)), https://www.europarl.europa.eu/ doceo/document/TA-9-2022-0244_EN.html (27.10.2022)

Landtag Baden-Württemberg 2016: Plenarprotokoll 4/2016, 4. Sitzung, 1. Juni 2016. https://www.landtag-bw.de/files/live/sites/LTBW/files/dokumente/WP16/Plp/16_ 0004_01062016.pdf (29.05.2022).

Landtag Baden-Württemberg 2017: Mitteilung des Ministeriums der Justiz und für Europa. Unterrichtung des Landtags in EU-Angelegenheiten; hier: Weißbuch zur Zukunft Europas, 26.04.2017, Drs. 16/1967. https://www.landtag-bw.de/files/live/ sites/LTBW/files/dokumente/WP16/Drucksachen/1000/16_1967_D.pdf (29.05.2022).

Landtag Baden-Württemberg 2022: Mitteilung des Staatsministeriums. Unterrichtung des Landtags in EU-Angelegenheiten; hier: Erste Bewertung der Ergebnisse der Konferenz zur Zukunft Europas durch die Europäische Kommission, 11.07.2022, Drs. 17/2857.

https://www.landtag-bw.de/files/live/sites/LTBW/files/dokumente/WP17/ Drucksachen/2000/17_2857_D.pdf (27.10.2022).

State Government of Baden-Württemberg 2019a: Anliegen der Landesregierung von Baden-Württemberg an die neue Europäische Kommission, 03.12.2019. https:// www.baden-wuerttemberg.de/fileadmin/redaktion/dateien/PDF/191203_Anliegen_ der_Landesregierung_BW_an_die_neue_EU-Kommission.pdf (29.05.2022).

State Government of Baden-Württemberg 2019b: State Government's Guiding Principles on Europe. https://stm.baden-wuerttemberg.de/fileadmin/redaktion/m-europ/intern/ epaper/guiding-principles-on-europe/epaper/ausgabe.pdf (11.05.2022).

State Government of Baden-Württemberg 2022: Contribution of the State of Baden-Württemberg to the Conference on the Future of Europe. https://www.baden-wuerttemberg.de/fileadmin/redaktion/dateien/PDF/Publikationen/220300_Broschuere_ Zukunftskonferenz_en.pdf (29.05.2022).

Austria in the Conference on the Future of Europe

Sarah Meyer/Lukas Böhm/Anna Dermitzakis/Leopold Kernstock/Oskar Kveton/
Patrick Steindl/Melina Weilguni/Jasmin Zengin[1]

1. Introduction

In past years, the European Union has continuously received criticism on its distant policy-making reflected in a lack of political accountability, responsiveness, and effective channels for citizen participation (Føllesdal/Hix 2006; Hobolt/Tilly 2014; Neuhold 2020). The EU democratic deficit thesis was fueled after the European Parliament elections in 2019, when EU heads of state or government departed from the – legally non-binding, but politically important – *Spitzenkandidatensystem* by nominating Ursula von der Leyen for president of the European Commission. However, this also paved the way for the Conference on the Future of Europe (CoFoE) that von der Leyen promised to launch in her attempts to obtain the necessary majority among members of the European Parliament (MEPs) to become Commission president.[2] It aimed to create a space for debate via European citizen panels, the Conference Plenary, a Multilingual Digital Platform as well as numerous events organized by a variety of actors, including member states, regional and local authorities, the European Committee of the Regions (CoR) but also civil society organizations.

Austria was represented in the Conference Plenary by two members of government and four delegates from the national parliament. As part of the delegation from the European Parliament, five Austrian MEPs (one from each parliamentary party) were also represented. Another Austrian delegate was nominated from the CoR as elected representative of a regional authority.[3] In this chapter, we provide a summary of Austria's involvement in the CoFoE, focusing on activities and, more importantly, policy positions taken by the Austrian government, by governing and opposition parties in the *Nationalrat* as well as the *Bundesländer*. These were represented either by members of regional governments and parliaments or the second chamber of the Austrian national parliament, the *Bundesrat*. We will, first, look at the political goals and EU policy claims that these actors pushed forward, then analyze whether these are in line with Austrian parties' overall EU positioning and party ideology, and finally identify (potential) differences in positioning towards the CoFoE between the governing parties ÖVP and Greens as well as between the federal and regional levels of government.

Austria is an interesting case in point for a member state given its comparatively early EU issue-salience in national elections (cf. Meyer 2012; Schoen 2010; Plasser/Seeber 2010) and governing actors who "must look over their shoulders when negotiating European

---

1   This chapter is the result of a joint research effort carried out within a seminar on the EU and Europeanization for bachelor students of political science at the University of Vienna under the lead of Sarah Meyer. The authors want to thank Denis Schintgen and Hanna Ciric for their contributions to the research.

2   For a discussion of the background and conflict over the CoFoE see introduction by Abels to this volume.

3   Further plenary members from Austria were delegates from the European Economic and Social Committee, Austrian social partnership organizations, and individuals from the citizens' panels.

119

issues" (Hooghe/Marks 2009: 5). In the initial 1994 referendum on joining the EU, roughly 67% voted in favor of accession. Ever since then, public opinion has gradually declined; Eurobarometer results show that the Austrian population consistently expresses higher levels of skepticism towards European integration and the EU project compared to the EU average (see section 2). Moreover, the current government coalition consists of the center-right ÖVP, which has moved away from its very pro-integrationist stance in recent years, and the Greens, one of the strongest supporters of further EU integration in the Austrian party system. This constellation bears the potential for intra-governmental dissent with a view to Austria's engagement in and positioning towards the CoFoE, which is why we would expect less enthusiasm of the government in terms of concrete activities and policy proposals due to a lack of consensus.

In line with other observers (cf. Bußjäger 2019), we further claim that for the last two decades, a general lack in strategy for a genuine Austrian European policy (*Europapolitik*) has existed in terms of a clear political vision or long-term policy goals. Rather, Austrian European policy has been driven by political parties' vote-seeking efforts and a comparatively Eurosceptical general public. These patterns can also be observed in the context of the CoFoE, despite nuanced differences resulting from recent changes in the composition of the Austrian government.

Our study is based on an analysis of 105 press releases issued by the Austrian Federal Chancellery, the Austrian parliament, and party groups between January 2020 and the end of June 2022 on the CoFoE. These documents are supplemented by a short online questionnaire among Austrian delegates to the CoFoE structures and three expert interviews.[4]

2. Public opinion and party conflict on European integration in Austria

Despite the comparatively high level of support for EU membership expressed in the 1994 accession referendum, public Euroscepticism is relatively high and stable in Austria. As Eurobarometer data show, support for membership is constantly below the EU average (see Fig. 1), with the Austrians even undercutting the notoriously Eurosceptic British, who meanwhile left the EU, in several years.

---

4 The questionnaire consisted of a total of ten questions, including open questions. It was sent to political representatives and staff from public administrations at federal and state level, who were directly or indirectly involved in the CoFoE. The survey yielded 14 complete responses, including representatives of all political parties, except for the FPÖ. Interviews were conducted with an Austrian MEP represented in the Conference Plenary as part of the EP delegation, a policy officer from the Austrian Federal Chancellery directly involved in intra-state policy coordination on the Conference, and a staff member from the state administration of Vorarlberg.

Fig. 1: Support for EU membership among citizens

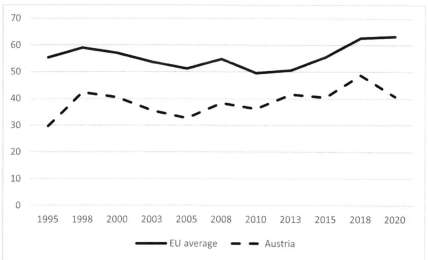

Source: Eurobarometer (EB): EB 44.1 (1995), EB 50.0 (1998), EB 54.0 (2000), EB 60.1 (2003), EB 64.2 (2005), EB 70.1 (2008), EB 73.4 (2010), EB 79.5 (2013), EB 84.1 (2015), EB 90.1 (2018), EB 94.2 (2020); EU average refers to the current EU member states at the time respectively (EU-15, EU-28 respectively EU-27).

Support for European integration follows clear, identifiable patterns: It differs between supporters and voters of the different political parties, with voters from the right fringes of the policy space being most critical while those of the libertarian parties are most supportive. Today's party-political landscape at the national level consists of five relevant parties currently represented in the *Nationalrat*: the traditional mainstream parties ÖVP (member of the EPP group in the European Parliament) and SPÖ (member of the S&D), the radical right FPÖ (member of ID), the Greens (member of the Greens/EFA), and NEOS (member of Renew Europe). Since the beginning of 2020, Austria has its first coalition government which includes the Greens: After the snap elections resulting from the so-called Ibiza scandal, the ÖVP did not renew its prior coalition with the FPÖ but formed a government together with the Greens. Agreement on EU issues between the two governing parties was higher in the previous ÖVP–FPÖ coalition (lasting from 2017 until 2019), which jointly called for the "doing less more efficiently" scenario during the post-Brexit EU future debate and repeatedly showed an intentionally anti-Brussels attitude. During this time, i.e. in the second half of 2018, Austria held the rotating EU Council Presidency.

The center-right government emphasized the principle of subsidiarity, which it often reframed as a re-nationalization of competences already delegated to the European level. Whereas such framing is not surprising for the notoriously Eurosceptic FPÖ, it clearly marks a departure from its previous pro-EU attitude on the part of the ÖVP. After Austria's EU accession, party-Euroscepticism for a long time was a monopoly of the radical right, whereas all other parties were very supportive of European integration and the EU (Pelinka 2004). According to data from the Chapel Hill Expert Survey (CHES, see Jolly et al. 2022), the

ÖVP was even the most pro-EU party. However, this changed over time (see Tab. 1). This came at a price: While intra-party dissent was very low in the late 1990s, it is highest for the ÖVP in 2019 compared to the other parties, climbing impressive 4.6 points (on an 11-point scale) in recent years. The Greens, in contrast, underwent the opposite shift in its positioning towards EU integration: Since the party announced to fully respect the Austrian population's yes-vote in the accession referendum, over time the Greens became strong and internally united supporters of EU integration.

Tab. 1: Austrian parties' intra-party dissent over European integration

	1999	2002	2006	2010	2014	2019
ÖVP	1,00	0,98	1,86	2,43	1,90	6,50
SPÖ	2,50	3,61	4,00	3,54	2,80	3,50
FPÖ	2,50	7,50	1,29	2,29	1,70	2,50
Grüne	3,50	3,20	4,00	2,54	2,40	2,00
NEOS (Liberals)*	1,00	2,22	1,67	-	2,22	1,50

* Data for LIF (Liberales Forum) between 1999 and 2006, NEOS since 2014.
Source: Chapel Hill Expert Survey (Jolly et al. 2022)

Austrian opposition parties are divided. On the GAL side of the spectrum is the youngest parliamentary party, NEOS, which entered the *Nationalrat* in 2013; ever since then it has become the strongest advocate for further EU integration and explicitly mobilizes for a federal vision of a *United States of Europe*. On the TAN side is the Eurosceptic FPÖ that strongly mobilizes against further integration and the EU, which is labelled as a centralistic threat to Austrian sovereignty and identity. The social democrats, SPÖ, are generally supportive of European integration, especially advocating progress towards a social union. However, there is also considerable intra-party dissent on the issue of Europe, and previous party leadership proclaimed significant shifts when the SPÖ was still in power (cf. Schoen 2010).

Austrian parties' general EU attitude is very much in line with expectations derived from the cleavage theory of party positioning towards European integration (Marks/ Wilson 2000), which argues "that European integration is assimilated into pre-existing ideologies of party leaders, activists and constituencies that reflect long-standing commitments on fundamental domestic issues" (ibid.: 433). The core argument is that parties are ideologically constrained in their response to the issue of Europe. Applied to the CoFoE context, we can thus expect the positions and claims expressed by political parties to correspond to their overall ideological fundament. Although strategic reflections certainly also play their part, parties are not simply vote-maximizing machines. As Marks and Wilson (2000: 345) put it, "although political parties exist in a competitive electoral environment, their policy position cannot [...] be predicted as an efficient response to electoral incentives". Rather, party response is mediated by the cleavages from which parties emanated, making party family the core explanatory factor for parties' engagement in and positioning towards the CoFoE.

Many scholars have shown that there is a decline in the traditional class-based cleavage, while at the same time a new, value- or identity-based cleavage has developed (Hooghe et al. 2002; Hooghe/Marks 2009; Kriesi et al. 2006, 2008; Kriesi 2010): whether labelled as the GAL-TAN (green/alternative/libertarian versus traditional/authoritarian/nationalist) dimension of conflict (Hooghe et al. 2002; Hooghe/Marks 2009) or as the integration-demarcation cleavage (Kriesi 2007; Kriesi et al. 2006, 2008), there is a powerful connection between a party's location on this new politics dimension and its positioning towards European integration, much stronger than on the economic left-right dimension. This new politics dimension can be understood as part of a broader structural conflict transforming the party systems in Western Europe, namely conflict between the winners and losers of globalization (Kriesi 2007). Integration into the European or global community and demarcation of the national community defines the poles of this new cleavage (ibid.: 85; see also Kriesi et al. 2006, 2008).

This conflict contains both an economic and a cultural dimension, which is also characteristic for conflict over European integration. Hence a party's response will also vary for the different issues discussed prior, during, and in the follow-up to the CoFoE, depending not only on the respective policy field, but also in relation to what facet of integration is prioritized in reform proposals – negative or positive, economic or political. Depending on the party family, different facets of integration may be in line or at odds with a party's overall ideological program (Marks/Wilson 2000: 437). For instance, social democrats competing on the traditional class cleavage can be expected to be reluctant to economic integration regarding the removing of market barriers, while they are highly supportive of measures towards a strengthening of social rights and the creation of a social and health union. The contrary applies to center-right parties favoring economic over political integration. Fig. 2 displays the location of Austrian parties on the GAL-TAN new politics dimension and party leadership support to European integration based on CHES data.

Fig. 2: Austrian parties on the GAL-TAN dimension (horizontal axis) and party leadership support for European integration (vertical axis) in 2019

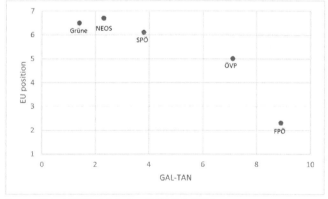

Source: Chapel Hill Expert Survey (Jolly et al. 2022).

3. Austrian activities in and positioning toward the CoFoE

3.1 Government involvement, activities, and initiatives

Like all member states, Austria was represented in the Conference Plenary with two members of government: the Minister for EU Affairs, Karoline Edtstadler (ÖVP), and the Minister for Climate Change, Environment, and Energy, Leonore Gewessler (Greens). The former was part of the Plenary's working group on migration, the latter was represented in the one on climate change and the environment. The government viewed the CoFoE essentially as an opportunity to listen to citizens' concerns and ideas rather than to come up with its own proposals or initiatives (Interview B, Online questionnaire 2022). Consequently, there was no pre-defined governmental agenda. Yet, certain concrete initiatives were taken, e.g. to include representatives of the Western Balkan states in the Conference structures. This was a joint initiative together with the Czech Republic, Slovakia, Hungary, and Poland, and strongly supported by the European Commission. It eventually succeeded in October 2021. Another priority was on youth participation.

In addition to the institutionalized European Citizens' Panels (EPCs), a number of dialogue events and formats took place in Austria in order to involve citizens as well as stakeholders. Already in summer 2020, and hence prior to the official launch of the CoFoE, Minister Edtstadler started touring the *Länder* for discussions with citizens all over Austria. At the start on 9 May 2021, a digital event with Minister Edtstadler plus several current and former political representatives from Austria, including from the *Länder* but also from other EU member states, kicked off the Conference. During the process, there were a number of other events, both online and in person (Bundeskanzleramt 2022: 8ff.). A special website was established that published events organized by the government and by stakeholders. On the part of the government, Minister Edstadler, among others, took part in many citizens' talks and various discussion rounds (ibid.: 34ff.). Both parliamentary chambers (*Nationalrat* and *Bundesrat*) contributed by organizing discussions and an event series called *democracy workshop*. The aim of this was to mobilize adolescents and young people for the CoFoE (ibid.: 50ff.). The *Länder* also organized congresses, discussions and events, or re-labelled existing formats to fit into the CoFoE format. An example is the *European Forum Wachau*, which is annually organized by the government of Lower Austria (ibid.: 77). There were also a number of events at the municipal level including EU municipal councils (*Europagemeinderäte*), a pioneering initiative established more than 20 years ago that regained attention throughout the Conference.

3.2 Government and party positions

As mentioned, the *government* and *governing parties* behaved somewhat reluctant. On the one hand, concrete initiatives were introduced, first, regarding the inclusion of representatives from the Western Balkan states in CoFoE bodies and, second, on the participation of young people in the process. On the other hand, there were not – and there still do not seem to be – any clear-cut positions on key issues of the CoFoE, including the general question of support for treaty change or, more specifically, the abandoning of unanimity in certain policy areas. Still, in the preparatory stage of the Conference, the Austrian government joined other member states in support of a non-paper demanding lean Conference structures that should not "duplicate or unduly interfere with established legislative processes" (Kingdom of the Netherlands 2021) in respect of the inter-institutional balance and current division of competences. In the follow-up to the Conference, however, there is yet no final Austrian position on key issues since – according to representatives of the Austrian Federal Chancellery – the process of reviewing recommendations from the Conference plenary has only started (Press release, 1/6/2022; Interview B). This is even despite the fact that the government already stated in its coalition agreement for 2020–2024 to promote an extension of qualified majority voting, referring to foreign policy as an example (Bundesregierung 2020).

The Austrian government's ambiguity in its positioning towards the Conference is most clearly visible on part of the governing ÖVP. While the Conference was, from the outset, labeled a great opportunity for further developing the EU (the official motto was "Our future – rethinking the EU"), there were few concrete demands put forward by the party. Emphasis was rather put on the participation of and dialogue with citizens and the inclusiveness with a view to the Western Balkans and young people. While there was consensus within the party, statements differed between party representatives on issues such as treaty change and the principle of unanimity. The abolishing of unanimity was referred to as "unrealistic" by Minister Edtstadler. Also, the new chancellor and ÖVP party leader Karl Nehammer saw no need for change and referred to unanimity as an important principle for medium-sized countries like Austria (Press release, 22/6/2022). Non-governmental party representatives, however, expressed their support for the introduction of qualified majority voting in areas such as Common Foreign and Security Policy: National MP Reinhold Lopatka, the party's spokesperson in EU affairs, referred to the end of blockade policy of countries like Hungary (Press release, 19/5/2022). MEP Otmar Karas, first Vice-President of the European Parliament, is known to be a strong advocate for the introduction of majority voting in many areas (Der Standard 2022).

A similar pattern can be observed on the general question of treaty change and the convening of a convention under Article 48 TEU. However, ÖVP members of government seem to have become more supportive towards the idea in the follow-up to the CoFoE. Still, the final national activity report issued by the Federal Chancellery neither mentions the idea of a convention nor treaty change. It refers to specific issues that should be "anchored" in the EU treaties, namely the *Spitzenkandidatensystem* and rule of law conditionality, as part of one of three priorities for reforming the EU as suggested by Minister Edtstadler (Bundeskanzleramt 2022). The other two priorities are a stronger focus on geopolitics and a return to the EU as an economic power. Claims put forward in these areas are in line with the overall party profile focusing on economic matters (removing barriers in the internal market, a return to the Maastricht criteria, pragmatic free trade agreements etc.) and, increasingly in recent years, security and migration issues (external border protection, stop of "illegal" migration, effective return and re-admission policy etc.). Strong party cohesion can be found on subsidiarity, which is labelled a guiding principle in Austria's European policy.

Unsurprisingly, many of the statements on the CoFoE came from EU Minister Edtstadler, who regularly provided updates in the national parliament and issued press releases on dialogue events with citizens. However, MEP Othmar Karas and national MP Reinhold Lopatka, both delegates to the Conference Plenary on behalf of the European Parliament and the *Nationalrat* respectively, also actively engaged in the debate. The former is known as a strong pro-integrationist who has repeatedly been deviating from the official party line in recent years. Accordingly, he proposed to link the next European Parliament elections with a referendum to let EU citizens vote on the implementation of the results of the CoFoE and treaty change (Der Standard 2022).

The Greens seemed to follow a pragmatic approach towards the Conference that reflected both their genuine strong support for further EU integration as well as their efforts to maintain government coherence. A recurring frame in statements by Green party representatives was that current global challenges could not be solved by member states individually, but required joint activities in a strong EU that needs to become a social and health union. Most public statements on the CoFoE were issued by MEP Monika Vana, delegate to the Conference Plenary on behalf of the European Parliament, who was very active throughout the whole process. She proposed a number of concrete claims in line with her party's general EU attitude. National MP Michel Reimon, a former MEP and the national party's spokesperson on EU affairs, also actively engaged in the debate and activities in Austria. Noticeably fewer – and less concrete – statements came from the Green Minister Leonore Gewessler, representing the government in the Conference Plenary. She maintained the governmental line during by emphasizing the CoFoE's participatory character plus the inclusion of the Western Balkan states and youth. This distribution of roles can be viewed as a decisive strategy in order to push for reforms without departing from the government line.

Claims raised by Green representatives included institutional reform claims (see below), environmental and social issues, but also human rights and anti-discrimination policy. In the run-up to the CoFoE, the party also called for debating the Euratom Treaty in order to stop subsidies for nuclear energy. The Green parliamentarians – both European and national – were also quite explicit in their critique of member states' governments and the Council of the EU for blocking necessary reforms. In our analysis we find several statements supporting qualified majority voting in the Council instead of unanimity and strengthening of the European Parliament, including the right of initiative and the introduction of transnational lists. More competences should also be transferred to the EU on health issues (Press release, 10/3/21, 19/5/2022). The results, including debates in the citizens dialogues and recommendations from the Plenary, were taken up to substantiate and further legitimize the party's reform claims in the follow-up process (Press release, 9/5/2022B). This includes claims for a true social and health union as well as climate protection.

What is the position of opposition parties? Austria's largest opposition party SPÖ took a positive stance; it criticized the government for its reluctance towards treaty change in the early stages of the CoFoE (Press release, 9/5/2021). Citizens' participation was viewed positively despite initial fears that it might not work out as planned (Interview A). Besides claims for institutional reforms (including a right of initiative for the European Parliament, less unanimity voting in the Council, and new competences for the EU), positions taken very much reflect the SPÖ's ideological profile with a strong focus on equal opportunities, prosperity, and social rights for a more social Europe. According to the SPÖ, the EU's social pillar is too weak compared to strong economic freedoms, which is why the EU needed to catch-up on the former. Questions related to climate protection and energy policy were also framed in connection with social policy (Press release, 9/5/2022A). Concrete reform claims include the implementation of minimum wages in all member states, measures against child poverty, investments in jobs, and taxes for millionaires.

After the end of the Conference, the party reaffirmed its claims for a social union and for results to be taken seriously by member states' governments. In this regard, MEP Schieder criticized the government for being largely inactive instead of taking the lead on issues where Austria could be seen as pioneer (Interview A). Generally, the CoFoE was viewed as the starting point for a structural debate on reforming the EU that would eventually need to come up with concrete proposals ready for adoption. The most active communicators were the SPÖ politicians Andreas Schieder and Eva-Maria Holzleitner. Both MEPs were delegates to the Conference Plenary and participated in the working groups on *Climate Change and the Environment* and *Digital Transformation*, respectively.

In line with its very pro-integrationist position, NEOS generally took a positive view on the CoFoE outcomes, although the "grand vision according to NEOS, had failed to materialize. The Conference was viewed as great opportunity to make the EU more tangible for citizens and to achieve a more effective and courageous Europe responsive to citizens' concerns (Press release, 25/5/2021, 19/6/2021). Even before the start of the CoFoE, MEP Claudia Gamon insisted that proposals and demands should actually be put into practice. The party connected the CoFoE to one of its central claims, namely the establishing of a United States of Europe, given that the world's major problems could only be solved together in a reformed Europe, which would especially benefit smaller countries like Austria (Press release, 15/1/2020, 7/10/2021A).

Over the course of the CoFoE, NEOS further clarified its wishes, making three key claims: First, a binding nature of the results should be warranted by putting results through a European referendum; second, the issue of climate change should be at the core of the Conference; and third, the Council of the EU, viewed as a blocker of reforms, should be abolished and the European Parliament transformed into a bicameral parliament. In the follow-up process, NEOS supported the recommendation for abandoning the unanimity principle for it would reduce future blockades or vetoes, yielding to faster and more efficient decision-making (Press release, 23/6/2022). The party's prestige project of the United States of Europe is repeatedly taken up and promoted. Compared to the other Austrian parties, NEOS' position on the CoFoE is unique due to its very concrete as well as far-reaching claims. Most of the party's statements were made by MEP Claudia Gamon, who was also member of the Conference Plenary. Furthermore, also individual MPs from the Austrian parliament (both *Nationalrat* and *Bundesrat*) repeatedly praised the process. Irrespective of who was speaking, all statements reflect the party's general attitude in support of a strengthening of the EU.

In the Austrian parliament, the FPÖ currently has a monopoly in its anti-EU stance. In line with this position, the CoFoE was opposed from the outset and labelled as a "show event" enabled by Brussels' elites. Whereas the FPÖ is a strong advocate for direct democracy, citizens' participation as implemented in the CoFoE was criticized for being pure entertainment whereas only referenda would be a sincere instrument for participation. Referring to various formats of citizens' involvement in the EU during the last ten years, the FPÖ stated that neither of these activities had any impact on decision-making. Even in the case of referenda, results would not be respected, as FPÖ speakers illustrated by referring to the initial No-vote of the Irish population on the Treaty of Lisbon in 2008 (Press release, 19/4/2021, 7/5/2021). Throughout the Conference the FPÖ reaffirmed its warnings against "even more EU centralism" and called for a return to key competences for the EU like international trade and traffic as well as security matters. Speakers repeatedly referred to the EU as being centralist and cautioned against it becoming even more masterminded by Brussels instead of the member states (Press release 3/5/2022).

In the follow-up to the CoFoE's closing event and the publishing of the concluding conference documents, the party framed the recommendations as a "wish list of EU centralists" that had nothing to do with citizens' preferences (Press release, 2/5/2022). FPÖ representatives heavily criticized claims for an abandoning of unanimity in foreign and security policy and called on the government to reject any initiatives for a convention on treaty change. Many statements come from the party's MEPs, but the FPÖ is also active in its opposition to the CoFoE in the Austrian parliament, were it proposed a motion for a resolution asking the government to support FPÖ demands regarding the issues of unanimity and treaty change (Press release, 19/5/2019).

3.3 Regions / Länder

Austria's federal structure was also reflected in the framework of the CoFoE. Both the Federal Council (*Bundesrat*) and the federal states (*Bundesländer* or *Länder*) expressed their own positions and held their own events. State parliaments (*Landtage*) were also active, with several activities by their presidents and respective European Affairs committees (EACs). The Austrian Länder were also directly represented in the Conference Plenary with two delegates (one member of the *Bundesrat* nominated as part of Austria's delegation from the national parliament and one delegate nominated by the Committee of the Regions as representative from local and regional authorities).

Not surprisingly, an important claim put forward by all regional-level actors focused on the strengthening of regions in the EU together with issues of subsidiarity and proportionality, also emphasizing the importance of federalism at the European level. At a joint event of the Federal Council and regional parliaments' EACs, the Federal Council President Christian Buchmann, for instance, criticized the increased adoption of regulations instead of directives, which would undermine the subsidiarity review process by excluding national and regional parliaments (Press release, 21/5/2021). At the same time, there was also affirmation that certain issues need to be dealt with at EU level, including foreign policy, climate policy, or democracy policy (Press release, 7/10/2021B). A frequent issue were questions related to security. Except for the FPÖ members of the *Bundesrat*, all parliamentary groups reviewed the results of the CoFoE positively. The same division appears regarding the abandoning of unanimity in the CFSP, which is vigorously rejected by the FPÖ (Press release, 1/6/2022).

In addition to activities by the Bundesrat, the federal states also developed their own positions. Most of the time, however, they joined forces in order to strengthen their position in the overall Austrian debate (Interview C). Important policy fields for the Länder were climate change and environmental questions, but also economic and social issues as well as values, rule of law, and security issues (Online questionnaire 2022). Consensus between the Länder was very high on most of these issues, with two exceptions (Interview C). First, Styria and Lower Austria slightly differed from the other states in their call for sufficient transition periods on climate protection measures due to the economic importance of the automotive industry in these states. The second difference seems to be more ideological, as the issue of minimum wages caused a split between SPÖ-governed and ÖVP-governed *Länder* (Interview C).

State parliaments also joined forces and continued their previously established cross-border cooperation with German-speaking regional parliaments from Germany, Belgium, and Italy. In a joint declaration, the presidents of these parliaments' honored the results of the CoFoE, emphasized the importance of the subsidiarity principle, called for a right of initiative for national and regional parliaments with legislative competences and a general strengthening of regional actors in EU decision-making, and demanded for a convention according to Article 48 TEU.

Overall, no major conflicts emerged in positioning towards and during the Conference between the federal and state levels. This indicates either a well-functioning cooperation between the two levels that worked to the satisfaction of the *Länder* (Interview C), or their limited participation efforts within the intra-Austrian coordination process led by the Federal Chancellery (Interview B). In any case, consensus can also be observed regarding the follow-up process: Expectations regarding the implementation of the Conference results are restrained, with representatives from both levels of government expecting implementation to be a long-term process that has only started. Still, Austrian *Länder* took the opportunity to call for a serious follow-up, illustrated for instance by the joint declaration of the state parliaments' presidents or state governments' statements after the conclusion of the CoFoE (Press release, 18/5/2022). Finally, they seemed to be prepared to agree to the holding of a convention under Article 48 TEU for the implementation of reforms suggested by the Conference Plenary.

4. Conclusions

After the official closing of the CoFoE in May 2022, the follow-up process is just in its early stages. On key issues, the Council still needs to find common positions, and the Austrian government only recently started its intra-state coordination process on these matters (Interview B). However, the domestic political debate in the run-up to and during the Conference displays certain patterns characteristic to Austrian government and party behavior on EU affairs.

Firstly, the CoFoE was no high salience issue for Austrian political parties. This might come as a surprise, given the high issue-salience that EU matters repeatedly have had in Austrian party contestation since accession in 1995 (cf. Meyer 2011). However, the continuously high level of public Euroscepticism together with the lack of consensus for reform among member states makes the CoFoE a difficult issue for parties supportive of further EU integration. This could explain why party leaders from all political parties represented in the national parliament refrained from getting actively engaged in the debate and left the field to parliamentarians from the national and European level.

Secondly, there was no clearly identifiable government strategy on the Conference, which did not seem to be a high priority issue for the governing coalition between the ÖVP and the Greens. There are three plausible explanations for this circumstance: (i) a general lack of a genuine Austrian European policy in terms of a clear political vision or long-term policy goals of Austrian governments since the implementation of the EU enlargement in 2004; (ii) a lack of agreement on the course of further EU integration between the two governing parties; (iii) political infighting at the domestic level caused by a number of scandals involving the governing ÖVP, which led to no less than three different Chancellors in Austria during the timeframe of the Conference. Instead of presenting its own political vision or policy agenda, the government consequently framed the CoFoE as a pioneering participatory exercise. Accordingly, governing representatives declared its mission to be to listen to citizens' concerns.

Thirdly, party positioning on the CoFoE and its key issues were strongly in line with expectations from the cleavage theory of party positioning on European integration (cf. Marks/Wilson 2000; Edwards 2009). This even holds true for the ÖVP and its repositioning on EU affairs commenced by former party leader and Federal Chancellor Sebastian Kurz, which was in line with a more general shift towards the TAN- or demarcation-side (cf. Hooghe et al. 2002, Kriesi 2007) of the policy space. Positions on the CoFoE and its key issues were also very much in line with the overall party ideology of Austria's other parliamentary parties.

Fourthly, federalism did not cause any major conflicts on the Conference between representatives from the different territorial levels in Austria. The *Länder* (including governmental and parliamentary actors) mostly called for a stronger involvement of regions, including regional parliaments, in EU decision-making but also supported the government line towards the Western Balkan states and other issues. Likewise, no serious conflicts were visible within political parties at the different levels.

Finally, instead of presenting its own political vision or policy agenda, the Austrian federal government consequently framed the CoFoE as a pioneering participatory exercise. Accordingly, governing representatives declared their mission to be listening to citizens' concerns. Whether this signifies a missed opportunity to develop a joint and tangible approach towards the future of EU integration is a matter of interpretation. It is, however, in line with attempts by previous governments not to upset the comparatively high share of Eurosceptics among the Austrian population. Whether the ÖVP will return to its previously supportive EU positioning and framing under its new leadership is an open question. Thus far, the debate on the Conference on the Future of Europe indicates a slight departure from parts of the populist Brussels-bashing applied under the former party leadership of Sebastian Kurz. The future will tell us whether this is a temporary phenomenon or a sustainable re-shift also in response to the radical changes in the global environment (pandemic, war, energy crisis etc.) that currently challenges (social) peace and welfare in European societies.

5. References

Bußjäger, Peter 2019: Gibt es überhaupt eine „österreichische Europapolitik"?, in: *Eppler, Annegret/Maurer, Andreas (eds.)*: Europapolitische Koordination in Österreich. Inter- und intrainstitutionelle Regelwerke, Funktionen und Dynamiken, Baden-Baden, pp. 63–76.

Bundeskanzleramt 2022: Die Konferenz zur Zukunft Europas in Österreich. Aktivitäten-bericht 2020–2022 (9/7/2022), Wien.

Bundesregierung 2020: Aus Verantwortung für Österreich. Regierungsprogramm 2020 – 2024, Wien.

Der Standard 2022: Karas: „Würde Europawahl gerne um Volksbefragung ergänzen", 22.01.2022. https://www.derstandard.de/story/2000132723986/karas-wuerde-europa wahl-gerne-um-volksbefragung-ergaenzen (09.08.2022).

Edwards, Erica E. 2009: Products of Their Past? Cleavages and Intra-Party Dissent over European Integration, Institute for Advanced Studies: Political Sciences Series, no. 118, Vienna. https://nbn-resolving.org/urn:nbn:de:0168-ssoar-245687 (08.08.2022).

Føllesdal, Andreas/Hix, Simon 2006: Why There is a Democratic Deficit in the EU: A Re-sponse to Majone and Moravcsik, in: Journal of Common Market Studies 44(3), pp. 533–562.

Hobolt, Sara/Tilly, James 2014: Blaming Europe? Responsibility without Accountability, Oxford.

Hooghe, Liesbet/Marks, Wilson/Carole J. 2002: Does Left/Right structure Party Positions on European Integration?, in: Comparative Political Studies 25(8), pp. 965–989.

Hooghe, Liesbet/Marks, Gary 2009: A postfunctionalist theory of European integration. From permissive consensus to constraining dissensus, in: British Journal of Political Science 39(1), pp. 1–23.

Jolly, Seth/Bakker, Ryan/Hooghe, Liesbet/Marks, Gary/Polk, Jonathan/Rovny, Jan/ Steenbergen, Marco/Vachudova, Milada Anna 2022: Chapel Hill Expert Survey Trend File, 1999–2019, in: Electoral Studies 75, pp. 1–8.

Kingdom of the Netherlands 2021: Non-paper on the Conference on the Future of Europe, 24.03.2021. https://www.permanentrepresentations.nl/documents/publications/2021/03/ 24/non-paper-on-the-conference-on-the-future-of-europe (16.08.2022).

Kriesi, Hanspeter 2007: The Role of European Integration in National Election Campaigns, in: European Union Politics 8(1), pp. 83–108.

Kriesi, Hanspeter 2010: Restructuration of Partisan Politics and the Emergence of a New Cleavage Based on Values, in: West European Politics 33(3), pp. 673–685.

Kriesi, Hanspeter/Grande, Edgar/Lachat, Romain/Dolezal, Martin/Bornschier, Simon/ Frey, Timotheos 2006: Globalization and the transformation of the national political space: Six European countries compared, in: European Journal of Political Research 45(6), pp. 921–956.

Kriesi, Hanspeter/Grande, Edgar/Lachat, Romain/Dolezal, Martin/Bornschier, Simon/ Frey, Timotheos 2008: West European politics in the age of globalization, Cambridge.

Marks, Gary/Wilson, Carole J. 2000: The Past in the Present: A Cleavage Theory of Party Response to European Integration, in: British Journal of Political Science 30(3), pp. 433–459.

Meyer, Sarah 2012: EU supporters at a disadvantage? Party politicization of European integration in Austria (Dissertation theses, University of Vienna), Vienna.

Neuhold, Christine 2020: Democratic deficit in the European Union (Oxford Research Encyclopedias, Politics), Oxford.

Pelinka, Anton 2004: Austrian Euroscepticism: The shift from the left to the right, in: European Studies 20, pp. 207–225.

Plasser, Fritz/Seeber, Gilg 2010: Wahlentscheidung in der Boulevard-Demokratie: Die Kronen Zeitung, News Bias und Medieneffekte, in *Plasser, Fritz (ed.)*: Politik in der Medienarena, Wien, pp. 273–312.

Schoen, Harald 2010: Mehr als ein Auslöser der Neuwahl? Die Europapolitik, die Kronen Zeitung und die Wahlentscheidung 2008, in *Plasser, Fritz (ed.)*: Politik in der Medienarena, Wien, pp. 313–337.

5.1 Primary sources

Press release, 19/5/2022, OTS0176: https://www.ots.at/presseaussendung/OTS_ 20220519_OTS0176 (10.08.2022).

Press release, 15/1/2020, OTS0065: https://www.ots.at/presseaussendung/OTS_ 20200115_OTS0065 (10.08.2022).

Press release, 10/3/2021, OTS0045: https://www.ots.at/presseaussendung/OTS_ 20210310_OTS0045 (10.08.2022).

Press release, 19/4/2021, OTS0126: https://www.ots.at/presseaussendung/OTS_ 20210419_OTS0126 (10.08.2022).

Press release, 7/5/2021, OTS0054: https://www.ots.at/presseaussendung/OTS_ 20210507_OTS0054 (10.08.2022).

Press release, 9/5/2021, OTS0004: https://www.ots.at/presseaussendung/OTS_ 20210509_OTS0004 (10.08.2022).

Press release, 21/5/2021, OTS0190: https://www.ots.at/presseaussendung/OTS_ 20210521_OTS0190 (10.08.2022).

Press release, 25/5/2021, OTS0150: https://www.ots.at/presseaussendung/OTS_ 20210525_OTS0150 (10.08.2022).

Press release, 19/6/2021, OTS0030: https://www.ots.at/presseaussendung/OTS_ 20210619_OTS0030 (10.08.2022).

Press release, 7/10/2021B, OTS0120: https://www.ots.at/presseaussendung/OTS_ 20211007_OTS0120 (10.08.2022).

Press release, 7/10/2021A, OTS0156: https://www.ots.at/presseaussendung/OTS_ 20211007_OTS0156 (10.08.2022).

Press release, 2/5/2022, OTS0116: https://www.ots.at/presseaussendung/OTS_20220502_OTS0116 (10.08.2022).

Press release, 3/5/2022, OTS0053: https://www.ots.at/presseaussendung/OTS_20220503_OTS0053 (10.08.2022).

Press release, 9/5/2022A, OTS0022: https://www.ots.at/presseaussendung/OTS_20220509_OTS0022 (10.08.2022).

Press release, 9/5/2022B, OTS0016: https://www.ots.at/presseaussendung/OTS_20220509_OTS0016 (10.08.2022).

Press release, 18/5/2022, OTS0116: https://www.ots.at/presseaussendung/OTS_20220502_OTS0116 (10.08.2022).

Press release, 19/5/2022, OTS0130: https://www.ots.at/presseaussendung/OTS_20220519_OTS0130 (10.08.2022).

Press release, 1/6/2022, OTS0236: https://www.ots.at/presseaussendung/OTS_20220601_OTS0236 (10.08.2022).

Press release, 22/6/2022, OTS0241: https://www.ots.at/presseaussendung/OTS_20220622_OTS0241 (10.08.2022).

Press release, 23/6/2022, OTS0098: https://www.ots.at/presseaussendung/OTS_20220623_OTS0098 (10.08.2022).

5.2 Interviews

Interview A: Austrian MEP Andreas Schieder, S&D/SPÖ, represented in the Conference plenary as part of the EP delegation. Zoom interview on 13.07.2022 (Leopold Kernstock).

Interview B: Policy officer in the Austrian Federal Chancellery directly involved in intrastate policy coordination on the Conference. Zoom interview on 28.07.2022 (Anna Dermitzakis, Patrick Steindl).

Interview C: Staff member from the state administration of Vorarlberg. Zoom interview on 25.07.2022 (Anna Dermitzakis, Patrick Steindl).

6. Appendix

Replication data for figure 1: Austrian parties' Intra-party dissent over European integration.
Chapel Hill Expert Survey (Jolly et al. 2020): approval of „EU-membership is a good thing".

Year	EU average	Austria
1995	55,4	29,7
1998	59	42,3
2000	57	40,4
2003	53,7	35,5
2005	51,1	32,6
2008	54,8	38,2
2010	49,5	36,1
2013	50,5	41,5
2015	55,6	40,4
2018	62,6	48,7
2020	63,2	40,7

Replication data for figure 2: Austrian parties on the GAL-TAN dimension (horizontal axis) and party leadership support for European integration (vertical axis) in 2019.
Chapel Hill Expert Survey (Jolly et al. 2020).

Party	EU_position	GAL-TAN
FPÖ	2,30	8,90
SPÖ	6,10	3,80
ÖVP	5,00	7,10
NEOS	6,70	2,30
Grüne	6,50	1,40

The Conference on the Future of Europe and the Autonomous Communities in Spain[1]

Mario Kölling

1. Introduction

The Conference on the Future of Europe (CoFoE) was a series of debates and discussions that ran from April 2021 to May 2022. A first analysis emphasised the innovative and the participatory elements as well as citizens' enthusiasm for taking part, in addition to the cooperation evident between the main EU institutions. Other observers have been less enthusiastic about the agenda and procedures of the CoFoE, especially since the final report presented in May 2022 included only one reference to the idea of multi-level governance and no reference was made to the role of subnational actors in EU policy-making. The reform proposals included in the final report regarding the Committee of the Regions contained the idea of encompassing "adequate channels of dialogue for regions if matters with a territorial impact are concerned" (CoFoE 2022: 36). These proposals are far removed from long-standing demands of the Autonomous Communities (ACs) regarding a stronger role in the EU decision-making process. This result came at a time when ACs were complaining about the lack of participation in the drafting of the National Recovery and Resilience Plan and an increasing centralisation of EU multi-level governance (Kölling 2022). But neither were the results a surprise, since the CoFoE was a bottom-up exercise for citizens and did not anticipate setting an agenda or framework to promote subnational institutional, cultural, or political objectives. According to a representative of the government of the Basque Country, the conference overlooked the fact that there are more than seventy regions in Europe with legislative powers, some with broad political competences, which are undoubtedly an asset for the better formulation and implementation of European policies (Elorza 2021). The disappointment is reflected in that comment, but it was not always like this.

Spain's EU membership has consolidated the Spanish decentralisation process and the role of ACs in policy-making. During the past decade, the ACs have developed numerous activities regarding the promotion of cultural and political objectives based on specific regional identities or autonomy demands at the EU level. But at the same time, the EU has developed public policies, which, in practical terms, have not only been decisive for the economic and social development of ACs but also determined and shaped their policy-making. In addition, ACs have become responsible for the implementation and management of important EU redistributive policies. These developments have been conceptualised by the theory of *multi-level governance* (MLG) which underlines the importance of sub-national actors within the EU. Multi-level governance refers to "the coordinated action

---

1 The text was elaborated within the research project: Institutional Reforms in Multilevel Systems: Paradigms, Constraints, Processes and Outcomes (PID2020-116659GB-I00).

135

by the European Union, the Member States and local and regional authorities, based on partnership and aimed at drawing up and implementing EU policies. It leads to responsibility being shared between the different tiers of government concerned and is underpinned by all sources of democratic legitimacy and the representative nature of the different players involved" (CoR 2009).

In this text, I will analyse the preferences of ACs and how the ACs could and did represent their interests at the domestic and supranational levels within the context of the CoFoE. Several studies have analysed the preferences and participation of the ACs in the decision-making process for European affairs, both at the domestic and the European level (Garcia Morales 2013; Carmona Contreras/Kölling 2013; Colino et al. 2014; Kölling 2015). In general terms, the literature differentiates internal and external participation in European affairs. While internal participation mainly concentrates on intergovernmental relations at the horizontal level or with the central government, external participation refers to the activities of the ACs at the European level (e.g., within the Committee of the Regions). I will follow this distinction in the following analysis. Firstly, I will introduce the institutional framework for the ACs' EU activities, secondly, I will analyse the preferences of ACs regarding the CoFoE, and thirdly, I will analyse how the ACs have used the institutional framework in order to defend their preferences.

The empirical data related to the preferences of the ACs regarding the future of the EU has been obtained by an analysis of written and audiovisual contributions submitted to the debate by the governments of the ACs and the central government. Further resources were parliamentary minutes, websites of (regional) government(s), and interviews. The empirical data related to the participation mechanisms for ACs in EU affairs has been obtained through semi-structured interviews conducted by the author in a previous research project (Kölling 2015).

The article contributes to three lines of research. First, and foremost, to the literature on the debate of the role of subnational actors in the institutional reforms of the EU. Secondly, it contributes to work on regional mobilisation in the EU. And finally, the article contributes to the research on the Spanish territorial model.

2. The ACs and EU integration – preferences and institutional framework

Spain is mostly like other Member States where the restructuring of the State has taken place from both 'above' and 'below'. This has been a consequence of both European integration and political decentralisation. Probably, both processes have reinforced each other, and Spain's EU membership has consolidated the role of ACs in the implementation of policy areas as relevant as regional development, environment, agriculture, or fishing policies (Baraibar/Arregui 2022: 135f.). At the same time, starting with the revision of Cohesion Policy in 1988, EU governance has increasingly involved the regional tier alongside Member States and EU institutions (Schakel 2020). As is the case with other regions, the mobilisation and preferences of Spanish subnational governments were driven by their interest in influencing EU policy and legislation with, among other things, the prospect of accessing or defending funding opportunities. But there was also a motivation in relation to promoting cultural or political objectives based on specific regional identities or autonomy demands (Callanan/Tatham 2014).

With regard to the first motivation, for decades Spain was one of the main beneficiaries of EU redistributive policies, and as far as the ACs were concerned, the financial resources coming from Brussels have represented an important source of income for their budgets and allowed them some independence from central government allocations. Although the financial relationship between Spain and the EU has changed over the past years, Spain is, with 140 billion euro in transfers and appropriations over the period 2021–2026, the second largest beneficiary of the NextGenerationEU (NGEU) after Italy. The ACs contributed only indirectly to the design of the National Recovery and Resilience Plan, but are the main actors responsible for its implementation. Given their diverse socioeconomic development and productive sectors, the ACs have different preferences regarding EU policies. The geographic or socioeconomic characteristics of certain ACs (e.g. the Canary Islands as an outermost region) or specific fiscal arrangements (e.g. the Basque County and Navarre) have also given rise to specific preferences.

The promotion of cultural or political objectives based on specific regional identities or autonomy demands also has a long tradition. Already by the 1990s, several ACs were pushing for a Europe of multi-level governance with the EU as a post-national union. In 2000, the network of Regions with Legislative Powers (REGLEG) was created in Barcelona and demanded a new role in the institutional architecture of the European Union for regions with legislative powers and for those that represent national realities (Pahl 2003). But following the proposal made by the former MEP Alain Lamassoure during the European Convention 2001–2004, there have also been specific demands, for example those of the Basque Government that relate to a unique status such as 'Partner region inside the EU'(Gobierno del País Vasco 2018). Finally, the territorial conflict between the Spanish government and some Catalan parties had an important European dimension. While the Spanish government understood the conflict as a domestic issue, the Catalan government was interested in internationalising it.

Regarding the institutional framework for EU activities, the ACs have traditionally carried out EU activities with different degrees of intensity. While the Basque Country and Catalonia were in the 'vanguard' during the 1990s, other ACs have only slowly become involved and did not prioritise activities at EU level until more recently. Although the ACs pursue different strategies to achieve their interests, since the beginning of the 21st Century they have been subnational actors with similar law-making powers and financial autonomy (with the exception of the Basque Country and Navarre, which also have fiscal autonomy). The EU activities of the ACs have provoked controversy and conflict between the central government and the ACs, since the latter challenged the central government monopoly over EU policy, but one can also observe long periods of cooperation and coordination, especially when minority central governments needed the support of regional parties in parliament (López Laborda et al. 2019). Since 2020, in an attempt to base intergovernmental relations in Spain on a cooperative approach, mechanisms of co-governance have been agreed between the ACs and the central government, also in relation to EU affairs. The mechanism of *co-gobernanza* is an attempt to ensure that the government levels cooperate in specific situations, especially in the case of unclear allocation of competences or special challenges. The term deliberately conveys a non-hierarchical connotation of cooperation, but what this actually means has remained unclear in practice thus far (Erkoreka et al. 2021).

At the domestic level, the ACs count on having only very weak constitutional participation mechanisms. Internal participation has mainly concentrated on (bilateral) intergovernmental relations with the central government. Nevertheless, for some years an increasing dynamic in intergovernmental cooperation at the domestic level can be confirmed and a quantitative and qualitative increase in the participation of the ACs in European affairs can also be traced (Castella/Kölling 2022; Colino 2022). However, the 'State of Autonomies' lacks a permanent institutionalised representation of regional interests at the national level. The Spanish Senate is a territorial chamber made up of 266 members, of whom only 58 are appointed by the subnational legislatures (Nohlen/Kölling 2020). Therefore, the Senate does not possess real participation or veto rights for subnational governments in central institutions (Colino 2013). Notwithstanding, the joint Congress of Deputies–Senate European Affairs Committee (EAC) has a remarkable role as consensus builder between political and territorial interests when it comes to Spain's EU policy (Closa/Heywood 2004). Since 2010, the subnational governments may appear before the EAC to provide information about the expected impact of EU initiatives. Within the multilateral transversal participation mechanisms, the Conference for European Union related Affairs (CARUE, after its initials in Spanish) has traditionally assumed a central role. CARUE is an inter-administrative body with the objective of fostering cooperation, consultation, and deliberation between the central government and the ACs. During the last few years, the Conference has lost relevance as the central body in which topics related to European affairs could be discussed on a broader basis between the different levels. Studies on the mechanisms of intergovernmental relations in Spain show that sectoral conferences have become decision-making bodies that reach common agreement on shared-cost programmes while coordinating policies in various sectors (Colino 2022). The sectoral conferences also assume an increasing role in securing participation in EU affairs by the governments of the ACs, whether for the coordination of a common position, or in order to determine the representation of the ACs in the specific Council meetings.

In 2004, the central government established an intergovernmental Premiers' Conference (*Conferencia de Presidentes*) in order to promote an institution that could potentially absorb some of the intergovernmental interaction usually debated in other arenas. With the outbreak of the Covid pandemic, the Premiers' Conference stood out as the main forum for coordination and consultation on several import issues. Although the conference is not a forum for joint decision making, it also is the highest level for intergovernmental relations in relation to the distribution and coordination for the implementation of NGEU.

External participation refers to the activities of the ACs at the European level. We can distinguish between direct activities when ACs participate individually, e.g., the Committee of the Regions (CoR), and indirect activities, when ACs participate in the name of other ACs or within the Spanish government delegation. The indirect participation of the ACs in EU institutions is coordinated by two Councillors for AC affairs at the Permanent

Representation of Spain to the EU. Since 2004, ACs have been able to take part in the national delegation at several Council meetings. The participation of the ACs within the CoR has a longer tradition. In fact, the CoR is the main institution for the participation at EU level of almost all ACs, both in relation to representing their interests in the thematic commissions and as a platform for coalition building with other Spanish or European regions. In the past, presidents of the ACs signed several declarations within the CoR (e.g., on the Cohesion Policy). The ACs also participated in a coordinated way, either through amendments in the plenary or within the thematic Commissions in the elaboration of reports and opinions of the CoR.

It is noticeable that, since 2000, an increasing number of ACs have also participated within European-wide interregional networks (e.g., the Conference of Peripheral Maritime Regions) and they have also been proactive in the promotion of these networks. In 1997, the Conference of European Regional Legislative Assemblies (CALRE) was founded in Oviedo. Its missions are to defend the values and principles of regional democracy and to reinforce links among regional legislative assemblies. As already mentioned, in 2000, the network of Regions with Legislative Powers (REGLEG) was created in Barcelona. All ACs actively participated in the REGLEG network demanding a stronger participation of regions with legislative competences in EU affairs and an active participation in policy formation in accordance with the principles of subsidiarity. Since 2018, four ACs, the Balearic Islands, Basque Country, Catalonia, and Valencia, have participated in RLEG, which is an initiative of regions with legislative powers that share a common basis of values and principles. Nevertheless, for some ACs the external participation did not evolve in line with their expectations.

3.   The AC and CoFoE – preferences and institutional framework

3.1   Preferences in the context of CoFoE

According to the Joint Declaration on the Conference on the Future of Europe, each EU Member State and Institution could organise events in line with their own national or institutional specificities and make contributions to the CoFoE (CoFoE 2022). Within this framework, in close cooperation during 2021/2022, the Ministry of Foreign Affairs and several Autonomous Communities organised several conferences (Gobierno de España 2022a). Although the objective of these conferences was to foster citizen consultation on the Future of Europe, during these events representatives from 15 AC governments (with the exception of the ACs Catalonia and Madrid) also expressed their preferences with regard to the CoFoE. These covered many thematic areas and often went beyond the thematic framework of the CoFoE.

On the CoFoE digital platform, most of the contributions in the area of European Democracy were from Spain, and comments made during the national and regional conferences also covered a wide range of issues.[2] Regarding the institutional design, some representatives offered positive opinions on the existing framework for AC participation in EU affairs: "There are always aspects to improve, but this system [participation in the Council] has allowed the Autonomous Communities to have a forum where we can meet to discuss and agree positions on the European legislation that interests and concerns us" (cf. Gobierno de La Rioja 2021). Other AC representatives demanded a stronger involvement in designing EU policies, e.g., through promoting access by subnational actors to different EU institutions – such as the European Council – as well as a stronger participation in the legislative process (Gobierno de España 2022a). In this regard, they highlighted the need to revise the nature and composition of the CoR. According to these contributions, the CoR should give regions with legislative authority greater qualitative weight in its adopted decisions (ibid.). Moreover, EU regulations regarding territorial cohesion and cross-border cooperation should meet with a favourable response from the CoR. In relation to this, a representative of the government of the Basque Country said: "I believe that the Committee of the Regions must be given greater weight, in general terms, that the work we do as a whole must have greater weight, and I believe that it is also necessary to recognise that, when we talk about regions, there are some very particular regions, [...], with special powers and special responsibilities, which are responsible for some of the powers exercised by the European Union. I believe that this also needs to be highlighted, and it will probably not be the CoR that does this." (Elorza 2021).

Moreover, the Basque and Catalan Government considered that the CoFoE should address the incorporation of a 'clarity' directive in EU legislation. In this regard, subnational actors that have clearly expressed the will to decide their political status (e.g., to decide on self-determination) within a Member State, should be able to consult their citizens on this question. Furthermore, the Basque Government, within a RLEG initiative, demanded that the EU Cohesion policy should be adapted to the needs and characteristics of the ACs which should remain as the central actors of this policy (Gobierno del País Vasco 2022).

Social and territorial Cohesion was also an important issue for most ACs in the consultations held during 2021 at the national and regional level.[3] In this regard many of the activities organised by ACs and the central government were devoted to specific topics for ACs, e.g., cross-border, outermost, mountainous and island regions, or demographic and intergenerational challenges. The AC of Extremadura and the Portuguese regions of Região do Centro and Alentejo expressed their support for preserving cross-border cooperation within the Euroregions. In an event on cross-border cooperation, the ACs of Navarre and the Basque Country emphasised the importance of standardising administrative procedures, in addition to seeking local solutions to citizens' day-to-day problems. Both ACs also demanded the strengthening of territorial and cross-border collaboration. In this

---

2 Events in the thematic area of European democracy have been organised by the ACs Aragon, Castilla-La Mancha, Castilla y León, the Valencian Community, the Balearic Islands and La Rioja.

3 Events in the thematic area of Social and territorial Cohesion have been organised by Aragon, Castilla-La Mancha, Castilla y León Cantabria, Asturias, the Basque Country, Navarre, the Balearic Islands, the Canary Islands and Galicia.

respect, both ACs and the New Aquitaine region in France underlined the continuity of the Euroregion. The Basque Government advocated the creation of an Atlantic macro-region.

Besides the special situation of border regions, the problems affecting certain territories with special characteristics, such as mountainous regions, were also raised. Islands and de-populated areas demanded special treatment from the European Union, as established in articles 349 and article 174 of the Treaty on the Functioning of the EU. In the case of the outermost region of the Canary Islands, the specific needs of this AC regarding the Common Agricultural Policy and the EU Cohesion Policy were highlighted, as were exceptions in taxation and state assistance.

The fight against climate change and the conservation of the environment and of bio-diversity was highlighted by several events, e.g., an event organised jointly by the AC of Castilla y León and the Central and Northern Regions of Portugal. Further concerns were raised on the impact of the energy transition and the impact of NGEU.

3.2 The institutional framework at the domestic level

As already mentioned, during 2021/2022, the central government and the ACs organised several consultations at the national and regional levels in close cooperation. In total, six national and 18 regional events were held. This cooperative approach between the two levels of government was emphasised by the workshop on 'The Role of Regions in the European Union' held in November 2021 in Seville, bringing together representatives from the Spanish Ministry of Foreign Affairs, European Union and Cooperation (MAEUEC) and several ACs. In this conference, the MAEUEC underlined the need to increase the participation of the ACs in the preference formation at the national level, as well as their participation in policy-making at the EU level. Although the conferences mainly concentrated on (bilateral) relations between one or two ACs and the central government and no common multilateral declaration was signed at the end of the consultation process, the central government confirmed the support for ACs with special status, e.g., the outermost region, or with specific preferences (Gobierno de España: 2022a).

Besides this consultation process, the formal institutionalised participatory mechanisms were used less. The sectorial Conference for European Union related Affairs did not meet in 2021 and 2022. Other sectoral conferences on EU affairs met regularly but did not include the CoFoE in their Agenda (Gobierno de España: 2022b). The Premiers' Conference (*Conferencia de Presidentes*) held three meetings during the deliberations of the CoFoE[4], but the Conference was not mentioned in the agendas of the meetings. A common declaration was adopted neither.

In June 2021, the joint Congress of Deputies–Senate European Affairs Committee (EAC) appointed four parliamentarians to represent the Spanish Parliament at CoFoE, among them a representative of the Basque Nationalist Party (PNV). The EAC also established a sub-committee and organised hearings on specific questions related to the

---

4   XXIVth Conference of Presidents, 30.07.2021; XXVth Conference of Presidents, 22.12.2021; XXVIth Conference of Presidents, 13.03.2022.

CoFoE. However, only one hearing out of seven was dedicated to the perspective of an AC.[5] On 12 November 2021, the Secretary General for External Action of the Basque Government presented the position of the Basque Country to the EAC. The Joint Committee for the European Union also set up a public e-mail for the submission of initiatives and proposals on the main issues discussed in the CoFoE. Nevertheless, there have been no submission from ACs on these specific issues.

3.3 The institutional framework at the EU level

Since 2019, the CoR has expressed its commitment of playing a significant political role in the CoFoE. It has already been active in the preparation of the CoFoE, setting up internal structures for discussion and developing ideas for how to strengthen the role of regions in the process and in the future of the EU (Abels et al. 2021). However, in accordance with the Joint Declaration, the CoR was only invited as an observer (CoFoE 2021).

The CoR has argued for a stronger and more active role for regional authorities, such as regional parliaments, in the future debate and has provided support structures for regional action. Among the 18 regional and local delegates proposed by the CoR, three represented the ACs, Isabel Díaz Ayuso, President of the AC of Madrid (EPP); Concepción Andreu Rodríguez President of the Regional Government of the AC of La Rioja (PES), and Paula Fernández Viaña, Minister for Interior, Justice and External Action, AC of Cantabria (RE). All three maintained a very low profile and none of them participated in the plenary debates and in only one joint a debate by video conference (Aldecoa: 2022). Other ACs had no direct access: "We made an express request to be part of the delegation of the Committee of the Regions to the plenary, but, [...] we have not been able to form part of this commission. However, through our political group, we are following very closely what these plenary sessions and the preparations for them are producing" (Elorza 2021). In this regard, although not all ACs could participate via the CoR in the CoFoE, some channelled their participation through the political groups at the EP. For example, several MEPs promoted the idea of an 'active subsidiarity'. Moreover, nine MEPs, including Carles Puigdemont, presented a proposal at the EP to include the debate on self-determination and on the Clarity Mechanism within the CoFoE.

Other ACs, such as Catalonia, presented their proposals to the CoFoE via civil society organisations, in this case the Catalan National Assembly. Their proposal on self-determination and the official status of the Catalan language, co-promoted by Junts with other parties and organisations, was presented in February 2022 as a topic which should be

---

5   Hearings by EAC: Marian Elorza, Secretary General for External Action of the Basque Government, 12.11.2021; Marta Arpio Santacruz, Director representing the Council at the Secretariat of the Conference on the Future of Europe, 25.03.2022; Francisco Aldecoa Luzárraga, President of the Spanish Federal Council of the European Movement 18.03.2022; Julia Fernández Arribas, President of Equipo Europa and member of the High Level Advisory Board of the Conference on the Future of Europe, 18.03.2022; Rafael García-Valdecasas Fernández, State Lawyer (retired), and former judge of the Court of Justice of the EU, 10.02.2022; José María Areilza Carvajal, Secretary General of ASPEN Institute Spain, 10.02.2022; Francina Esteve García, Professor of International Public Law and Director of the Europe Direct-Universitat de Girona, 12.11.2021.

discussed in CoFoE. Neither proposal received enough votes to be included in the final plenary.

3.4 Transregional activities

Earlier, in May 2021, several RLEG members, among them the Balearic Islands, Basque Country, Catalonia, and Valencia Region, had sent a joint letter to the presidents of the European Commission, European Parliament, European Council and the Council of the EU requesting a greater involvement of regions with legislative powers in the CoFoE (RLEG 2021). According to the letter, these regions should participate in the plenary body as well as in the decision-making and governance of the implementation process of the CoFoE outcomes. The undersigned expressed their commitment to organise a high-level event on effective multi-level governance.

Several ACs (the governments or regional assemblies of Cantabria, Canarias, Rioja, Madrid, Andalucía, and Murcia) belonged to a group of 31 frontrunner regions whose long-term political objective is to enhance the regions' political impact at the European level on matters with direct relevance to the work of local and regional authorities. In June 2021, the 'Alliance of Regions for European Democracy' (2021), together with CALRE/CoR and the Assembly of European Regions (AER), signed the Declaration on 'The place of regions in the European Union architecture in the context of the Conference on the Future of Europe'. The Declaration called for the CoFoE to discuss the role of regions in the EU institutional architecture, in particular those with legislative powers. Gustavo A. Matos Exposito, President of the Parliament of the Canary Islands and President of CALRE, said during the presentation of the Alliance: "The regional parliaments and legislative assemblies of the EU represent the citizens of their regions, through their elected representatives, therefore they are fundamental tools to achieve the involvement of citizens in the process of redefining the EU" (CoR 2021). In the same context the President of La Rioja added: "The participation of regional administrations in European affairs should be included in the national and regional legal systems. La Rioja is reforming its Autonomy Statute and one of the proposals is the region's participation in the European legislative process" (Gobierno de La Rioja 2021). However, in contrast to the RLEG declaration, the signatories stated that the European Committee of the Regions is a valuable way of representing their institutional and political objectives.

4. Conclusions

The Conference on the Future of Europe was a novel and innovative process. It was a citizen-focused, bottom-up exercise for Europeans to have their say on what they expect from the European Union, and not a framework for addressing the specific demands of subnational actors. The conference report was published in May 2022 and only one reference on multi-level governance was included.

We found a wide range of shared preferences among ACs regarding the future of the EU, with several preferences linked to the socio-economic characteristics of the ACs. It is too early to draw conclusions, but it looks as if we can identify three groups of ACs. The first one makes serious demands for institutional reform of the EU beyond the CoR, including demands for greater autonomy and the right of self-determination; the second group mainly demands a stronger role for regions with legislative competences in the EU and a reinforced CoR, while a third group comprises the ACs that are not affiliated to either of the two 'blocs'.

Nevertheless, all ACs maintained a low profile with regard to the Conference on the Future of Europe. This may be explained by the 'policy first' approach of the conference, the procedures which concentrated on citizen consultation, and the dominance of the council vis-à-vis other EU institutions, as well as the international context in which the conference went on. Finally, at the national level, the debate on the implementation of the NGEU was a much stronger issue. The framework of events in partnership with civil society and stakeholders at the European, national, regional, and local level, in a wide variety of formats, did not satisfy AC demands to have a specific role as regions with legislative competences, among them several ACs, immediately raised the need for a more specific conference. Regarding the participatory mechanisms at the domestic and EU level, the ACs did not employ the mechanisms with a view to influencing the conference, even though the institutional framework governing the role of ACs in the EU has expanded over the past 20 years

Spain will assume the Presidency of the Council of the European Union in the second half of 2023. It will be interesting to see if the cooperative relationship between ACs and the central government can also lead to initiatives which may foster the role within the EU of regions with legislative powers. Considering the increasingly complex policy challenges, ranging from climate change, demographic pressures, rising inequalities and discontent, successful responses will require integrated approaches to policy-making. The Committee of the Regions emphasises that local and regional authorities implement 70% of climate change mitigation measures and 90% of adaptation measures, so in this regard regional authorities should also take part in the decision-making.

5. References

Abels, Gabriele/Große Hüttmann, Martin/Meyer, Sarah/Lenhart, Simon 2021: The Committee of the Regions and the Conference on the Future of Europe, in: *Abels, Gabriele (ed.)*: From Takers to Shapers? Challenges for Regions in a Dynamic EU Polity, EZFF Occasional Papers Nr. 43, Tübingen, pp. 23–44.

Aldecoa, Fransisco 2022: Conferencia sobre el futuro de Europa: Participación de los ciudadanos en la federalización y democratización de Europa, Federalistes d'Esquerres – UEF Catalunya, 29.01.2022.

Alliance of Regions for European Democracy 2021: Declaration on "The place of regions in the European Union architecture in the context of the Conference on the Future of Europe", June 2021. https://cor.europa.eu/en/engage/pages/declaration-place-of-regions-in-the-eu-architecture.aspx (31.05.2022).

Baraibar Molina, Javier/Arregui, Javier 2022: European Union Regional Policies: A Convergence Point of Spanish Regions towards the EU? BACES Working Papers No. 08-2022.

Callanan, Mark/Tatham, Michaël 2014: Territorial interest representation in the European Union: Actors, objectives and strategies, Journal of European Public Policy 21(2), pp. 188–210.

Carmona Contreras, Ana M./Kölling, Mario 2013: La participación de las CCAA en la negociación de la política de cohesión ¿Ambitions beyond Capacity?, Revista de Estudios Politicos, No.161, pp. 239–278.

Castellà Andreu, Josep M./Kölling, Mario 2022: Intergovernmental Relations and Communal Tensions in Spain, in: *Fessha, Yonatan T./Kössler, Karl/Palermo, Francesco (eds)*: Intergovernmental Relations in Divided Societies. Comparative Territorial Politics. Palgrave Macmillan, Cham, pp. 159–182.

Closa, Carlos/Heywood, Paul M. 2004: Spain and the European Union, New York.

CoFoE 2021: Joint Declaration of the European Parliament, the Council and the European Commission on the Conference on the Future of Europe Engaging with citizens for democracy – Building a more resilient Europe, 05 March 2021. https://eur-lex.europa.eu/legal-content/EN/TXT/?uri=CELEX%3A32021C0318%2801%29 (31.05.2022).

CoFoE 2022: Report on the final outcome, May 2022.

Colino, Cesar. 2013: Intergovernmental Relations in the Spanish Federal System: In Search of a Model, in: *López Basaguren, Alberto/Escajedo, Leire (eds)*: The Ways of Federalism in Western Countries and The Horizons of Territorial Autonomy in Spain. Vol. 2, Berlin/Heidelberg, pp. 111–124.

Colino, Cesar/Molina, Ignacio/Hombrado, Angustias 2014: Responding to the new Europe and the crisis: The adaptation of subnational governments' strategies and its effects on intergovernmental relations in Spain, Regional & Federal Studies 24(3), pp. 281–299.

Colino, Cesar (ed.) 2022: Retos de la gobernanza multinivel y la coordinación del Estado autonómico: de la pandemia al futuro Instituto, Madrid, Nacional de Administración Pública.

Committee of the Regions 2009: White Paper on Multilevel Governance, CONST-IV-020, 80th plenary sesión, 17 and 18 June 2009.

Committee of the Regions 2021: Regional leaders commit to launch an 'Alliance of Regions for European Democracy' to enhance regions' political impact at EU level, Press release. https://cor.europa.eu/en/news/Pages/ALLIANCE-REGIONS-EURO PEAN-DEMOCRACY.aspx (31.05.2022).

Elorza, Marian 2021: Comparecencia de doña Marian Elorza, Secretaria General de Acción Exterior del Gobierno Vasco, para que informe sobre el objeto de la Ponencia relativa a la Conferencia sobre el Futuro de Europa. Comisión Mixta para la Unión Europea (12.11.2021).

Erkoreka, Mikel/Grau Creus, Mirea/Kölling, Mario 2021: Decentralisation and Covid-19: the Spanish territorial system under pressure, in: *Steytler, Nico (ed.)*: Comparative Federalism and Covid-19, London, pp. 33–50.

García Morales, Maria Jesus 2013: Intergovernmental Relations in Spain and the Constitutional Court Ruling on the Statute of Autonomy of Catalonia: What's Next?, in: *López Basaguren, Alberto/Escajedo, Leire (eds)*: The Ways of Federalism in Western Countries and The Horizons of Territorial Autonomy in Spain, Vol. 2, Berlin/Heidelberg, pp. 83–109.

Gobierno de España 2022a: Spanish Framework for Citizens' Consultations on the Future of Europe - Conclusions. https://www.exteriores.gob.es/es/Comunicacion/Noticias/Documents/NOTICIAS/202203/Conclusions%20COFoE_Spanish%20Framework%20for%20Citizens%27%20Consultations.pdf (31.05.2022).

Gobierno de España 2022b: Reuniones de Conferencias Sectoriales. https://www.mptfp.gob.es/portal/politica-territorial/autonomica/coop_autonomica/Conf_Sectoriales/Conf_Sect_Reuniones.html (31.05.2022).

Gobierno de La Rioja 2021: La presidenta Andreu asegura que la Conferencia sobre el Futuro de Europa servirá para que la ciudadanía debata sobre políticas que le afectan. https://actualidad.larioja.org/noticia?n=not-la-presidenta-andreu-asegura-que-la-conferencia-sobre-el-futuro-de-europa-servira-para-que-la- (31.05.2022).

Gobierno del País Vasco 2018: Visión del futuro de Europa. https://www.irekia.euskadi.eus/uploads/attachments/11343/Vision_del_Futuro_de_Europa.pdf?1520589969 (31.05.2022).

Gobierno del País Vasco 2022: Lehendakari Iñigo Urkullu: RLEG Initiative, contribution to the Future of Europe. https://bit.ly/3KnVZBs (31.05.2022).

Kölling, Mario 2015: Subnational Governments in the Negotiation of the Multiannual Financial Framework 2014–2020: The Case of Spain, Regional & Federal Studies 25(1), pp. 71–89.

Kölling, Mario 2022: El impacto de NGEU y del MFP 2021-2027 en el Sistema de Gobernanza Multinivel de la UE, Gestión y Análisis de Políticas Públicas (GAPP), (29), 11–22.

López-Laborda, Julio/Rodrigo, Fernando/Sanz-Arcega, Eduardo 2019: Consensus and dissent in the resolution of conflicts of competence by the Spanish Constitutional Court: the role of federalism and ideology, in: European Journal of Law and Economics 48, pp. 305–330.

Nohlen, Dieter/Kölling, Mario 2020: Spanien. Wirtschaft, Gesellschaft, Politik, Wiesbaden.

Pahl, Marc-Oliver 2003: Die Rolle der Regionen mit Gesetzgebungskompetenzen im Konvents-Prozess, in: *Europäisches Zentrum für Föderalismus-Forschung (ed.)*: Jahrbuch des Föderalismus 2003, Baden-Baden, pp. 462–479.

RLEG 2021: RLEG calls for a greater involvement of regions with legislative powers in the policy-making and implementation process in the EU - https://rleg.eu/news/rleg-calls-greater-involvement-regions-legislative-powers-policy-making-and-implementation (31.05.2022).

Schakel, Arjan H. 2020: Multi-level governance in a 'Europe with the regions', The British Journal of Politics and International Relations 22(4), pp. 767–775.

6. Annex

Framework for Citizens' Consultations on the Future of Europe

01 Extremadura: Relations between the European Union and Latin America and the Caribbean, a revamped agenda and a recovery programme within the Sustainable Development Goals. Cuacos de Yuste, 23 July 2021.

02 Valencian Community: Europe and Health: A New Era. Valencia, 27 October.

03 Basque Country and Navarre: CrossBorder Cooperation and the Conference on the Future of Europe. Pamplona, 28 October.

04 Region of Murcia: Transportation and Smart, Sustainable, Resilient Mobility. Cartagena, 29 October.

05 Cantabria: Citizens' Dialogue on Values and the Law. Santander, 2 November.

06 Castilla y León: Innovative Responses to Cross-border Cooperation on Climate Change. Zamora, 3 and 10 November.

07 Canary Islands: The Future of the Outermost Regions in the Future of Europe. Las Palmas de Gran Canaria, 5 November.

08 Canary Islands and the Basque Country: Migralantics: Meeting of Atlantic Migrations. Las Palmas de Gran Canaria, 10 and 11 November.

09 Balearic Islands and Valencian Community: The Mediterranean and the EU: A Basin for Cohesion. Palma de Mallorca and Valencia, 18 November.

10 Navarre: New European Bauhaus. Pamplona, 19 November.

11 Andalusia: Andalusia, a Neighbourhood Model in the EU. Seville, 24 November.

12 Principality of Asturias and Cantabria: Territorial and Demographic Disparities in the EU: The Challenge of Mountain Regions. Argüeso, 24 November.

13 La Rioja: Youth Social Forum on Gender Violence within the Framework of the Conference on the Future of Europe. Logroño, 24 November.

14 Galicia: All the Opportunities in the Sea: Advancing the Blue Economy. Vigo, 24 November 2021. • Autonomous Cities of

15 Ceuta and Melilla: A Vision of Europe from North Africa. Ceuta and Melilla, 23- 25 November.

16 Balearic Islands: Island Citizenship and the EU. Ibiza, Artá, Ciudadela and Mahón, 8 and 29 October and 24-25 November.

17 Extremadura and Castilla-La Mancha: The Contribution of Spain's Autonomous Communities to the Ecological Future of Europe. • Citizenry and Sustainable Tourism in Inland Rural Destinations. Garrovillas de Alconétar and Cáceres, 30 November. • The Energy Transition. Mérida, 29 November. • Environmental sustainability. Toledo, 2 December.

18 Aragon, Castilla-La Mancha, and Castilla y León: Response to the European Depopulation Challenge. Teruel, Cuenca and Soria, 10 December.

Italian perspective on the Conference on the Future of Europe

Susanna Cafaro

1. Introduction

The Conference on the Future of Europe (hereinafter CoFoE) – launched in May 2021 and closed on 9 May 2022 – marks a turning point in the procedure for the revision of the European treaties, when and if it will be followed by a Treaty revision. Yet, even if it will not, it will nonetheless represent a significant evolution in the relation between the Union and its citizens and maybe even lead to some adjustments in its democratic formula.

Before the entry into force of the Lisbon Treaty in 2009, the convening of an intergovernmental conference was necessary for the revision called ordinary in Article 48 of the Treaty on European Union (TEU). Since 2009, Article 48, para 3 TEU provides for the convening of a convention composed of representatives of national parliaments, Heads of State or Government of the Member States, the European Parliament, and the Commission. The convention examines the draft amendments and limits itself to presenting a recommendation, adopted by consensus, to the intergovernmental conference which therefore remains the main hub of the procedure for treaty revisions – with all that it entails in terms of method and decisional procedure (consensus). A simplified revision procedure is also foreseen for the Treaty on the Functioning of the EU (TFEU), Part. III, detailing competences and policies.

In 2020, the Commission asked for, and obtained, a leap forward with an uncertain outcome: before an intergovernmental conference or even a convention is convened, the European institutions set out to listen to the voice of citizens through a double channel: a platform online and four panels of citizens, each made up of 200 people randomly chosen from the 27 Member States, representative of the diversity of the Union by geographical origin (citizenship and urban/rural context), by gender, age, socio-economic context and level of education. One third of each panel was made up of young people aged between 16 and 25.[1] The aim pursued by this double exercise in participatory democracy is to further develop the concept of democracy to shorten the distance between the European citizens and the Union, and to compensate for the gap that is inevitably created between elections to the European Parliament in the 5-year electoral cycle.[2]

Participatory bodies and procedure are usually less formal than the traditional structures of representative democracy, and they are intended to complement them. While the deliberative process is not removed by its legitimate locations, the convention and the following ratification process, the citizens' assemblies called European Citizens' Panels (ECPs) were

---

1 For a more detailed history of the origin and development of the CoFoE see introduction to this volume as well as the contributions by *Metzger* and *Torres-Ader* as well as by *Aras* in this volume.

2 In Commission President von der Leyen's agenda as of 2019 we can read: "I want Europeans to build the future of our Union. They should play a leading and active part in setting our priorities and our level of ambition. I want citizens to have their say at a Conference on the Future of Europe, to start in 2020 and run for two years. The Conference should bring together citizens, including a significant role for young people, civil society and European institutions as equal partners" (von der Leyen 2019:19).

established to make the voice of the citizens heard, to increase the awareness of political elites about their specific needs and perspectives and, in the end, to deliver recommendations. Yet, little is achieved by this tool if the participatory processes are not really participated in.

Italy hosted a session of the European Citizens' Panel on "European democracy, values and rights, rule of law, security", its third and final one, in the setting of the European University Institute (EUI) in Florence, Italy, and remotely. Citizens of different ages and backgrounds, from all Member States, adopted 39 recommendations for the future of Europe in the fields of European democracy, values and rights, rule of law and security.[3] The panellists focused on ensuring rights and non-discrimination; protecting democracy and the rule of law; reforming the EU; building European identity; and strengthening citizen participation (Mackay/Nicolaidis 2021).

The second tool, the online CoFoE platform was, nonetheless, the focus of the national strategies to shorten the distance between Italian citizens and European institutions. The platform – multilingual and multitopic – enabled participants to elaborate and share their ideas with just a few clicks, allowed them to like other citizens' posts and to promote their own events on the topics listed. To declare this exercise a success or a failure, the only effective criterion is in numbers: How many uploads, clicks, sharing, are really required? And how to get the citizens informed about the platform and its scope, aware about its importance and willing to participate?

In every EU Member State this participatory democratic exercise has been shaped differently and it has been, ultimately, in the hand of national governments to promote or ignore this process, spreading effective information and providing real encouragement to induce citizens to get involved in it. However, in several Member States regions were also actively involved in the CoFoE.

The final numbers are not exceptionally good, neither do they show a complete failure – an honest appraisal is somehow in the middle. Close to 5 million individual visitors, over 750,000 participants, 18,000 ideas debated, and over 6,500 events organized are not really that many for a Union of about 450 millions of citizens. Yet, they are not so few as to make their voice irrelevant.

2. The governance structure promoting the participation of Italian citizens

In Italy, this participatory process started with the Government itself taking a stance for European reforms, through an informal document called "non-paper" (Government of Italy 2020). The Italian Government made itself abundantly clear that it was in favour of a substantial revision of the European treaties as a follow-up of the CoFoE.

To comply with the mission of making Italian citizens' voice heard, the Government established two temporary bodies dedicated to amplifying the European invitation to join the double-track CoFoE and especially the online platform, since the EPCs were directly estab-

---

3 Recordings of the two-day session are available online on the website of the Multimedia Centre of the European Parliament. See https://multimedia.europarl.europa.eu/en/package/conference-on-the-future-of-europe_17609 (05.12.2022).

lished at European level. This governance framework was created by Decrees of the Head of Government[4] establishing a Scientific Committee for the Future of Europe, an Organizational Committee – co-chaired and co-managed by the Foreign Affairs Ministry and the European Policies Department – and a Technical Secretariat.

The 35 Scientific Committee members were selected showing due attention not only to gender balance and geographical differentiation, but also to interdisciplinary academic representation, alongside the involvement of renowned think tanks and relevant civil society groups. The intergenerational balance was less good with just one from a youth organization: Young European Federalists (JEF). The two co-chairs, a man and a woman, had a diplomatic back-ground, ambassador Ferdinando Nelli Feroci, respectively and academic background, professor and lawyer Paola Severino.

As a first step, the Scientific Committee split into four thematic working groups dedicated to foreign policy and international projection of the EU; institutional affairs; economic governance and social policy; and climate, energy and health. The goal of the first group meetings in August to September 2021 was to discuss and recognize the relevant issues in each of the four areas in relation to the CoFoE. The four topics have been articulated in points; issues were identified to give orientation to potential citizens' discussions, and to develop accessible material to encourage debates and events. Even if every group has interpreted this specific role differently, the documents – as informal and unofficial as they were – were circulated in the plenary of the Scientific Committee and shared with the Organizational Committee. They are published in the book *Conferenza sul futuro dell'Europa. Relazione sul contributo del Governo italiano* (Conferenza 2022)

With a certain degree of approximation, we can say that the topics the four working groups worked on reflected to a certain degree the ones of the four transnational EPCs officially established by the CoFoE. This first exercise, nonetheless, proved to be not significant for the activities of the Scientific Committee in the following nine plenary meetings. These meetings were held monthly and mostly online. The discussions provided input as well as feedback to the Organizational Committee which carried out the work on the ground. Hence, in the end the Scientific Committee served as an advisory body – reacting, commenting, and suggesting, sometimes even ratifying – the choices and activities conducted by the governmental body.

The latter was co-chaired and co-managed by the Department for European Policies, which in Italy is a department under the Presidency of the Council of Ministers, and by the Ministry of Foreign Affairs and International Cooperation. Together, representatives from these two administrations joined forces as members of the technical secretariat. Yet half of the members of the Organizational Committee were representing local authorities: the Conferences of regions, of provinces, of municipalities and of mountain communities.

In general terms, the Government wanted to stimulate the debate at all levels and aimed for a significant participation of students, both from universities and high schools, local authorities, and civil society. Although the discussion on the topics of the CoFoE was open to all citizens, the privileged interlocutors were young people, considered to be the protago-

---

4   Decreto del Presidente del Consiglio dei Ministri (DPCM) of 20 April 2021, modified on 2 July 2021, and DPCM of 15 July 2021, online as annex 2, 3 and 4 (see Conferenza 2022).

nists of the consultation. The involvement of young people also had an international dimension thanks to bilateral initiatives. On specific topics, two events were designed to involve young people from the Western Balkans and from the Southern Neighbourhood. All these initiatives were also intended in the spirit of highlighting the general objective of the European Year of Youth.

3.   Targets and Specific initiatives

3.1. Schools

On 14 October 2021, the announcement of the competition "Europe is in your hands!" was published, which aimed at upper secondary school students, with the intention to stimulate reflection on the future of the EU through a language suitable for the new generations. Participants could send a product (digital presentation, video or other content specifically fitted for social media) aimed at creative contributions on the future of the EU, from young Europeans standpoint. A Joint Commission composed of representatives of the Directorate General for Students, Inclusion and Scholastic Guidance of the Ministry of Education, of the Department for European Policies and of the Ministry of Foreign Affairs and International Cooperation evaluated the contributions and finally selected 21 winning classes. The competition registered a large participation, with 350 works presented. The total cost of 147,000.00 Euros, supported by the Department for European Policies, was split into prizes of 7,000.00 Euros for each class, for the purchasing of teaching material or for the implementation of training initiatives related to Europe. Additionally, four webinars dedicated to the CoFoE themes were held with teachers and students at secondary schools, which were attended by over five thousand students.

3.2. Universities

On 10 December 2021, the call "University 4 EU – Your future, our Europe" was published, targeted at universities and other higher education institutions. A wide discretion was left regarding eligible initiatives. Once again, creativity was encouraged (audiovisual, textual, multimedia contents, commercials, conferences, etc.), the involvement, together with the students, of citizens, and civil society – or, at least, the impact on them - was a requirement for eligibility. The evaluation committee was composed of officials representing the Ministry of University and Research, the Department for European Policies, and the Ministry of Foreign Affairs and International Cooperation. Considering the high quality of the submitted 64 projects, the committee considered them all eligible for the 4000 Euros prize, to encourage an even larger dissemination than intended, financing 14 more initiatives in addition to the first 50 ones as planned.

The initiatives had a dual purpose: they contributed directly to the visibility of the CoFoE, and they were also posted on the online platform for further outreach. In many cases they were also apt to generate more entries in the online platform as proposals and contributions to the debate. Several projects had a creative and artistic side, as laboratories, architectural planning, digital/virtual spaces, photographs, graphic designs. The more recurrent topics were climate change, solidarity, circular economy, energy, social inclusion, gender equality, and cultural heritage. Others addressed more directly the political challenges of democracy and European integration.

Another initiative, which was officially developed by the Department for European policies, but substantially carried out by volunteering universities, was the series of events called "let's meet in ... to talk about the future of Europe" (*Incontriamoci a ... per parlare del future dell'Europa*). The nine events – with a local outreach – were organized in nine cities from north to south[5] and had different thematic foci related to the CoFoe topics. All of them involved, jointly with university students, civil society organizations, local authorities, and other relevant guests.

All of the meetings followed the same format: a first session with one of more panels with guests, and a second one consisting of debates and teamworking among students with the objective to produce original content to be then uploaded on the CoFoE digital platform.[6] Finally, two particularly relevant events closed the series. On 11 April 2022, a big wrap-up conference was organized by the Department for European Policies, the Foreign Affairs Ministry and the Rome municipality in collaboration with the European Parliament and the European Commission. This conference was held in a highly symbolic place, i.e., in Campidoglio. This is where the Treaty establishing the European Economic Community (EEC) was signed in 1957. The wrap-up conference hosted over 150 university and high school students. The series was concluded by a symbolic event in Ventotene on the eve of Europe Day, 8 May.[7]

Another four events, which also involved young people, were organized in cooperation with the local Europe Direct offices. According to calculations more than 1,000 students participated in in these 9 plus 4 events. Further events were organized with the Youth National Council specifically involving youth associations.

As already mentioned, the Ministry of Foreign Affairs and International Cooperation organized two events aimed at encouraging the involvement of young people across borders. Firstly, the EU-Balkan Youth Forum took place in Rome in November 2021, organized in collaboration with the Regional Cooperation Council, the Regional Youth Cooperation Office, the Center for International Political Studies and the Observatory Balkans Caucasus Transeuropa. In this event, students from all EU Member States and from the six Western Balkan countries participated. The students discussed in working groups, addressing enlargement and institutions; identity and reconciliation; environmental challenges; economic integration; European digital space (EU-Balkan Youth Forum 2021). The second event, in

---

5   The cities were Venice, Milan, Bologna, Lecce, Teramo, Pavia, Catania, Florence and Padua.

6   See https://futureu.europa.eu/.

7   The Ventotene Manifesto (Italian: *Manifesto di Ventotene*) – original name *For a Free and United Europe. A Draft Manifesto (Per un' Europa libera e unita. Progetto d'un manifesto)* – is a political statement written by Altiero Spinelli together with Ernesto Rossi and Eugenio Colorni while they were imprisoned on the Italian island of Ventotene during World War II as political dissidents of the fascist regime. Completed in June 1941, brought clandestinely to Switzerland and then printed, the Manifesto became the founding text of the European federalist movement. In it, European Federalism and World Federalism are presented as ways to prevent the insurgence of nationalism in the future and the only ways to prevent future wars. See also European Observatory on Memories 2021.

December 2021, was held in the framework of the Youth forum of Med Dialogues[8], dedicated to climate, environmental sustainability, and green economy. The future of Europe – and of the European relations with the Southern Neighbourhood Countries – was discussed in a session specifically dedicated to a shared green agenda.

3.3. Socio-economic Actors

Specific dialogues were hosted by the National Council of Economy and Labor (CNEL).[9] The CNEL, which is a body enshrined in article 99 of the Italian Constitution, started on this occasion, a collaboration with the Department for European Policies. This collaboration might continue to flourish, hopefully, even beyond the CoFoE, in order to involve the economic stakeholders more in the discussion of European policies. En passant, we note that this Department has taken the opportunity offered by the CoFoE to dialogue with numerous institutional and non-institutional actors, thus enlarging the dimension of its activity, which promises to bring more of the European perspective in the Italian political sphere in the future.

The CNEL had a specific session on the CoFoE to discuss four proposals with a socio-economic focus, which were the outcome of previous meetings. In January and February 2022, two meetings were held with youth representatives of organizations represented at the CNEL, promoted by the EU Policy Commission and International Cooperation, and in collaboration with the Department for European Policies. A second stream of activity launched by the Department for European Policies and conducted since spring 2021 was a collection of hearings of representatives of political and economic entities as well as of civil society. Again, there was a specific focus on youth organizations.[10]

3.4. Communication Strategy

Much could be said about the communication strategy implemented by the Organizational Committee. The main actions were, once again, targeted at young people, even if with a wider focus. A commercial was realized – very "young" in its videoclip conception[11] – commissioned through a public selection. It was broadcasted on national TV about half dozen times per day. While this is little compared to the usual visibility of commercials on TV, it was, however, considered to be a relevant investment. A social media strategy flanked the commercial, showing coloured cards on topics and idea from the CoFoE. A social media campaign was created on TikTok and Instagram by two influencers, who were in charge of

---

8 MED – MEDITERRANEAN DIALOGUES is the annual high-level initiative promoted by the Italian Ministry of Foreign Affairs and International Cooperation and ISPI (Italian Institute for International Political Studies) in Rome (https://med.ispionline.it/).

9 The CNEL, based in Rome, is made up of a president (appointed by the President of the Republic) and 64 members, who remain in office for a five-year term: 48 representatives of productive categories; 10 experts (8 appointed by the President of the Republic, 2 proposed by the Prime Minister); and 6 representatives from non-profit organizations.

10 The recording of the hearings is available at https://www.politicheeuropee.gov.it/it/conferenza-sul-futuro-delleuropa/audizioni/ (12.12.2022).

11 See https://www.politicheeuropee.gov.it/it/comunicazione/progetti-e-campagne/campagne-radio-tv/la-tua-parola-conta/ (12.12.2022).

producing content to engage followers on the topics of the CoFoE.

Nevertheless, the repeated pleas of the Scientific Committee members to go on air to provide information and in-depth analysis and commentary in TV programs on current affairs had no follow-up. The CoFoE was the focus of very few programs along the year. Unfortunately, a large majority of Italian citizens remained completely unaware of the CoFoE as well as of the campaign described above. Yet, Italy was not an exception: media attention on the CoFoE was low in other Member States as well (HLAG 2022).

4. The Political Outcome

The Italian government presented, at an early stage of the CoFoE, a positioning non-paper titled *Using the Conference on the Future of Europe to shape a real European political discourse* (Government of Italy 2020). It was approved by the Interministerial Committee for European Affairs on 14 February 2020. The Italian proposal suggested two strands for European reforms: (1) institutional innovations that could help improve the functioning of the Union, in a supranational perspective, and (2) political priorities for the EU. It can be described as a bold progressive text.[12] How its assertiveness was partly due to the awareness that it was the starting point of a tough negotiation with much less pro-integration countries, we cannot say for certain.[13]

The Italian Parliament carried out a fact-finding survey to stimulate debate. In addition, it held parliamentary hearings involving members of the civil society as well as representatives of national and European institutions. Furthermore, on 27 April 2022 both the Senate and the competent Commissions of the Chamber of Deputies adopted guidelines calling on the Government to support the proposals emerging from the CoFoE, through ordinary Treaty revisions. In May 2022, the Italian government then supported a non-paper issued jointly with Germany, Belgium, Luxembourg, the Netherlands, and Spain calling for treaty reforms and for implementing the proposals derived from the CoFoE (Non-Paper 2022). Italy was also involved in a joint dialogue among regions, involving France, Poland, the Czech Republic, Italy, Spain and the Danube River region to promote the development of "pan-European visions on the future of Europe".[14]

In the main events of the campaign, which culminated in the *Stati Generali della Conferenza sul futuro dell'Europa* held in Rome on 15 June 2022, all ministers and undersecretaries responsible for foreign and European affairs took a strong stance in favour of an outspoken and courageous position of Italy. In their position they promoted a bold revision

---

12 The first strand included the strengthening the role of European Parliament (and the European dimension of its elections through the transnational lists for a quota of members), especially where it is lacking, such as in the economic governance, reinforcing the citizens' initiative, introducing a pan-European referendum, starting a debate on the possibility of direct election of the President of the European Commission; shifting from unanimity to qualified majority voting in the Council in areas as social security and protection, anti-discrimination measures, taxation and the common foreign and security policy; developing stronger EU external action in support of its internal policies, Regarding the political priorities, the Italian government's proposals focused on environmental issues and the green economy, on the completion of the fiscal union, on the establishment of a migration and asylum policy based on solidarity.

13 See also the in-depth discussion of the conflicts in the Council of the EU in the introduction to this volume.

14 See the chapter on Germany in this volume.

of the treaties, to strengthen the supranational institutional dimension through the abolition of the unanimity vote, the transition to a more decisive common dimension in fiscal policy and in the common foreign and security policy and in developing weak competences, such as migration, social policy, or healthcare.

These positions, many of which were shared with the European institutions, were later on vigorously presented before the European Parliament by Prime Minister Mario Draghi in a speech delivered on 3 May 2022. Draghi was the first EU leader to address the European Parliament on the CoFoE. He announced:

"We need a pragmatic federalism, embracing all areas affected by the ongoing transformations – from the economy to energy to security. If this requires the start of a path that will lead to the revision of the Treaties, embrace it with courage and confidence. If we know how to draw the strength to take a step forward from the tragic events of these years; if we know how to imagine a more efficient functioning of the European institutions that allows for timely solutions to citizens' problems; then we will be able to hand over to them a Europe in which they can recognise themselves with pride" (Draghi 2022; translated with DeepL.com).[15]

However, the CoFoE does not seem to have found a significant echo in the Italian political debate outside the places strictly reserved to it. We can only speculate if the new Government, resulting from the elections held on 25 September 2022, will maintain such strong commitments, although the radical change in the political forces – with a centre-right coalition firmly holding the majority – is not particularly promising. Even if Prime Minister Giorgia Meloni confirmed the Government's commitment to support the European Union, it does not imply a progressive position on the evolution of the European integration.

The contributions uploaded on the CoFoE platform by the Italian citizens, nonetheless, show a strong pro-European and integrationist attitude, just as those collected during the campaign events. Young people and civil society actors stressed in various ways the need for a more social Europe, a strong commitment to the environmental goals, and a migration policy including sharing burdens among Member States, and paths to integrate migrants into society. Citizens have more ambitions and expectations than politicians towards European integration. They are more concerned about policies than institutional matters – even if it is quite clear to experts and political leaders how the two area are interrelated. Only a genuine supranational decision-making process grants the European Union the tools to adopt common policies. Conversely, critics are mainly concerned with the lack of efficiency or the inadequate response of the Union to critical subjects, resulting from weak competences, intergovernmental processes, and unanimous vote requirements.

One could explain such outcome with the scarce participation of euro-sceptics in the consultation, the events and maybe the entire process.[16] This could be a partial justification, given that they could access the platform and open events to express their own critical views,

---

15 The original reads: "*Abbiamo bisogno di un federalismo pragmatico, che abbracci tutti gli ambiti colpiti dalle trasformazioni in corso – dall'economia, all'energia, alla sicurezza. Se ciò richiede l'inizio di un percorso che porterà alla revisione dei Trattati, lo si abbracci con coraggio e con fiducia. Se dagli eventi tragici di questi anni sapremo trarre la forza di fare un passo avanti; Se sapremo immaginare un funzionamento più efficiente delle istituzioni europee che permetta di trovare soluzioni tempestive ai problemi dei cittadini; Allora potremo consegnare loro un'Europa in cui potranno riconoscersi con orgoglio.*"

16 This is, indeed, a regular accusation by right-wing populists against CoFoE. We can see this in the Austrian and the German cases very clearly. See the chapters on Austria and Germany in this volume.

but maybe they simply lacked the genuine interest in doing so. Yet, when the opportunity arises for a comprehensive debate, it seems that not Europe per se is the object of many of its critics, but the model of Europe and the policies it implements.

As it happened in other national consultations[17], it seems that proposals stemming from local and national consultations were in the end not so different from each other and from the results of the CoFoE. The concerns raised and the positions expressed show that a European political sphere or at least a significant number of shared views do exist. Especially among young citizens, there is a widespread attention for environmental goals as there is for employment, inclusion, and social justice.

5.   Lights and shadows of the Italian campaign

Despite a governance structure and a dedicated budget, the Italian campaign has not fully achieved its goals. It had followed two different aims: (1) uploading of a significant number of contributions from Italy onto the platform and organizing many events; (2) spreading awareness of the democratic exercise underway in the population so that, even without any specific solicitation, anyone interested – individuals, civil society and other intermediate bodies of society – could on their own initiative contribute in the ways and forms they deemed appropriate. The first target was successfully achieved, thanks to the number of schools and universities involved and the many events solicited and organized: In fact, Italy was in second place among the Member States in terms of number of events (750 out of a total of 6,600). Yet, the campaign overlapped with several initiatives which would have taken place anyway, i.e., even without the funding provided by the Government. This is all those events organized with and by the European movement, the European federalist movement and other organization promoting European integration, the events involving the Europe Direct network and all those initiatives such as conferences and seminars planned and managed in the universities by the chairs in European studies, including the Jean Monnet chairs. What was certainly positive, and innovative for the Italian political experience, was the focus on the younger segment of the population.

The second goal of spreading awareness also had its own dedicated tools – despite the assumption that it would have also been the result of successfully fulfilling the first goal. The toolbox included TV commercials, hiring the influencers, and developing and implementing a social media strategy. Yet, this goal was largely missed: the CoFoE did not make its way through the wall of the main information channels as TV and radio; the impact at large was vastly disappointing. Not only was a general awareness about the platform lacking, but close to nothing was reported on the panels' activity on the news and the current affairs programs. This seems to reflect a more general European deficit in communication, as reported by the Eurobarometer[18] (Michailidou/Trenz 2022; see also HLAG 2022). On average

---

17 See e.g. the chapter on France in this volume.

18 See the 2022 Special Eurobarometer 517. It has to be specified that the Eurobarometer covering the topic was released in March 2022 and covered the period September–October 2021. When asked "Have you recently read in the press, seen on the Internet or on television or heard on the radio something about the

only 1 in 4 Europeans report to have heard about the CoFoE. Hence, the lack of media reporting and public awareness is not just an Italian problem, or maybe it is the addition of many similar national deficits.

The absolute inadequacy of media attention throughout the entire process is not surprising, given that in general little space is dedicated to European decision-making and policies. It remains a major missed opportunity, since a team of high-level ministerial officials and a significant number of experts, plus a dedicated budget, had been tasked with achieving a goal that could lead to giving more substance to European citizenship even beyond the specific occasion. The lesson learned is therefore striking: the paramount role of media in building (or non-building) a genuine political sphere.

That said, my personal experience, as a member of the Italian Scientific Committee and above all as a professor of European law, has been largely positive. I had the opportunity to be involved in two initiatives in my university supported as part of the campaign: (i) an event as part of the "Incontriamoci a ..." series and (ii) a series of podcasts called "Voci per il Futuro".[19] Furthermore, I made an interesting first-hand experience as part of my course of European Union Law. The direct involvement of students – carried out through four labs in which students were free to imagine, suggest and upload "their own" reforms on the CoFoE platform, signed with their own name – generated a great enthusiasm in expressing and arguing their ideas. Beyond the result of more than fifty uploads, all stemming from working groups in the EU Law classes, I had the huge gratification of realizing, when the time of exams came, that I had the most motivated and learned class in twenty years. My personal takeaway from this experience is that participatory democracy tools are also great didactical tools. Luckily, in the area of European studies we have aplenty: discussing and signing European citizens initiatives, contributing to the European Commission's online consultations or drafting petitions are all opportunities we can use to foster active European citizenship, building awareness along with competences and skills. Indeed, participation appears to be an effective means not only for combating the lack of interest in European democratic life, but also for legitimizing or for questioning the major political orientations and decisions taken by the European institutions and eventually for training young people in active citizenship.

The Conference on the Future of Europe, to the extent that it has reached citizens, can be qualified as the largest consultation ever carried out on a European scale and a step forward in that "demos in the making", which constitutes the heart of the "ever closer Union" objective emphasized in the European treaties. Yet, the fact that the CoFoE did not reach out to the majority of citizens is, sadly enough, a wasted opportunity.

Conference on the Future of Europe", on average 1 in 4 replied (EU average 23%) "Yes, but don't really know what it is about" (Eurobarometer 2022, QA6).

19 Created on the initiative of my colleague Claudia Morini as part of the initiatives of the universities supported by the Italian Government through the competition mentioned above and available on all the main platforms for podcasts.

6. References

Conference on the Future of Europe 2022: Report on the final outcome, 09.05.2022. https://futureu.europa.eu/pages/reporting?locale=en (12.07.2022).

Conferenza 2022: Conferenza sul futuro dell'Europa, Relazione del Governo sul contributo italiano. https://www.politicheeuropee.gov.it/media/6373/futuroeuropa_volume_web.pdf (03.12.2022)

Draghi, Mario 2022: Discorso del Presidente Draghi alla Plenaria del Parlamento Europeo* Strasburgo, 3 May 2022. https://www.astrid-online.it/static/upload/disc/discorso-presidente-draghi-plenaria-pe-3.5.2022.pdf (03.12.2022).

Eurobarometer 2022: Future of Europe 2021. Special Eurobarometer 517, January 2022. https://europa.eu/eurobarometer/surveys/detail/2554 (06.12.2022).

European Observatory on Memories 2021: Ventotene 80. 80th anniversary of the Draft Manifesto for a Free and United Europe 1941–2021. https://europeanmemories.net/stories/ventotene-80/ (12.12.2022).

Government of Italy 2020: Using the Conference on the Future of Europe to shape a real European political discourse. Italian Non-Paper for the Conference on the Future of Europe, 14 February 2020. https://www.esteri.it/mae/resource/doc/2020/03/paper_conf_futuro_europa_post_ciae_14_febbraio_-_clean.pdf (12.12.2022).

HLAG 2022: Conference on the Future of Europe: What worked, what now, what next?, High-Level Advisory Group Report, Conference on the Future of Europe Observatory, 22 February 2022, https://conference-observatory.eu/wp-content/uploads/2022/03/High_Level_Advisory_Group_Report.pdf (05.12.2022).

Mackay, Jamie/Nicolaidis, Kalypso 2021: What's in an Experiment? Participatory Democracy Comes to Town, la Repubblica, 7 December 2021. https://firenze.repubblica.it/dossier/firenze-europa/2021/12/07/news/what_s_in_an_experiment_participatory_democracy_comes_to_town-329263801/ (03.12.2022).

Michailidou, Asimina/Trenz, Hans-Jörg 2022: The Future of Europe debate needs the intermediary power of journalism, EUI transnational democracy blog, 7 March 2022. https://blogs.eui.eu/transnational-democracy/the-future-of-europe-debate-needs-the-intermediary-power-of-journalism/ (03.12.2022).

Non-paper 2022: Non-paper submitted by Germany, Belgium, Italy, Luxembourg, the Netherlands, and Spain on implementing the proposals of the Plenary of the "Conference on the Future of Europe" 2022, 13.05.2022. https://twitter.com/alemannoEU/status/1526922932970262528 (02.08.2022).

von der Leyen, Ursula 2019: A Union that strives for more: My agenda for Europe. Political Guidelines for the Next European Commission 2019–2024, Brussels.

EU-Balkan Youth Forum 2021: "What is Europe?", 22–26 November 2021. https://www.eubalkanforum.org (03.12.2022).

Conference on the Future of the EU in Czechia: Achievements and setbacks

Jarolím Antal

1. Introduction

The Conference on the Future of Europe (CoFoE), a joint initiative of the main EU institutions, was established to enable and engage citizens in May 2021. Due to the pandemic and various restrictions in the EU member states, a vast number of events had to be moved online or was held in a hybrid format. The central role played a multilingual digital platform, where citizens could insert their ideas and contribute to the CoFoE. Despite this common framework for the whole EU, the flavor of the debate on the future of the EU has been different in each country – in terms of its activities, intensity and nature of the engagement of citizens. This is very much linked to the attitude of citizens towards the EU, political ownership (communication of the CoFoE by political leaders), and activity of the stakeholders in contributing to the whole debate on the CoFoE.

Czechia is a case of an EU member state which entered the Union in 2004 and became an "adult" in terms of its age – as of 2022, Czechia's membership in the EU celebrated its 18th birthday. When talking about the economic dimension the EU membership, even after all these years, the attitude of Czech citizens remains rather ambivalent despite of the huge economic impacts of the EU membership and the beneficiary position of the country to the EU budget. This together with low interest of Czech political elites in stimulating and supporting the CoFoE project serves as a quite case for analysis of the project – its presence, reactions, and outcomes.

This contribution discusses the CoFoE in Czechia. It attempts to identify the main challenges during the CoFoE and, last but not least, tries to frame the outcomes of the CoFoE's final report in the expectations and the reality of understanding the EU issues among the Czech public. This paper is structured as follows: Firstly, the context of CoFoE in the country is analyzed. Further, the paper investigates the CoFoE in Czechia in regard to the activities, their focus, and outcomes. The attitudes of the Czech citizens are then discussed in relation to the reflections of the final report presented in May 2022. As Czechia held presidency in the Council of the EU between July-December 2022, the ambition of the Czech presidency in the relation to the CoFoE is also captured.

Due to very limited data and information available on this matter, the literature mainly builds on available documents of the Czech government, think-tanks and other materials that have been produced as outputs of events organized under the CoFoE-umbrella.

2. Context of the CoFoE in Czechia

Czechia is a medium size EU member. As a country located in Central Europe, it is naturally benefiting from its relations with its neighbors in the region. Particularly its trade profile, focusing predominantly on export to the EU, indicates enormous benefits for the prosperity of the country. Given its post-communistic history, the country went through an economic transformation. However, in terms of its economic performance (as well as other Central and Eastern European countries), it still lags behind the old EU members.

One would expect that the benefits of the EU single market, impacts of the cohesion policy and in general net beneficiary position of the country in relation to the EU budget[1] contribute to the positive perception of the EU, but this is not exactly the case. The attitude of Czech citizens towards the EU remains mixed. Several reasons can be drawn in this regard. One of them is a historical experience and the desire to protect one's own territory and to keep control over it, as under the communist regime civic freedoms have been suppressed. This eventually created a certain sentiment, which drives the public opinion and contributes to doubts about supranationalism (powers of the EU institutions) and the role of the European integration process. The explanation is linked to the ideology of euroscepticism represented by Vacláv Klaus, who was president when Czechia joined the EU[2], and he remained the strongest voice of the anti-EU currents. Several new political parties and movements build on this legacy and further reject the EU and governance from "Brussels". Some authors describe the development of party and non-party euroscepticism as the most prominent phenomena in Czech political history in the last decade (Havlík/Mocek 2017). As Figure 1 shows, despite the fact that trust in the EU has been growing during the last years, it only reaches 50%. Interestingly however, Czech citizens trust the EU more than the national government or the parliament.

Fig. 1:   Trust of Czech citizens in selected institutions

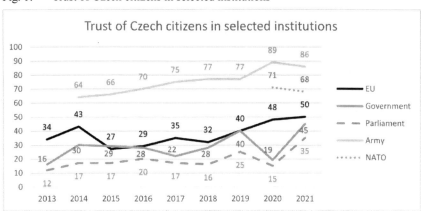

Source: European Commission 2022a.

---

1   Czechia has been a net beneficiary of the EU funding since its accession. Since 2004 the country received app. 38 bil. EUR from EU budget, in 2021 the country received around 3,45 bil. EUR (Ministry of Finance, Czechia 2021).
2   Václav Klaus was President of Czechia between 2003–2013.

3. Main actors and expectations of the government from the CoFoE in Czechia

Czechia is a unitary parliamentary republic, where powers are divided between the national government and 13 regions (*kraje*) plus the capital city of Prague. The regions have their own regional councils, led by governors (*hejtman*). The powers of the regions are limited to certain areas such as management of secondary schools, hospitals and social facilities, maintenance of roads, organization of transport infrastructure in their territory, and cooperation in the implementation of projects funded by the EU.

Given the Czech political system and the roles of both parliamentary chambers, it is essential to elaborate on the interest of legislative bodies in the CoFoE. During the preparatory phase of the CoFoE, the Chamber of Deputies was, through its Speaker, part of the *Slavkov/Austerlitz Declaration of the Speakers* (Austria, Czechia, Slovakia) where the leaders expressed a need for inclusive debates and "shared ownership of the EU institutions, including national parliaments" (Slavkov/Austerlitz 3 2020). Later, the Chamber of Deputies and the Czech Senate both recognized the importance of the CoFoE with respect to the role and involvement of national parliaments. As reaction to the COSAC[3] meeting in 2021 in Zagreb, speakers of 24 national parliaments signed a letter to the President of the European Parliament; expressing the need that national parliaments must be involved in the governing bodies of CoFoE and must also participate in establishing the programme. They claimed that the European parliament and national parliaments should have an equal number of participating representatives in the CoFoE. Czechia joined this initiative as the Chairmen of the Committee for European Affairs, the Chamber of Deputies, and the EU Committee of the Czech Senate signed the letter (Francová 2020: 8).[4]

In a resolution from 17 March 2021, the Committee for EU affairs of the Chamber of Deputies regretted that, despite the participation of national parliaments in the Executive Board, representatives from national parliaments would only have observer status (Francová 2021: 9).

The coordination of the CoFoE in Czechia was managed by the Office of the Government. This institution provided an umbrella for activities and also organized some of the events in Czech regions. The department for Communication of the EU agenda, which was in charge of the CoFoE, has also worked actively with local representations of the EU institutions (European Commission and European Parliament), national institutions, and stakeholders.

The Czech government aimed to involve citizens and raise awareness about the EU. The Secretary of State for EU Affairs, Milena Hrdinková, pointed out that the government had no willingness to push for reforming the EU treaties and supported the current setup of weights of powers among member states through CoFoE. Regarding the CoFoE and facili-

---

3 COSAC is the Conference of Parliamentary Committees for Union Affairs of Parliaments of the European Union.

4 A similar letter was initiated by the Chairman of EU Committee of Portuguese Assembleia da República Luís Capoulas Santos. This letter was sent to presidents of EU institutions, this was also supported by other EU member states, among others by chairmans of EU committies of Czech Chamber of Deputies and Czech Senate.

tation of the debates with citizens, the government had an ambition to assess the needs of the citizens. The government approached the CoFoE through the focus of the New Strategic Agenda.[5] According to Hrdinková, the Czech government's main aim was to verify whether the opinions of citizens complied with this document. In addition, the debate on national and regional level should mainly focus on topics such as the Green Deal, environmental issues, and their impacts on prosperity. Another essential area was the EU internal market and its digital dimension. Rather than looking and discussing general aspects of the EU and its institutional affairs, the government wanted to seek out ways on how to target specific policies and bring the benefits of the European integration process closer to the citizens, so they would better understand the EU and could formulate their opinions on how the EU can better contribute to their life. The main ambition was to facilitate the debate within the CoFoE in Czech regions, particularly with the assistance of stakeholders and the parliament (Hrdinková 2021).

One of the key platforms for discussing EU affairs among experts is the National Convention. It includes various stakeholders, who are regularly attending meetings and are engaged in the discussions. Outputs in the form of recommendations serve as material for the government and are further subject for discussion at the Committee for EU affairs of the Chamber of Deputies. Two roundtables have been dedicated to the CoFoE. The first one on this topic highlighted that the CoFoE was an opportunity for engaging citizens in EU matters. According to the recommendations of the roundtable, Czechia should enable a wide range of actors on national, regional, and local levels to enter the debate. Given the overall rather skeptical attitude of Czech citizens, the CoFoE could contribute towards a better understanding of the EU and eventually raise awareness on the upcoming Czech Presidency in the Council of the EU (Bartovic et al. 2020: 6).

In the second roundtable dedicated to this matter (3 July 2022), the Convention concluded that the CoFoE has been successful, as it engaged citizens and triggered discussion. The platform, in this regard, played a crucial role, and therefore should remain active (Faktor 2022).

4.   A closer look at the CoFoE activities

The CoFoE in Czechia has been kicked off by an opening event organized by the Office of the Government. Among panelists was the Vice-President of the European Commission, Věra Jourová, Vice-President of the European Parliament Dita Charanzová, experts, and stakeholders. The government has been represented by Secretary of State for the EU, Ms. Milena Hrdinková. No member of the government attended the event, which was later a subject of criticism. Tomáš Pesczinsky compared the opening event to the approach of Slo-

---

5   The New Strategic Agenda was adapted by the European Council in June 2019. It sets priorities of the European Council and provides guidance to other EU institutions. According to this document, the EU should focus on protecting citizens and freedoms, developing a strong and vibrant economic base, building a climate-neutral, green, fair and social Europe, as well as promoting European interests and values on the global stage.

vakia, where a similar event has been attended by Prime Minister and the President of the country. According to him, Czech citizens don't perceive the importance of EU issues and neither do the politicians, regardless the period of a political cycle. Zuzana Stuchlíková shares a similar view, which highlights how tough it is to communicate EU issues to the citizens for political leaders, parties, and also public administration (Zichová 2021).

The Office of the Government has used its wide network of Eurocentres, which serve as regional information channels for the communication of EU issues. This network played an essential role under the CoFoE. The audience of the events mainly consisted of students, seniors, and the general public. Of the 10 main topics that were structured in the platform of the CoFoE, six resonated mostly during the discussions organized by the Office of the Government. These were:

- EU in the World;

- Education, Culture, Youth and Sport;

- Stronger Economy, Social Justice and Jobs;

- Digital Transformation;

- Climate Change and Environment;

- European Democracy.

By November 2021, Czech citizens inserted 86 ideas and 339 comments. At the end of the CoFoE, 114 events have registered at the platform (Blahušiak 2021). Around 40% of the events have been organized in Prague, the rest in other regions of the country (Conference on the Future of Europe 2022).

Besides the events under the Office of the Government (7 regional flagship debates), three transnational debates have been organized. One of them took places under the cooperation of the German and Czech Ministries of Foreign Affairs and the Czech-German Fund for Future. This debate focused on topics such as Education and Youth, Climate Change and Environment, and Values and Rights. Another specific transnational event was organized under the Prague European Summit with a program for young professsionals (Prague European Summit's Future European Leaders Forum). Also, a series of simulation games about the EU institutions, "Decide about Europe", was organized at various Czech high schools.

The CoFoE was also a subject of a unique cross-regional dialogue initiated by Grand Est (France), Baden-Württemberg and Saxony (Germany), Województwo Dolnoslaskie (Poland), and Karlovarský kraj and Ustecký kraj (Czechia). At first, citizens participated in dialogues organized online in their regions. Based on the results and topic that had been raised, three topics were selected for a dialogue among citizens of all involved regions. The goal was to enable a discussion of citizens among the participating regions on EU topics (Landesregierung Baden-Württemberg 2021).

During the CoFoE, 4 citizens panels in the country took place.[6] These panels revealed unique observations on 4 selected topics, where participants discussed benefits and issues related to the future of the EU.

(1) Democracy, Values, Rule of Law, Law and Security

According to the panel participants, it is important to focus on the problems of environmental protection, combating climate change and solving the energy crisis. Building a strong economy that will be built on the highest possible food and energy self-sufficiency is another expectation emphasized among participants of the panel (Buchtík et al. 2022).

In its foreign policy, according to the participants, the EU must focus on strengthening the position of the EU in the world and the bloc must be able to compete and have a strong say in negotiations with other great powers (such as USA, Russia, China). Specifically, it is essential to pay attention towards resolving relations with Russia. Security is also important for positive development in the future, minority rights, compliance with the principles of the rule of law, modern education, and the fight against misinformation (ibid.).

(2) Climate Change, Environment and Health

The most significant challenges that were mentioned are the impacts of climate change, further extensive pollution from industries, agriculture, transport, and the role of humans. Excessive consumption accompanied by the production of excessive amounts of waste is also perceived negatively. Czechia and the EU should focus on the diseases of civilization such as stress, diseases resulting from an unhealthy lifestyle, oncological diseases, or viral epidemics with global impact (ibid.).

(3) Economy, Social Issues, Sport, Culture and Digital Transformation

The economic impacts and benefits of the Czech Republic's membership in the EU are mostly understood positively. Restrictions on the Czech industry and consumers are subject to criticism. According to the respondents, the EU should guarantee equal rules for agricultural producers and should not favor producers of specific commodities in selected states. The EU should focus on the competitiveness of its own products at world markets. At the same time, with the help of protectionist measures, the EU should develop its own production in strategic sectors in such a way as to ensure its power and economic independence (ibid.).

(4) EU in World and Migration

Among the Czech public there is only a minimum of those who express a pro-Russian support for security and only some are "open" to the idea of balancing the relations and an openness of Czechia to both directions – to the EU and to Russia. The Czech public

---

6   The panels were organized under similar rules as panels organized on the EU level. The research was conducted by STEM Empirical Research for Democracy under a Research Project funded by the Technological Agency of Czechia, conducted for the Office of the Government of Czechia.

thoroughly perceives the EU as a suitable representative of Czech interests in the world, because the power of a bloc provides a stronger voice and a better bargaining position. The majority of the Czech public agrees with its European neighbors on the meaning that it is attributed to the EU as an association of states built on common values. Furthermore, part of the public would like to see the EU as a guarantor of basic human rights. According to the Czech public, NATO represents a key guarantor of European security. At the same time, the Czech public has long been inclining to strengthening military cooperation within the EU. The decreasing dependency is thus considered a key measure in light of security threats on strategic raw materials (ibid.).

5.   Czech expectations vs. recommendations of the CoFoE final report

The presented results of the CoFoE in its final report include 49 recommendations that are further structured in 325 more detailed points. The proposed ideas are, in the institutional relations, demanding more integration and strengthening the role of the EU, more exclusive competences, and facilitation of the decision-making process. This would obviously require a reform of the treaties. For Czechia, this might be problematic. Not only for the political representations, but also citizens are, in comparison to Germans, more skeptical towards more common decision-making at the EU level. On the contrary, Czechs would welcome more transparency and easing of the decision-making process. Nevertheless, this is not only the case for Czechia. In a non-paper signed by Bulgaria, Croatia, the Czech Republic, Denmark, Estonia, Finland, Latvia, Lithuania, Malta, Poland, Romania, Slovenia, and Sweden it becomes clear that these countries stand together and point out the fact that a „Treaty change has never been a purpose of the Conference". Their view builds on the current capability of the EU that is being challenged by COVID-19 and Russia's aggression against Ukraine. These challenges „have clearly shown how much the EU can deliver within the current Treaty framework" (Permanent Representation of Sweden to the European Union 2022).

Climate change is generally perceived as a crucial issue that needs action to be taken by the EU. Czech citizens, however, see the Green Deal as a threat to prosperity and jobs. Accepting gas and nuclear energy as an eligible part of the energy mix is another sensitive issue. Some of the recommendations might be too ambitious in this regard.

Despite the fact that the economic benefits from the EU single market are significant for Czechia, support for adopting the common European currency is low. Czech attitudes towards economic and social affairs oppose some of the recommendations of the CoFoE in these areas. Strengthening the powers of the EU in social affairs and eventual more integration in the tax could be therefore sensitive in the eyes of Czech citizens.

Some overlapping areas are present in the common foreign and security policy. Czechs perceive NATO as a guarantor of security but would like to see more cooperation in the military sector and favor building more European capacities.

6. Czech Presidency and next steps in shaping the CoFoE

The Priorities of the Czech Presidency promise to actively work with the CoFoE outcomes, as the Presidency "will work on making use of these ideas and the creation of a space for the continuation of the debate", particularly focusing on improving involvement of young people in the political/policy process in light of the European Year of Youth (Czech Presidency of the Council of the European Union 2022). Nevertheless, the context and very turbulent circumstances resulting from the Russian invasion of Ukraine, dictate that this will be anything but easy. In addition, the rather skeptical position of the Czech government towards opening the debates on treaty reforms on the EU level gives Czechia a comfortable position during its Presidency for being not too active in this regard. Apart from this, leading complex negotiations on this matter is timely demanding and will definitely exceed the duration of the presidency. Nevertheless, Ursula von der Leyen, President of the European Commission indicated in the European Parliament that she will present some of the proposal in her speech on the State of the Union (European Commission 2022b).

In general, the Czech Presidency has been focusing on the implementation of the CoFoE report and negotiating with the GAC and other sectoral Councils. At this stage, concrete steps are now a subject for negotiations among the EU member states. More progress could eventually be brought through a follow-up event, which is planned in December 2022.

7. Conclusions

Czech society has a mixed attitude towards the EU. This influences the communication of EU issues to the citizens. Political parties often lack courage to focus on topics related to the EU, as the eurosceptical sentiment present in the Czech society might threaten their position in the political campaigns. Public administration and departments in charge of the communication of EU affairs have, without stronger political ownership, limited the impact on shaping the public opinion on the EU. Varying regional attitudes also serve as a challenge. Whereas Prague as the capital, is traditionally pro-EU, particularly under-developed regions (such as Ústecký kraj) have concerns about issues such as effects of the Green Deal (loss of jobs). The knowledge on the functioning of the EU among citizens is another issue.

The CoFoE in Czechia had various forms. At the top political level, the topic has not been very much articulated. This was due to the lack of ownership, as the government during the CoFoE was not in favor of active stimulating and directly contributing from the highest political level. At the same time, the interest coming from the legislative bodies was more intense in the preparatory phase of the CoFoE with the activities organized by the Office of the Government and the stakeholders. These two were the driving forces of the debates and engaging the citizens. In total, 114 events have been organized under the CoFoE-umbrella in Czechia. In addition, 4 citizen panels consisting of citizens took place.

The CoFoE offered to Czech citizens an opportunity for reflections on the state and future of the EU. Nevertheless, its success has been limited. On the EU level, Czechia is supposed to be the driving force of further progress during its Presidency. Its real power, however, remains questionable, not only due to the external circumstances, but particularly due to the complexity of the debate on eventual treaty changes and reforms of the EU institutions among member states.

8. References

Bartovic, Vladimír/Havelka, Vít/Kasáková, Zuzana 2020: Konference o budoucnosti Evropy z pohledu České republiky [Conference on Future of Europe from the perspective of Czechia], Recommendations, Praha. https://narodnikonvent.cz/wp-content/uploads/sites/5/2021/12/Podklad_Konference-o-budoucnosti-Evropy.pdf (07.07.2022).

Blahušiak, Igor 2021: Výsledky regionálních debat pod Konferencí o budoucnosti EU [Results from Regional Debates under the Conference on the Future of EU], 06.12.2021, Presentation, Prague University of Economics and Business.

Buchtík, Martin/Komasová, Sarah/Uhrová, Jitka/Horejš, Nikola 2022: Národní občanské panely Konference o budoucnosti Evropy: shrnutí a analýza debat [National Citizens Panels Conference on Future of Europe: Summary and Analysis of Debates]. https://www.vlada.cz/assets/evropske-zalezitosti/analyzy-EU/7b_Vyzkumna_zprava_COFE_synteza_konsorcium_EUROPEUM.pdf (07.07. 2022).

European Commission 2022a: Standard Eurobarometer 2021-2022. Czechia, April 2022. https://europa.eu/eurobarometer/api/deliverable/download/file?deliverableId=81539 (07.07.2022).

European Commission 2022b: Statement by President von der Leyen at the joint press conference with President Metsola and Prime Minister Fiala on the presentation of the programme of activities of the Czech Presidency of the Council of the EU. https://ec.europa.eu/commission/presscorner/detail/en/STATEMENT_22_4346 (07.07.2022).

Conference on the Future of Europe 2022: Czechia. https://futureu.europa.eu/pages/czechia (07.07.2022).

Czech Presidency of the Council of the European Union 2022: Priorities. https://czech-presidency.consilium.europa.eu/en/programme/priorities/ (07.07.2022).

European Council 2019: A new strategic agenda 2019–2024. https://www.consilium.europa.eu/en/press/press-releases/2019/06/20/a-new-strategic-agenda-2019-2024/ (07.07.2022).

Faktor, Žiga 2022: Závěry a implementace výstupů Konference o budoucnosti Evropy Shrnutí a doporučení vyplývající z diskuze kulatého stolu Národního konventu o EU konaného dne 3. června 2022 [Conclusions and implementation of the outputs of the CoFoE from the debate of Roundtable of the National Convention on the EU, 3 June 2022]. https://www.europeum.org/data/articles/kulaty-stul-nk-3-6-doporuceni.pdf (07.07.2022).

Francová Jana 2020: Konference o budoucnosti Evropy Příprava konference o budoucnosti Evropy na půdě klíčových unijních institucí a pozice národních parlamentů, včetně Parlamentu ČR [CoFoE, Preparations of the CoFoE in the key EU institutions and position of national parliaments in including the Czech Parliament], 5/2020. https://www.psp.cz/sqw/text/orig2.sqw?idd=169718 (07.07.2022).

Francová Jana 2021: Informační podklad ke sdělení Plánování konference o budoucnosti Evropy [Information Material to the Communication on planning of the CoFoE], Parlamentní institut, March 2021. https://bit.ly/3ckVsmY (07.07.2022).

Havlík, Vratislav/Mocek, Ondřej 2017: Václav Klaus as Driver of Czech Euroskepticism, in: *Hashimoto, Tom/Rhimes, Michael (eds.)*: Reviewing European Union Accession: Unexpected Results, Spillover Effects, and Externalities, Leiden, pp. 96–112.

Hrdinková, Milena 2021: Strategie vlády ČR pro přípravu Konference o budoucnosti Evropy [Strategy of the Government in the Preparations of the COFE], Speech transcript, 18.06.2021, Conference Perspectives of Czechia in the EU. https://www.eapncr.org/sites/default/files/obrazky/zaznam_proslovu_mileny_hrdinkove.pdf (07.07.2022).

Landesregierung Baden-Württemberg 2021: Dokumentace výsledků dialogu 6 regionů o přeshraniční spolupráci a budoucnosti Evropy, 21.12.2021. https://beteiligungsportal.baden-wuerttemberg.de/fileadmin/redaktion/beteiligungsportal/Dokumente/211221_Dokumentace_6_Regions_Dialogue_2021.pdf (07.07.2022).

Ministry of Finance, Czechia 2021: Čistá pozice ČR vůči EU dosáhla v roce 2021 bezmála 89 mld. Kč [Net position towards the EU reached in 2021 almost 89 bil. CZK]. https://www.mfcr.cz/cs/aktualne/tiskove-zpravy/2022/cista-pozice-cr-vuci-eu-dosahla-v-roce-2-46333/ (07.07.2022).

Permanent Representation of Sweden to the European Union 2022: Non-paper by Bulgaria, Croatia, the Czech Republic, Denmark, Estonia, Finland, Latvia, Lithuania, Malta, Poland, Romania, Slovenia, and Sweden on the outcome of and follow-up to the Conference on the Future of Europe, 09.05.2022. https://twitter.com/swedenineu/status/1523637827686531072 (07.07.2022).

Slavkov/Austerlitz 3 (Austria, Czechia, Slovakia) 2020: Speakers of Parliaments Meeting – Declaration on Conference on the Future of Europe, 13 February 2020. https://www.psp.cz/sqw/detail.sqw?id=6165&z=13684 (07.07.2022).

Zichová, Kateřina 2021: Konference o budoucnosti Evropy budí velká očekávání, zapojení občanů však pokulhává [The conference on the future of Europe raises high expectations, but the participation of citizens falters], in: EURACTIV, 12.07.2021. https://euractiv.cz/section/budoucnost-eu/news/konference-o-budoucnosti-evropy-budi-velka-ocekavani-zapojeni-obcanu-vsak-pokulhava/ (07.07.2022).

Authors

Prof. Dr. Gabriele Abels: Jean Monnet Professor for Comparative Politics & European Integration, Institute of Political Science, University of Tübingen; Speaker of the Board, European Center for Research on Federalism, Tübingen.

Mgr. Jarolím Antal Ph.D.: Director of the Centre for European Studies, Faculty of International Relations, Prague University of Economics and Business, Czechia.

Muhterem Aras: President of the State Parliament of Baden-Württemberg; Delegate of the European Committee of the Regions to the Plenary of the Conference on the Future of Europe and Member of the Working Group on Climate Change and Environment.

Lukas Böhm: Student of Political Science, University of Vienna.

Prof. Susanna Cafaro: Full Professor of EU Law at Università del Salento (Lecce, Italy), Jean Monnet Chair on "Legal Theory of European Integration: a Supranational Democracy Model?"; Member of the Scientific Committee for the Future of Europe established by the Italian Government.

Vasco Alves Cordeiro: President of the European Committee of the Regions.

Anna Dermitzakis: Student of Political Science, University of Vienna.

Leopold Kernstock: Student of Political Science, University of Vienna.

Mario Kölling: Assistant Professor, Department of Political Science, Universidad Nacional de Educación a Distancia (U.N.E.D); Senior Researcher and Project Manager, Fundación Manuel Giménez Abad, Zaragoza, Spain.

Oskar Kveton: Student of Political Science, University of Vienna.

Servane Metzger: Assistant Director of Public Affairs Europe & Impact, France Digitale; former Policy Advisor, Private office of the Minister Delegate for Europe, Ministry for Europe and Foreign Affairs, France.

Dr. Sarah Meyer: Research Associate at the Department for European Policy and the Study of Democracy; Principle Investigator for the REGIOPARL research project, University for Continuing Education Krems, Austria.

Timo Peters: Unit for citizens' participation, State Ministry Baden-Württemberg.

Wolfgang Petzold: Former Deputy Director for Communication at the European Committee of the Regions, Brussels (until 2022); Official in different social and regional policy Directorates-General of the European Commission, Brussels (until 2008); Part-time lecturer (1999–2022).

Prof. Min Reuchamps: Professor of Political Science, Institute de sciences politiques Louvain-Europe, Université catholique de Louvain (UCLouvain); involved in the design of the deliberative commissions in Brussels at the request of the combined bureau of the Brussels Regional Parliament and the French-speaking Brussels Parliament; Member of the scientific committee for the deliberative commissions organised by the region of Wallonia.

Ann-Mireille Sautter: PhD Fellow in Democracy Studies at the Fund for Scientific Research (F.R.S. – FNRS); Institute de sciences politiques Louvain-Europe, Université catholique de Louvain (UCLouvain).

Patrick Steindl: Student of Political Science, University of Vienna.

Mattéo Torres-Ader: Policy advisor, Private office of the Minister Delegate for Europe, Ministry for Europe and Foreign Affairs, France.

Melina Weilguni: Student of Political Science, University of Vienna.

Jasmin Zengin: Student of Political Science, University of Vienna.

Florian Ziegenbalg M.A.E.S. (Bruges): Unit for European Policy, State Ministry Baden-Württemberg.

Annex I: Timeline of the Conference on the Future of Europe

13 February 2019	The European Parliament adopts a resolution "on the state of the debate on the future of Europe".
4 March 2019	French President Emmanuel Macron proposes the launch of a Conference on the Future of Europe during the electoral campaign for the 2019 European Parliament election.
16 July 2019	Ursula von der Leyen favours the organisation of a CoFoE in her speech as presidential candidate for the European Commission in the European Parliament.
10 September 2019	von der Leyen's Political Guidelines for the new European Commission 2019–2024 include a plan to launch a CoFoE.
Autumn 2019	The European Parliament sets up a special high-level working group.
27 November 2019	A Franco-German Non-Paper on key questions and guidelines is published presenting a proposed structure and timetable for a CoFoE.
1 December 2019	In the Mission Letter to Commissioner Šuica Commission President von der Leyen puts her in charge of leading the Commission's work on the CoFoE.
4 December 2019	AFCO has a committee hearing concerning the Future of Europe.
10 December 2019	AFCO presents an opinion in which it argues for a "leading role" for the European Parliament.
12 December 2019	The summit conclusion of the European Council addresses the CoFoE.
15 January 2020	The European Parliament adopts a resolution outlining its position on the CoFoE.
22 January 2020	The European Commission adopts a communication arguing that citizens' participation must be at the heart of the CoFoE.
12 February 2020	The European Committee of the Regions adopts a Draft Resolution on the CoFoE.
17 April 2020	In a resolution on the COVID-19 pandemic the European Parliament expresses the need to convene the CoFoE.
18 June 2020	The European Parliaments adopts a resolution on the CoFoE regarding the COVID-19 situation urging the Council to adopt a position.
24 June 2020	The Council adopts its position.
17 December 2020	The institutions agree on their legislative priorities for 2021 and commit themselves to citizens' participation in the CoFoE.
3 February 2021	The Council adopts its revised position.
23 March 2021	A group of 12 member states publishes a non-paper arguing that the CoFoE should not entail legal obligations.
10 March 2021	The three institutions sign the Joint Declaration of the Conference on the Future of Europe.
25 March 2021	The Executive Board meets for the first time.

19 April 2021	The multilingual digital platform launches.
9 May 2021	The inaugural event of the CoFoE takes place in Strasbourg.
26 May 2021	The Executive Board approves the timetable of events.
17 June 2021	The first European Citizens' Event is hosted in Lisbon.
19 June 2021	The Conference Plenary meets for the first time in Strasbourg.
24 June 2021	The Council of the European Union adopts its position.
17–19 September 2021	The first European Citizens' Panel is held.
8–9 October 2021	The European Youth Event takes place.
25–27 February 2022	The final European Citizens' Panel is held.
4 March 2022	The CoR adopts the "Marseille Manifesto of local and regional leaders: Europe starts in its regions, cities and villages".
2 May 2022	The Conference Plenary agrees on the final set of proposals.
4 May 2022	The European Parliament adopts a resolution declaring that treaty change is necessary to implement the proposals.
9 May 2022	The CoFoE concludes its work. The final CoFoE report is published. A group of 13 member states publishes a non-paper emphasizing that treaty change is not the purpose of the Conference.
13 May 2022	A group of six member states publishes a non-paper declaring that they are open to treaty changes in principle.
9 June 2022	The European Parliament adopts a resolution calling on the European Council to activate the process for treaty reforms.
10 June 2022	The European Council publishes a preliminary technical assessment of the Conference proposals.
17 June 2022	The European Commission issues a communication setting out a first analysis of the proposals of the CoFoE and outlining the organisation of the follow-up.
23–24 June 2022	The Conclusion of the European Council Summit entails a short reference to the CoFoE.
29–30 June 2022	The CoR adopts a resolution emphasizing that many recommendations of the CoFoE refer to an active involvement of the regions.
14 September 2022	Commission President Ursula von der Leyen delivers her State of the Union speech.
2 December 2022	The European Commission hosts a feedback-event for the citizens who participated in the transnational citizens' panels.

Annex II: List of Key Documents

CoFoE 2021: Conference on the Future of Europe: Conference Charter. https://futureu. europa.eu/uploads/decidim/attachment/file/3997/Conference_Charter_en__2_.pdf (10.09.2022).

CoFoE 2021: Rules of Procedure of the Conference on the Future of Europe, May 2021. https://futureu.europa.eu/uploads/decidim/attachment/file/9340/sn02700.en21.pdf (10.09.2022).

CoFoE 2022: Multilingual Digital Platform of the Conference on the Future of Europe, Final Report, May 2022. https://bit.ly/3BLErNe (08.08.2022).

CoFoE 2022: Report on the final outcome, May 2022. https://futureu.europa.eu/pages/ reporting (02.08.2022).

Committee of the Regions 2020: Draft resolution on the Conference on the Future of Europe, RESOL VII/003, 138th plenary session, 11-12 February 2020. https://cor. europa.eu/en/news/Documents/Draft%20Resolution%20Conference%20Future%20of %20Europe.pdf (02.08.2022).

Committee of the Regions 2020: Resolution on the Conference on the Future of Europe, Brussels, 29.04.2020.

Committee of the Regions 2021: CoR delegation ready to represent 1 million regional and local elected politicians at the Plenary of the Conference on the Future of Europe. Press release, 16 June 2021. https://cor.europa.eu/en/news/Pages/CoFoE-plenary-19-June. aspx (02.08.2022).

Committee of the Regions 2021: Resolution on the Conference on the Future of Europe, Interactio – Remote – 144th CoR plenary session, 27.07.2021.

Committee of the Regions 2021: The Conference on the Future of Europe: Putting Local and Regional Authorities at the Heart of European Democratic Renewal, October 2021.

Committee of the Regions 2022: Citizens, local politicians and the future of Europe. Final Report. Brussels, February 2022.

Committee of the Regions 2022: The outcome and follow-up on the Conference on the Future of Europe, Resolution adopted on 30 June 2022. https://memportal.cor.europa. eu/Public/Documents/MeetingDocuments?meetingId=2182079&meetingSessionId=22 27831 (04.07.2022).

Council of the European Union 2020: Conference on the Future of Europe, 9102/20, Brussels, 24.06.2020.

Council of the European Union 2021: Conference on the Future of Europe – revised Council position, 5911/21, Brussels, 03.02.2021.

Council of the European Union 2022: Conference on the Future of Europe - Proposals and related specific measures contained in the report on the final outcome of the Conference on the Future of Europe: Preliminary technical assessment, 10033/22, Brussels, 10.06.2022.

European Commission 2019: A Union that strives for more. My agenda for Europe. Political guidelines for the next European Commission 2019–2024. https://ec.europa. eu/info/sites/default/files/political-guidelines-next-commission_en_0.pdf (10.09.2022).

European Commission 2020: Communication from the Commission to the European Parliament and the Council: Shaping the Conference on the Future of Europe, COM(2020) 27 final, Brussels, 22.01.2020.

European Commission 2021: Conference on the Future of Europe – Joint Declaration. https://ec.europa.eu/info/sites/default/files/en_-_joint_declaration_on_the_conference_on_the_future_of_europe.pdf (02.08.2022).

European Commission 2022: Communication from the Commission to the European Parliament, the European Council, the Council, the European Economic and Social Committee and the Committee of the Regions, Conference on the Future of Europe: Putting Vision into Concrete Action, COM(2022) 404 final, Brussels, 17.06.2022.

European Commission 2022: Annex to the Communication, Conference on the Future of Europe: Putting Vision into Concrete Action, COM(2022) 404 final, Brussels, 17.06.2022.

European Council (EUCO) 2019: Conclusions of European Council meeting, EUCO 29/19, Brussels, 12.12.2019.

European Council (EUCO) 2019: A new strategic agenda for the EU 2019–2024. https://www.consilium.europa.eu/en/eu-strategic-agenda-2019-2024/ (02.08.2022).

European Council (EUCO) 2022: Conclusions of the European Council meeting (23 and 24 June 2022) – Conclusions, EUCO 24/22, Brussels, 24.06.2022.

European Economic and Social Committee 2021: A New Narrative for Europe: The EESC Resolution on the Conference on the Future of Europe, Brussels, April 2021. https://www.eesc.europa.eu/sites/default/files/files/qe-08-21-138-en-n.pdf (10.09.2022).

European Economic and Social Committee 2021: Resolution of the European Economic and Social Committee on 'A New Narrative for Europe — The EESC resolution on the Conference on the Future of Europe', Brussels, 16.07.2021.

European Parliament 2020: European Parliament resolution of 15 January 2020 on the European Parliament's position on the Conference on the Future of Europe, P9_TA(2020)0010, Strasbourg, 15.01.2020.

European Parliament 2020: European Parliament resolution of 17 April 2020 on EU coordinated action to combat the COVID-19 pandemic and its consequences, P9_TA(2020)0054, Strasbourg, 17.04.2020.

European Parliament 2020: European Parliament resolution of 18 June 2020 on the European Parliament's position on the Conference on the Future of Europe, P9_TA(2020)0153, Strasbourg, 18.01.2020.

European Parliament 2022: Future of Europe: Conference Plenary ambitious proposals point to Treaty review. Press release 30 April 2022. https://www.europarl.europa.eu/news/en/press-room/20220429IPR28218/future-of-europe-conference-plenary-ambitious-proposals-point-to-treaty-review (07.05.2022).

European Parliament 2022: Resolution of 4 May 2022 on the follow-up to the conclusions of the Conference on the Future of Europe, P9_TA(2022)0141, Strasbourg, 04.05.2022.

European Parliament 2022: Parliament activates process to change EU Treaties, Press Release 9 June 2022. https://bit.ly/3Y4yunq (02.08.2022).

European Parliament Research Service (EPRS) 2019: Preparing the Conference on the Future of Europe, EPRS Briefing, PE 644.202 – December 2019.

European Parliament/Committee on Constitutional Affairs (AFCO) 2019: Opinion on the Conference on the Future of Europe, adopted 10 December 2019. https://www.europarl.europa.eu/cmsdata/194307/Adopted%20opinion%20CoFoE_10122019-original.pdf (02.08.2022).

Franco-German non-paper 2019: Conference on the Future of Europe: Franco-German non-paper on key questions and guidelines. https://www.politico.eu/wp-content/uploads/2019/11/Conference-on-the-Future-of-Europe.pdf (30.04.2022).

General Secretariat of the Council of the EU 2022: Conference on the Future of Europe - Proposals and related specific measures contained in the report on the final outcome of the Conference on the Future of Europe: Preliminary technical assessment, 10033/22, Brussels, 10.06.2022.

Macron, Emmanuel 2019: For European renewal, 04.03.2019. https://www.elysee.fr/en/emmanuel-macron/2019/03/04/for-european-renewal (20.04.2022).

Non-paper 2020: Using the Conference on the Future of Europe to shape a real European political discourse: Italian Non-Paper for the Conference on the Future of Europe (2020-2022), 28.02.2020. https://www.esteri.it/mae/resource/doc/2020/03/paper_conf_futuro_europa_post_ciae_14_febbraio_-_clean.pdf (10.09.2022).

Non-paper 2021: Conference on the Future of Europe: Common approach amongst Austria, Czech Republic, Denmark, Estonia, Finland, Ireland, Latvia, Lithuania, Malta, the Netherlands, Slovakia and Sweden. https://www.permanentrepresentations.nl/binaries/nlatio/documenten/publications/2021/03/24/non-paper-on-the-conference-on-the-future-of-europe/Non-paper.+Common+approach+to+the+Conference+on+the+Future+of+Europe..pdf (23.07.2022).

Non-paper 2022: Non-paper submitted by Germany, Belgium, Italy, Luxembourg, the Netherlands, and Spain on implementing the proposals of the Plenary of the "Conference on the Future of Europe" 2022, 13.05.2022. https://twitter.com/alemannoEU/status/1526922932970262528 (02.08.2022).

Official Journal 2021: Joint Declaration of the European Parliament, the Council and the European Commission on the Conference on the Future of Europe – Engaging with citizens for democracy – Building a more resilient Europe, OJ C 91 I/01, Brussels, 18.03.2021.

Permanent Representation of Sweden to the European Union 2022: Non-paper by Bulgaria, Croatia, the Czech Republic, Denmark, Estonia, Finland, Latvia, Lithuania, Malta, Poland, Romania, Slovenia, and Sweden on the outcome of and follow-up to the Conference on the Future of Europe, 09.05.2022. https://twitter.com/swedenineu/status/1523637827686531072 (07.07.2022).

von der Leyen, Ursula 2019: A Union that strives for more: My agenda for Europe, Brussels.

von der Leyen, Ursula 2022: A Union that Stands Strong Together. 2022 State of the Union Address, 14.09.2022.

Annex III: Charter for citizens and event organisers participating in the CONFERENCE ON THE FUTURE OF EUROPE

I will contribute to the debate and deliberations on the priorities for our common future, together with citizens from all backgrounds, walks of life and all corners of the European Union.

As a participant in the Conference, I commit to:

- Respect our European values, as set in Art. 2 of the Treaty on the European Union: human dignity, freedom, democracy, equality, the rule of law and respect for human rights, including the rights of persons belonging to minorities, which is part of what it means to be European and to engage respectfully with each other. These values are common to all EU Member States in a society in which pluralism, non-discrimination, tolerance, justice, solidarity and equality between women and men must prevail.

- Contribute to the Conference with constructive and concrete proposals, respecting the opinions of other citizens and building Europe's future together.

- Refrain from expressing, disseminating, or sharing content which is illegal, hateful or deliberately false or misleading. In this context, I will always refer to credible and reliable sources when I share content and information to support my ideas.

- My participation in the Conference is voluntary and I will not try to use the Conference to pursue any commercial or exclusively private interests.

As a party organising events under the umbrella of the Conference, I commit to:

- Put citizens at the centre of any event and allow them to express their voice freely.

- Promote events that are inclusive and accessible for all citizens, including by publishing the details of any event on the Conference multilingual digital platform.

- Respect the **principles as set out in the Joint Declaration** on the Conference on the Future of Europe and ensure that citizens are able to discuss the topics that matter to them.

- Encourage **diversity in the debates**, by actively supporting the participation of citizens from all walks of life, irrespective of gender, sexual orientation, age, socio-economic background, religion and/or level of education.

- **Respect freedom of speech**, giving space to competing opinions and proposals – as long as they are neither hateful nor illegal.

- Whenever possible and relevant, favour the **cross-board participation** of citizens and the use of **different EU languages** in the events.

- Guarantee **full transparency**. Following any event, I will **report openly on debates and recommendations** formulated by citizens on the Conference multilingual digital platform. I will **stream and/or broadcast events**, whenever possible.

- When providing participants with **information on topics for debate** (e.g. digital, print or audio-visual material), ensure that is accurate, reliable, accessible and has traceable references.
- Ensure compliance with **EU data protection** and privacy rules.
- Use only the authorised **Conference visual identity** for communicating the event.